# CROSSING THE ATLANTIC

# Crossing the Atlantic

## Comparing the European Union and Canada

*Edited by*
PATRICK M. CROWLEY
*Texas A&M University-Corpus Christi*

Routledge
Taylor & Francis Group

LONDON AND NEW YORK

First published 2004 by Ashgate Publishing

Reissued 2018 by Routledge
2 Park Square, Milton Park, Abingdon, Oxon, OX14 4RN
605 Third Avenue, New York, NY 10017

First issued in paperback 2021

*Routledge is an imprint of the Taylor & Francis Group, an informa business*

ISBN 13: 978-0-815-38835-7 (hbk)
ISBN 13: 978-1-351-16056-8 (ebk)
ISBN 13: 978-1-138-35678-8 (pbk)

DOI: 10.4324/9781351160568

# Contents

**Part IV: Policies for Nation-Building**

# List of Contributors

**Patrick M. Crowley** is an associate professor of economics at Texas A&M – Corpus Christi. His published research mainly involves EU studies, NAFTA studies, but his other interests and research monographs in economics relate to international macroeconomics, international trade, applied statistics, and Austrian economics. He recently published an edited volume for Routledge entitled "Before and Beyond EMU", and has papers in journals such as the Journal of Common Market Studies, Contemporary Economic Policy, International Trade Journal and Current Politics and Economics of Europe. In 2004/2005 he will be a visiting research scholar at the Bank of Finland in Helsinki.

**Donald Barry** is a professor of political science at the University of Calgary. His publications include *Toward a North American Community? Canada, the United States and Mexico* (1995); *Regionalism, Multilateralism, and the Politics of Global Trade*, with Ronald C. Keith (1999), and *Icy Battleground: Canada, the International Fund for Animal Welfare, and the Seal Hunt* (forthcoming).

**Geneviève Bouchard** is a research director in the field of governance at the Institute for Research on Public Policy in Montreal, Quebec, Canada. She holds a BA and an MA in Political Science from Laval University and in November 2000 she completed a Ph.D. in comparative public policy at McMaster University. She has held several positions as teaching assistant and part-time instructor in different universities in Canada and in the United States (Laval University, McMaster University, University of Saskatchewan and Duke University) and she has working experience in the provincial and federal civil service. She was responsible for the preparation of the strategic plan at the Quebec Ministry of International Relations and she has worked as an analyst at the Immigration and Refugee Board in Ottawa.

**Paul Bowles** is Professor of Economics at the University of Northern British Columbia. He has published extensively on the topics of globalisation and regionalisation as well as on the political economy of China's reforms. He is currently working on a book on national currencies.

**William Chandler** is a Professor of Political Science at the University of San Diego, California, USA. His research is on federalism and party politics in the EU. He has published numerous articles in both journals and other edited collections.

**Osvaldo Croci** is Associate Professor in the Department of Political Science at Memorial University (St. John's, Newfoundland, Canada) where he teaches international politics. He has published numerous journal articles and book chapters on European integration, European foreign policies, and transatlantic relations.

**John Erik Fossum** is a Senior Researcher at ARENA – Advanced Research on the Europeanisation of the Nation State at the University of Oslo, Norway.

**Joseph F. Jozwiak, Jr.** is an Associate Professor of Political Science at Texas A&M University in Corpus Christi, Texas, USA. He is an active researcher on EU issues, most notably environmental and competition concerns.

**Brian K. MacLean** is an associate professor of economics at Laurentian University who specializes in macroeconomic policy analysis. He is co-editor of *The Unemployment Crisis* (McGill-Queen's, 1996), editor of *Out of Control: Canada in an Unstable Financial World* (Lorimer, 1999), and co-author of *Principles of Macroeconomics* (McGraw-Hill Ryerson, 2003) and *Principles of Microeconomics* (McGraw-Hill Ryerson, 2003). He speaks Japanese and has been a visiting professor at Hokkaido and Saitama Universities in Japan.

**Edelgard Mahant** is Professor of Political Science at York University's Glendon college. She has published a number of books and articles on European and North American integration.

**J. C. Robin Rowley** is a Professor of Economics at McGill University in Montreal, Canada. He has had over 60 articles published in a wide variety of journals (including the American Economic Review), and other outlets and his main fields of interest include econometrics, history of economic thought, statistics and international economics.

**John B. Sutcliffe** is an Assistant Professor in the Department of Political Science at the University of Windsor. His research interests include the place of local government in the European Union and Canada and Scottish devolution. His articles on these and other topics have been published in *Regional and Federal Studies* and the *Journal of European Public Policy* among others.

**Amy Verdun** is Associate Professor of Political Science (with tenure) and Director of European Studies at the University of Victoria, Canada and currently visiting fellow at the Max Planck Institute in Cologne Germany. She holds a Jean Monnet Chair in European Integration Studies in Victoria B.C.. She earned her Ph.D. in Political Science at the European University Institute in Florence, and her Bachelor and Master's level degrees in Political Science at the University of Amsterdam, the Netherlands. She was a Jean Monnet Fellow in the European Forum of the Robert Schuman Centre, European University Institute, in 1997. She has also been a lecturer at Leiden University and a post-doctoral research fellow in the Department of Government, University of Essex UK. Verdun is the author and editor of many journal articles, book chapters and books in the field of European integration studies and International Political Economy.

Chapter 1

# Apples and Oranges: The Habilitation of Continental Comparativism

Patrick M. Crowley

## Introduction

Every day in our lives we make comparisons. We compare such things as food prices, people, destinations, houses, cars, countries and political leaders. Usually when we make these comparisons we make these comparisons within certain classifications. The question arises though as to how big these classifications can be? Can we compare different types of apples? Of course – they are all one type of fruit. Can we compare oranges and apples? Yes, on a certain level we can, as although they are markedly different fruits, they are, nevertheless, both fruits, so have certain common properties. What properties might these be? Well they both contain vitamin C, they both contain fructose, and they both are good for you. Can we compare broccoli and apples? Well, they are different food categories, and so we can compare them as foods in terms of nutrition values and vitamin content. Can we compare cars and apples? Clearly an everyday comparison would now be absurd. Apples and cars are not really two items that would be worthy of comparison in everyday life, as there are no real commonalities between the two on which to base a comparison. Of course, scientifically there might be some basis for comparison in terms of, for example, evaluating the force needed to crush an apple versus the force needed to crush a car, their weight as objects, or some other scientific measurement which one might imagine. But for everyday purposes, comparisons require an overarching classification which both of the articles fall within. Without this classification comparisons become meaningless.

    Clarkson (2000) first brought the issue of apples and oranges in the context of continental comparisons and argued that although apples and oranges are substantially different, they can both be compared as different fruits. He argues that cognitively and normatively their comparison is academically useful, in the sense that our understanding of how these two fruits differ, and how their commonalities can be measured, is a useful pursuit. In the same way, Clarkson also argues that comparing the European Union (EU) and the North American Free Trade Agreement (NAFTA) is also useful, despite the fact there are large differences between the two forms of regional integration.

Up until the last decade of the last century, it was not popular or even seen as academically respectable to make more than a cursory comparison between continental systems in virtually any subject. Indeed, the organization where most of the papers presented in this volume first saw the light of day, the European Community Studies Association – Canada, tended only to discuss European Union (EU) issues up until their 2001 meetings in Toronto. So what prompted this habilitation of continental comparativism?

I believe the first reason has to do with the ongoing developments on both sides of the Atlantic relating to regional integration. Up until the Maastricht Treaty of 1990, and the completion of the single market at the end of 1992, the EU had essentially been a customs union with aspirations for deeper integration in the future. The same could be said of NAFTA, which came into being as an extension of the Canada-US Free Trade Agreement in 1994. These regional agreements were based on Article 24 of the General Agreement on Trade and Tariffs (GATT), which states that countries are allowed to form preferential trading blocs as long as they continue to abide by all the rest of the rules of the GATT. But in the 1990s, these regional trading agreements were supplemented by further integration measures, taking them beyond their original free trade foundations. This integration dynamic was common to all continents, and has continued apace not only in Europe and North America, but also in South America, South East Asia, Australasia and now Africa as well. In the initial stages, there was little reason to compare the actual structures of integration, but as time has elapsed, these different dynamics have obviously become clearer and now warrant investigation.

The second reason for this study of comparative study of continental systems was prompted by general political and economic developments in the 1990s. The Blair government, after it's stunning election victory in 1997, adopted a policy approach of "best practice", whereby government policy would not be made until a full evaluation had been made of political, economic and social policies elsewhere. This led to much greater awareness of policies being enacted in other parts of the developed world, and therefore a greater audience for academics that do such comparative work.

The third and final reason for the habilitation of comparative study of regional integration agreements relates to the future. The integration dynamic, by its very nature, incorporates so-called political "spillover effects" – that is, regional integration in one area can lead to a greater necessity to treat other policy areas at a regional level, at minimum in terms of coordinating these different national policies, or at the most, the need for these policies to be moved to a supranational or international level of governance. Learning the lessons of what happened, what worked and what did not work elsewhere can obviously guide politicians and policymakers to understand the nature and the dependencies of the integration dynamic at play, and so prepare for future issues and problems that are likely to arise.

**The Comparisons**

Comparing the EU and the NAFTA might seem an obvious exercise to an academic interested in the integration dynamic, and certainly it can be justified based on Balassa's steps of integration (Balassa, 1961). Of course one of the major problems with this type of comparison is that the two regional integration agreements are very different in nature, given that one (the EU) was based on a customs union, which can be used as part of deepening integration ( – a common market, for example, incorporates a customs union), where the other (NAFTA) was constructed around a free trade area agreement. The free trade area configuration for trade integration doesn't naturally lead to a common market. Some of these issues have been explored by Crowley (2002).

The question arises as to whether it is makes sense to compare the EU with the U.S. or Canada. These two countries are obviously bound by the rules governing NAFTA, and yet within NAFTA there is still no common market, economic union or monetary union. So perhaps more appropriate comparisons might be made between the EU and the U.S. or Canada. Most U.S. academics interested in the EU have chosen to make the comparison with the U.S., and indeed the same can be said of many EU academics as well. Certainly it would be difficult to make a case that comparisons with Canada are more appropriate or justified than those between the EU and the U.S. on every level, but there clearly are likely to be certain areas where an EU – Canada comparison could be not only justified, but also more appropriate. This volume does not contain any direct comparisons between the EU and the U.S. – instead, if comparisons are not made with NAFTA, then the focus tends to be on comparisons between the EU and Canada, as most of the academics who contributed to this volume are Canadians or have close ties with Canada.

So what are the likely differences implied from such comparisons with the EU and Canada rather than with the US? Well these differences obviously need to be analysed from several different perspectives – at the minimum from political, economic and demographic/societal perspectives, and perhaps one could also add historical and legal perspectives to this list ( – although this is not done here).

Without providing an exhaustive list of considerations under each of these headings, let us consider some of these different perspectives in a highly selective manner. From a political perspective the U.S. is a federation of states, where as Canada started as a confederation of provinces ( – although the confederation is now blurred as Canada possesses a federal government). Interestingly though, the U.S. went through its Civil War to establish its federation, where as Canada has evolved from a confederation into what largely constitutes a federation too, but notably by peaceful means and also with the maintenance of some of the vestiges of a confederal country ( – for example, the notwithstanding clause, and the requirement of unanimity when changing the constitution). Leaving aside the issue of war as the catalyst for federations, the EU, with its emphasis on intergovernmentalism and consequent unanimity on important changes to the

Treaties, but with the incorporation of permitted abrogations from key Treaty sections certainly mirrors the Canadian experience more closely. Indeed, when Quebec separatist politician Lucien Bouchard was asked what type of arrangement with the rest of Canada they would favour, he specifically mentioned the EU's economic and political arrangements as being particularly desirable.

In economic terms, Canada and the U.S. appear to have a similar economic structure on the surface, and yet when studied more closely, it is apparent that there are quite large ideological differences between the two countries. First, within their democratic systems, there have been systematic efforts made to improve the economic status of the poorer states/provinces. But the methods adopted to achieve this end differ significantly. In the U.S. resource redistribution is accomplished through an informal allocation of government resources to the poorer states (military installations, federal government agencies, government programs), where as in Canada the redistribution is achieved through an formula-driven process (equalization) as well as through the more informal approach. In the realm of monetary policy too, there are stark differences between U.S. policy and Canadian policy. In Canada, price stability is not just an economic ideology, but it also comes with an operationalised price stability framework whereby Bank of Canada policy is tied to inflation targeting. In the U.S., the Federal Reserve still operates a looser policy of eschewing a nominal anchor for monetary policy – that is, policy is operated on largely a discretionary basis. In both the above cases the EU clearly mirrors Canada much more closely than the U.S. Obviously there are many other interesting economic parallels between the EU and Canada that can be pursued – parallels such as the federal role in sales taxes, the larger role that government has in both economies (with some exceptions), and perhaps a much greater emphasis on the interaction between the economy and the environment.

Turning to demographic and societal aspects, Canada and the U.S. are markedly different. Canada is a multicultural country by design, where as the U.S. is multicultural by default. Canada's policy of allowing the cultural identities of immigrant communities to persist, and embedding difference as a societal asset, stands in direct contrast to the U.S. "melting pot" model, where the American identity is maintained and stamped on immigrants as a means of inculcating a sense of belonging. Second generation U.S. immigrants rarely refer to themselves by the racial origins, whereas the term "Italian Canadian", for example, is used freely by second and third generation Canadians of Italian origin. Indeed the officially "bilingual" ( – but in practice multilingual) nature of Canadian society marks out Canada's policy difference with the U.S., where bilingualism, despite the overwhelming Hispanic populations in South Texas and other southern border states, is largely rejected. In Canada, Quebec obviously stands alone as the only jurisdiction in Canada where the French language dominates English – but French is also spoken in many other provinces as well, as the migration of French language speakers to these provinces means that it is not uncommon to hear the language in British Columbia or in Newfoundland. Similarly in the EU, although English will likely become the *lingua franca* of the continent, many languages are spoken not just in their main countries of origin, but also in other parts of the EU.

Once again, the Canadian similarities with the EU are striking and suggest further exploration.

Clearly a justification for a comparison between Canada and the EU can only go so far though. Indeed, one might make further comparisons that could further justify the comparison between Canada and the EU, and some of these similarities are explored in this volume of papers. But obviously there are also substantial differences between the two entities as well which shouldn't be ignored either. Perhaps the most obvious difference between either Canada or the U.S. and the EU is cultural. In the EU the number of languages is obviously large, and has become much larger with the expansion eastwards in May 2004. Language and culture are obviously associated, so in the EU there is really a myriad of cultures, which of course is not the case in Canada or the U.S., unless immigrant culture is counted, and even if it were, it is rarely confined to one geographical locale in North America. Of course there are other large differences between Canada and the EU in other spheres as well – perhaps most notably in political terms the form of the conception of both entities, in economic terms the geographical nature of income distribution in the EU is markedly different from that of Canada's, and in societal terms, apart from the cultural aspects explored above, perhaps the degree of labour mobility is what distinguishes the two entities most.

## The Benefits

The case for comparing Canada and the EU has hopefully been satisfactorily made above, and so has convinced the reader that there are intellectual gains to be made by doing such comparisons. The next issue that needs to be addressed here is what benefits are expected to accrue from such an exercise? Certainly it would be foolhardy to suggest that significant policy implications would result from such an exercise, and nor can any claims of new methodologies be developed from this approach. The benefits, if and when they accrue are rather more indirect than direct.

One clear benefit from using a comparativist perspective is that the nature of political, economic and social developments can be better understood in terms of how dynamics operate. The integration dynamic, as mentioned above, is one area where better understanding of different countries and regions experience this dynamic can shed light upon how the dynamic operates in different circumstances. Crowley (2002) attempted this in a paper comparing different regional integration agreements, and studied how the different forms of integration flow from one into the next, as well as the pre-conditions from moving from one form to the next.

Other benefits that accrue from the comparativist perspective are less tangible but are nonetheless real: explaining the form of policies by comparing policy differences between entities can often shed light on the factors that mould these policies, explaining differences in economic performance by examining the institutional differences between entities can often shed light on economic and social rigidities, and lastly comparing political power structures can sometimes illuminate the reasons why international cooperation might be limited in certain instances. Obviously this is not an exhaustive list, but it nonetheless gives the flavor of the benefits of taking a comparativist perspective.

## The Contributions

The contributions for this book come from a variety of sources. Many of the papers, though, were first presented at the European Community Studies Association – Canada in Toronto in the summer of 2001. All the papers have some comparativist perspective in them, some to a large extent and some to a lesser extent – this is what essentially binds this diverse volume together. The contributions are multidisciplinary as well, coming from both political science and economics – and hopefully the reader will see this as a strength of the volume. All too often, economists talk about political science concerns as determining outcomes, and similarly political scientists often treat economics in the same manner. Putting economics contributions together with political science contributions, can, I feel, only positively impact a diverse collection of papers such as this.

The book is divided into 4 parts. The first deals with the EU-Canada nexus – that is, the comparison of the entities and the relationship between the two entities. John Erik Fossum's chapter (chapter 1) first extends and explores some of the issues from the first part of this introduction. In particular the chapter focuses on various strategies for comparing the two entities, laying out the various pros and cons of each strategy. The chapter concentrates on the political element in this comparison, and concludes that two particular strategies dominate the others. Chapter 2 by Donald Barry looks at the transatlantic relationship between the EU and Canada. In one sense the commonalities between the two entities should encourage certain types of linkages, but in fact, as Barry explores, these have been limited to a degree by the importance to both of the political and economic relationship with the United States. One of the issues common to both is the development of some kind of transatlantic free trade agreement, and this is explored in some depth in the chapter.

The next part of the book (Part II) contains two chapters on governance in the EU, and what the EU can learn from Canada. In the fourth chapter, Amy Verdun deals with the development on political and economic governance in the EU, and in particular, on issues of fiscal sovereignty and other fiscal arrangements, using Canada as an appropriate example of fiscal arrangements in a democratic state. In the following chapter in this section, John Sutcliffe compares intergovernmental relations between the EU and Canada, but focuses more on comparisons of the place and influence of local government in the governance structure of both entities. Very little research has been done on this important area for comparison, and Sutcliffe uses the UK as a good indicator in the EU, and compares this with the situation of local government in Canada.

Part III of the book contains three chapters specifically comparing the EU and Canada and what Canada and NAFTA can learn from the EU. The first contribution in this part (chapter 6) looks at EU and NAFTA environmental policies. In the NAFTA framework, environmental policy was the only policy to be given special priority at a supranational level, with the formation of an institution to oversee environmental policies in the NAFTA countries. Joe Jozwiak and Patrick Crowley do an institutional comparison of environmental policy between the EU and NAFTA, and then take two waste disposal case studies to explore and evaluate some of these differences. Apart from the obvious comparison of environmental policy between the two entities, the issue of monetary union has been very prominent in Canada since the launch of the euro, as various suggestions for monetary union in North America have been discussed and debated in the Canadian media and by North American politicians and central bankers generally. In chapter 7, Paul Bowles, Osvaldo Croci and Brian MacLean look at the arguments for a single currency that were used in the North American context, and show how most of these differed from the arguments and context that caused the inception of the euro in the EU. Chapter 8 rounds out this part of the book by considering the various options for exchange rate arrangements in NAFTA, considering that if integration in the North American continent is to be deepened, then as the option for adopting a single currency could be thought of as one possibility, there may be intermediate options worth evaluating. Patrick Crowley and Robin Rowley do exactly this in this chapter, and in particular consider a North American version of the exchange rate mechanism (ERM) from the EU experience, naming it a NAERM.

The fourth and final part of the book looks at policies for nation building in both the EU and Canada. In chapter 9, Edelgard Mahant looks at national identity from both a European and Canadian perspective. She considers cultural policy in Canada, Ireland, Luxembourg and the European Union as a whole, and draws from it some interesting conclusions about the future of the EU as an entity. The final chapter of the volume, contributed by Geneviève Bouchard and William Chandler, explores another aspect of nation building – that of immigration. In this contribution Bouchard and Chandler compare the evolution and state of immigration policy in France, Germany and Canada. They note that there has been some convergence in immigration policies between these three countries, but they also pose the question as to whether immigration should not be treated as an EU problem given the expansion of the EU eastwards and the lack of restrictions on labour mobility between most of the current member states.

## Acknowledgements

First and foremost I would like to thank the European Union Studies Association – Canada, for allowing me do this edited volume. Although it appears a largely thankless task, it has been a rewarding experience for me, as I have gained a lot more knowledge about the different approaches to comparative analysis. Many of the contributors to this volume I have now known for nearly a decade, and as a wayward economist, not completely accepted in my own domain, I am greatly honored to be still associated with them. Second, I would like to thank my research assistant at Texas A&M University – Corpus Christi, Rebecca Basquez, who has spent a lot of time editing and checking the papers – certainly up and beyond the call of duty. Last but not least, I would like to thank the staff and editors at Ashgate, who had sufficient faith in my proposal to take on this project.

## References

Clarkson (2000), "Apples and Oranges: Prospects for the Comparative Analysis of the EU and NAFTA as Continental Systems", EUI Working Paper RSC 2000/23.
Crowley (2002), "European Integration after EMU: What next?" in Crowley, Patrick (ed.) *Before and Beyond European Monetary Union*, Routledge, London, UK, pp.157-180.

# PART I

# THE EU-CANADA NEXUS

Chapter 2

# Why Compare Canada and the European Union – and How?

John Erik Fossum

## Introduction

This chapter evaluates the usefulness of comparing Canada and the European Union, and for this purpose the chapter is divided into two parts. In the first part a number of reasons are sketched as to *why* such a comparison is warranted by contrasting the two with the U.S. In the second part of the paper the question of *how* we might compare Canada and the European Union is discussed. The two questions of *why* and *how* are clearly related. The second part also provides supplemental or more in-depth information on some of the reasons presented in the first.

## Why Compare Canada and the European Union?

The most commonly used entity to compare with the EU is the U.S. An obvious practical reason for preferring Canada to the U.S. is that Canada is far less well known. That is hardly a satisfactory reason, though. Other, more compelling reasons for preferring to compare the EU with Canada, as opposed to the U.S. are; first, that both Canada and the EU are widely held to be multinational and polyethnic entities, whereas the US, despite its complex cultural make-up, has been touted as the 'first new nation'. Canada has two major official languages, whereas the EU has 11 official languages. The US still only has one. In their self-conceptions, Canada and the EU, are closer to the notion of 'vertical mosaic', in contrast to the U.S. notion of the 'melting pot'. Of course in all cases the reality is more complex – but it is apparent, however, that in official statements and policy programmes, Canada and the EU emphasise the need for diversity awareness – including protection of distinctive *national* and regional and group-based identities, whereas the U.S. tends to emphasise this less. For all three entities, their complex ethno-linguistic and cultural make-ups are to some extent officially recognised so as to give the politics of identity and language high prominence. But this is more pronounced in Europe and Canada than in the U.S., maybe because in the former two entities distinct identities exist on more clearly demarcated territories.

Second, in both entities, there is a strong traditional focus on social solidarity through a significant public presence. Social policy has been seen as a vital means of fostering a sense of community and solidarity. Despite significant neo-liberal onslaughts, Canada is still a welfare state with a far more 'European' orientation to social justice than has the U.S. The EU is made up of welfare states. The EU has also not seriously challenged the European welfare state ethic as there are also strong counterbalancing forces in Europe that are intent on instilling a much stronger social orientation on the EU. This can be seen in the emphasis on social solidarity in the Treaties and in the Charter Declaration. Recently we have also seen it in the Convention on the Future of Europe, where there was a working group on social issues.

Third, and related to the above, in both Canada and the EU there appears to be a stronger penchant for a peaceful and deliberative approach to conflict settlement than in the U.S. This applies to the domestic scene, where for example Canada and the EU reject the death penalty, but the U.S. does not. It also applies to the international scene. In a recent provocative article, Robert Kagan noted that the Europeans and Americans diverge in their views of the world. For example, on the question of power,

> Europe is turning away from power it is moving beyond power into a self-contained world of laws and rules and transnational negotiation and cooperation. It is entering a post-historical paradise of peace and relative prosperity, the realization of Kant's "Perpetual Peace." The United States, meanwhile, remains mired in history, exercising power in the anarchic Hobbesian world where international laws and rules are unreliable and where true security and the defense and promotion of a liberal order still depend on the possession and use of military might (Kagan 2002).

While this certainly overstates the difference in practice, it does capture some of the difference in sentiment, although this clearly varies across Europe. Similarly, Canada's foreign policy approach, with its commitment to human security and multilateralism is closer to that of Europe than to that of the US.

Fourth, the difference in approach in terms of handling conflicts also shows up in the way in which the tension between unity and difference is handled. This is apparent in the role and status of federalism in Canada and the EU, versus its role and status in the U.S. There are various aspects of this concept which make it more rewarding to Europeans to look to Canada and vice versa, than for either to look to the U.S. In Canada, the challenge was to create a sense of nationhood, without eradicating multiple (national) identities. In the U.S. "the issue was how to create a large country without destroying individual liberty and local initiative" (LaSelva 1996: xii). The federal system, to James Madison, was a vital safeguard against the tyranny of faction. In Canada, to George-Étienne Cartier, federalism "accommodated distinct identities within the political framework of a great nation. The very divisions of federalism, when correctly drawn and coupled with a suitable scheme of minority rights, were for him what sustained the Canadian nation" (LaSelva 1996: 189). This difference in emphasis has been reflected in federalist theory and debate: "American federalist theory has focused on the kind of government the nation should have; Canadian federalist theory has concerned itself with whether there is a nation at all" (LaSelva 1996: 38). Clearly, the EU must grapple with a challenge that is quite similar to that facing Canada, namely to create a sense of community, without eradicating multiple national identities. This is expressed in the treaties in the Charter and in the Convention's Draft Treaty, establishing a Constitution for Europe.[1]

The challenges of political identity and nationhood have left deep marks on both Canada and the EU. A fifth point is that neither has reached a final equilibrium or resting place. In fact, both Canada and the EU have long lived with what may be termed 'territorial insecurity'. This stands in some contrast to the U.S., which has no serious challenge(r) neither to its territorial integrity nor to its being a national community, however hard it may be to define its specific national traits. Canada has for decades faced the spectre of Quebec secession and possibly even a consequent unravelling of the rest of the country. In such a scenario there are also fears of eventual engulfment of parts of Canada into the U.S. In Europe, the European Union has gone through numerous bouts of enlargement, since its inception. At present it is faced with the largest yet and the one that includes the greatest diversity of states. These changes raise questions as to its ability to coalesce, given the relatively weak nature of the EU institutions.

Finally, again in contrast to the U.S., Canada and the EU have long been grappling with the fundamental question as to how to found the entity on a popular footing that is accepted by all those affected (states, would-be states, nations, regions and groups). In other words, in both entities there is a deep tension as to what are the core sources of legitimacy. Further, whilst this question remains unresolved in both places, their approach to *how* to resolve it shows remarkable similarity for two entities that are otherwise so different. It is also important to underline that the U.S. has resolved this question as to where sovereignty is ultimately located. The U.S. has had an agreed-upon constitution for a long time, and this constitution enjoys a great measure of legitimacy. In the following I will spell out in some further detail the nature of this similarity between Canada and the EU.

*The Search for Legitimacy*

The question of who are the ultimate sources of legitimacy remains contested in the EU and in Canada. Whereas the U.S. has long had a system of government based on an explicit popular sanction, formally speaking the constitutional systems of Canada and the EU have only had a *derivative* status. In formal terms, final say on Canada's constitution (pre-Constitution Act 1982) ultimately rested in the UK. In real terms, of course, final decision-making power rested in Canada. However, the notion that Canadians until 1982 had not yet constituted themselves as a people (Russell 1993: ix) carried with it great symbolic importance. The patriation of the Constitution in 1982, therefore, was a turning point. However, Quebec's failure to sign the Constitution Act signalled that there was no easy transition to popular sovereignty. Rather the patriation of the Constitution took place in a period of 'mega-constitutional politics' (Russell, 1993) and where different visions of the polity – its founding principles and their institutional manifestations – went through an unprecedentedly profound and intense debate:

> Constitutional politics at the mega level is distinguished in two ways from normal constitutional politics. First, mega constitutional politics goes beyond disputing the merits of specific constitutional proposals and addresses the very nature of the political community on which the constitution is based. Mega constitutional politics, whether directed towards comprehensive constitutional change or not, is concerned with reaching agreement on the identity and fundamental principles of the body politic. The second feature of mega constitutional politics flows from the first. Precisely because of the fundamental nature of the issues in dispute – their tendency to touch citizens' sense of identity and self-worth – mega constitutional politics is exceptionally emotional and intense. When a country's constitutional politics reaches this level, the constitutional question tends to dwarf all other public concerns (Russell 1993: 75).

From the late 1970s, Canada went through three major efforts at constitutional change: the patriation of the Constitution in 1982, the Meech Lake Accord of 1987 and the Charlottetown Accord of 1992. The first was not signed by the province of Quebec, the second rejected by two provinces and the third was rejected in a nation-wide referendum. Canada is quite unique in that it has been involved in mega constitutional politics for such a long period of time (from the mid-1960s on). Mega constitutional politics, although it certainly can take place within an established constitutional framework, is more appropriately labelled constitution-making than constitutional change, as in principle the entire constitutional system is at stake.

In the case of the EU, its constitutional system – insofar as it can be deemed as such[2] – was forged through the Member States' acts of treaty-making and change and through a teleological interpretation of the Treaties by the Court of Justice. Its democratic legitimacy was indirect and was derived from the democratic quality of the Member States, as well as based on performance (Beetham and Lord 1998, Fossum 2000). The Treaty of Maastricht (1991) was the first clear sign of change. The establishment of Political Union and Union citizenship signalled a move in the direction of, whilst clearly not reaching, direct legitimation. The Treaty of Amsterdam (1997) and the Nice Treaty (2000) and the Charter Declaration (2000) are further steps in that direction. The EU has thus also long been involved in an almost continuous and ongoing effort at polity-building a process, which is now referred to as constitution making. But the EU has still not settled the issue of where its legitimacy resides.

*Common Departures in Terms of Handling the Process of Constitution-making/change*

Canada and the EU not only grapple with the same general problems in terms of constitution-making/change – also the process through which these problems have been handled exhibits similar traits. This applies both to the initial elitist manner of organising the process *and* to how it has changed in response to popular challenge. The basic character of the initial system in both entities and the change it has undergone is only briefly covered here.

In both entities, the executive officials (heads of governments and their supportive staffs) have played a most important role in fashioning comprehensive changes of a constitutional nature (Macmillan and Laureshen 1990, Fossum 1998, 2000). From a democratic constitutional perspective, in its clearest and sharpest form, this approach to treaty/constitution making has had an element of 'constitutional avoidance' built into it.[3] In the EU, up to the most-recent round (which was due to result in a (constitutional) treaty in 2004), treaty changes are handled in Intergovernmental Conferences, so-called IGCs (albeit the Convention has opened this up, and if adopted the method would be modified). During an IGC the heads of government from each member state come together in the European Council (EC) at meetings 2-3 times a year and, as a body, is responsible for treaty changes. Despite its obvious and recently strengthened supranational features, in the EU, treaty changes are conducted by what largely amounts to a 'diplomatic' intergovernmental approach. Every member state is equipped with a veto. Thus, although the EU is involved in constitution-making, treaty changes are negotiated by executive heads of government and their respective staffs, in a formal system of summitry, with the European Council at its apex, rather than in specifically designated constitutional conferences. Ratification procedures vary, from parliamentary ratification to popular referendum. In formal terms, the European Parliament has no role in the process.[4]

The system of treaty change that has emerged in the EU, finds an obvious parallel in the initial Canadian approach to constitutional change (pre-Charlottetown), although the two are not synonymous. Here the heads of government – from the federal and each provincial government – come together in a system termed the First Ministers' Conference (FMC). It is this body that has played the most important role in the numerous efforts to fashion constitutional change in Canada. In Canada there has never really been agreement on how constitutional changes should be organised. Despite this, the mainstay of the system, in particular up until 1980 was the First Ministers' Conference (FMC). Since then, the process of Canadian constitution making has become more complex, but the executive heads have never relinquished their role as the core actors in constitutional change. The Canadian parallel to the European Council is the First Ministers' Conference, which is based on a similar logic to that of the EU, insofar as each participating government is popularly elected; each First Minister is held accountable by the relevant legislative assembly; and each First Minister has the *de facto* power to veto a proposal.[5]

*Opening Up the Processes*

The acrimonious atmosphere and lack of real results at Nice (2000) and more recently again in Brussels (December 2003), has exacerbated the imminent challenge of large-scale enlargement. It took the Laeken European Summit in December 2001 for the heads of government to acknowledge that the questions facing the EU were of a constitutional nature (cf. Laeken Declaration). This declaration also contained the decision to establish the Convention on the Future of Europe. This Convention has now been dubbed the *Constitutional Convention*. Its mandate was sufficiently broad for it to forge a proposal for a European constitution. Such a result, as initially expressed by its Chairman, Valerie Giscard d'Estaing,[6] was embraced by most of the Convention members, was adopted by the IGC as the proposal to be discussed, but failed to obtain unanimous support in Brussels in December 2003, with a final decision likely by Fall of 2004.[7]

The Convention on the Future of Europe was set up to serve as a preparatory body for treaty change. But it was a far more representative body than those used in the previous IGCs. It resembles the Convention that forged the Charter of Fundamental Rights of the European Union in terms of composition (it is made up of a majority of parliamentarians: 46 out of 66 voting members, and 26 out of 39 from the candidate countries). Its deliberations were public, and so were the relevant documents.[8] It organised links to civil society organisations and was open to inputs and submissions from civil society actors. The Convention was a far more open body than any previous such kind used in matters of a constitutional nature in the EU. There was wide agreement among the participants that the Convention obtained more in the constitutional sense than would any IGC.[9] But a critical issue that marked its work and that still remains is how much of its work will be embraced by the masters of the treaties, the Member State executives. The question that still remains is whether the Convention will leave any significant impact on the deliberations of the subsequent IGC, given the breakdown of the European Council talks in December of 2003 in Brussels.

The Convention's Draft contained the complete Charter (in Part II, the constitutional part). If adopted, the Charter will then be part of the EU's Constitutional Treaty.[10] The European Charter, insofar as this happens, can be construed as one means of equipping the EU with a direct and rights-based mode of legitimation.[11] Given that the Convention's Constitutional Treaty differs from a state-based democratic constitution, this could open up the prospect of a significant Charter-infused change in the constitutional make-up of the EU.[12]

The patriation of the Constitution and the inclusion of the Charter in the Constitution Act 1982 could be construed as similar efforts to entrench the Canadian constitution, in a more explicit sense, in the notion of popular sovereignty. When viewed in retrospect, the Canadian Charter has led to a significant transformation of the Canadian constitution, the Canadian political landscape and Canadian political culture (Cairns 1988, 1991a, 1992, 1995, Morton and Knopff 1999, Taylor 1993).

In Canada the question of how comprehensive constitutional changes should be organised has been one of the most widely debated and fought over political issues since the late 1970s. Opposition to what has come to be seen as an elitist process of constitutional change has included a wide range of demands. This includes, for instance, (a) demands from various interest-groups and so-called constitutional stake-holders for access to the process so that their interests be protected in the different stages of the process (for instance women's groups, aboriginals, and disabled people); (b) demands for a more prominent role for deliberative bodies in the process of change, (c) demands for direct participation in the process of constitutional deliberation by hitherto excluded groups – in particular aboriginals or first nations groups; (d) demands for a truly consultative and open process, that is, one that is based on debates and deliberations at all stages of the process, and (e) demands for a popular referendum to sanction the proposed changes. At various stages and points in time, many of these demands have been addressed and some have been met. The Charlottetown Accord process "reversed the stages of the Meech round: this time public discussion of constitutional options – lots of it – preceded negotiation of an agreement" (Russell 1993:157). The Citizens' Forum engaged 400,000 Canadians in discussions on the future of the country.   In the Forum open parliamentary hearings and five 'mini-constituent assemblies' were organised over five weekends (Russell 1993:177) prior to the intergovernmental negotiations.

In sum, both entities have undergone lengthy and protracted processes of constitution-making, where the very notion of how to *organise the process* has become highly contested. Both have gone from constitution making being conducted by executive officials, in closed settings with a highly elitist flair to far more open and inclusive processes. These examples reveal that the search for an acceptable process of forging the constitution is vitally important and is considered an intrinsic part of the legitimacy of the resultant output. The two examples also reveal an unusually high degree of experimentation as to process, over time, and in response to various demands.

## How to Compare the Two Entities?

In the above it has been shown that the EU and Canada both grapple with fundamental questions. The requisite solutions may not be compatible with those available from the nation state as organisational form and mode of association. To shed further light on this, a comparative approach can be useful. But this requires thinking carefully through how we use comparison. As Francis Castles notes "comparison is not merely a means of explanation or hypothesis testing, but also a mode of locating and exploring a phenomenon as yet insufficiently understood, and … these two functions can and should be iterative in character" (Castles 1989, 9). If we think of comparison not merely as method, but also as *strategy*, in other words, as an integral part of theorising, we can use it to get a better sense of the magnitude and direction of transformation that these entities go through and respond to.

This work draws on Charles Tilly's strategies of comparison. Tilly's approach permits us to use comparison as strategy so as to assess the multiplicity of *forms* that a phenomenon takes. This ranges from single – meaning that common properties are shared among all instances of a phenomenon – to multiple –

meaning that there are many forms of the phenomenon. The other dimension, that of *share*, ranges from one single instance – where the objective is to get the characteristics of the particular case right – to all instances – where the objective is to get the characteristics of all cases right. When combined in a four-fold table these two dimensions yield four *strategies of comparison*, individualising, universalising, variation-finding, and encompassing.

MULTIPLICITY OF FORMS[13]

|  |  | SINGLE ⟶ MULTIPLE | |
|---|---|---|---|
| SHARE OF ALL INSTANCES | One | Individualizing | Encompassing |
|  | All | Universalizing | Variation-Finding |

**Figure 2.1    The Four Strategies for Comparison**

The strategies differ in terms of what aspects of transformation they focus on. They also differ with regard to the relevance of the comparison of Canada with the EU.

**The Individualising Strategy**

An individualizing strategy is intended to "contrast specific instances of a given phenomenon as a means of grasping the peculiarities of each case" (Tilly 1984, 82). When the entity in question is not well enough understood this is a very useful strategy. Much of the debate on the EU has been focused on how to conceive of the entity as a political system or as a polity. Many analysts underline its uniqueness and hence underline the need for an individualising strategy of comparison. An obvious point of departure here is that the European Union is a highly complex entity, and holds a number of features that set it apart from any nation state (Schmitter 1992, 1996, Preuss 1996, Weiler 1995). Consider further the statement by The Reflection Group that was set up to prepare the EU for the IGC-96. In its report it stated that "(t)he Union is not and does not want to be a super-state. Yet it is more than a market. It is a unique design based on common values. We should strengthen these values [...]" (SN 520/95 and 5082/95 in EP White Paper I: 154, 29).

The EU also does not have a clearly defined territory. Some analysts find it better to think of it as marked by variable geometry. It does not have a clearly established centre of authority. Its institutional make-up is marked by a complex mixture of supranational, transnational and international features and therefore includes both intergovernmental and federal elements. Its complex nature is reflected in the sheer range of institutional forms and depictions that analysts have resorted to. Analysts portray the EU variously as (a) a system of *multi-level governance*, such as a multi-level polity (Marks et al. 1996), or a mixed commonwealth (Bellamy and Castiglione, 1997); or *condominio consortio* (Schmitter, 1992, 1996); or as *some form of transition*, such as partial polity (Wallace, 1993: 101); or as post-national entity (Curtin 1997, Eriksen and Fossum 2000, Habermas 1998a, Habermas 1998b, Habermas 2000); or in *globalist terms*, such as cosmopolitanism (Held 1993, 1995, Linklater 1996, 1998). The complex question of labelling this entity has prompted some analysts to designate the EU as an *objet politique nonidentifié* (Schmitter 2000: 2).

Similarly, the debate on the Canadian constitutional experience has also been quite introspective, with very few real efforts at comparison. There are some comparisons of Canada and other states,[14] but few efforts to tease out in a more systematic manner whether Canada is unique or represents something new in polity terms.[15]

The individualising strategy, in its pure form, "treats each case as unique, taking up one instance at a time, and minimizing its common properties with other instances" (Tilly 1984: 81). The academic issue at present appears to be less that of establishing the uniqueness of the EU and more that of establishing what it resembles. But it should also be noted that the EU has developed very rapidly and has established a political system, however inchoate. Thus the fast pace of change makes it very interesting to clarify the direction in which the EU has moved and that makes comparison even more essential. With regard to the EU, then, there appears to be a clear need for more rather than less comparison with other types of entities. On Canada, it seems important to establish its status. Perhaps this is best done through more rigorous comparisons with other states and entities. The individualising strategy is clearly useful but needs supplementing.

## The Universalising Strategy

The universalising strategy "aims to establish that every instance of a phenomenon follows essentially the same rule" (Tilly 1984: 82). The question then is what are the relevant rules? Since the EU and Canada hold traits that might set them apart from some of the tenets of the nation state, their status could be further clarified through examining how they relate to the rules pertaining to the process of nation-building and state formation. To study the EU and Canada in relation to this process, the point of departure would be to spell out the necessary and sufficient *conditions* for nation-state formation and also to try to identify various *stages* or *sequences* of this process. If our assumption is that the EU will eventually become a state, at some point it would have to pass through the same process or stages that all states have gone through. For instance, Stein Rokkan has identified four stages, as part of state formation and nation building: penetration, standardisation, participation, and redistribution.[16] For this to constitute a truly universal process, all states would have to pass through all these stages, in the same sequence. But this scheme could be modified so as to talk of the need to go through all stages, but not that all entities have to go through the stages *in the same sequence*. This is also how Stein Rokkan used his model.

The universalising strategy could be used to try to establish the extent to which the EU and Canada comply with the rules we can establish as characteristic of state formation and nation building. The EU, from its early beginnings was barred from developing those traits that are characteristic of states in their infancy, namely military and extractive apparatus.[17] It started out as an economic type of organisation with a very limited ability to control the territory, which it encompasses. Thus, if it becomes a state, it will clearly have reversed the sequencing of stages. At present, however, it is still an entity in the making and is no less subject to the threat of unravelling, reversal, and fragmentation, as is Canada. This uncertainty has also made it imperative to understand the specifics of this entity. Therefore, alternatives to the universalising strategy had to be developed and so the individualising one has been frequently used as a basis for comparison.

Applying the universalising strategy to the Canadian case, we note that Canada has not yet succeeded in becoming a unified nation-state. Northrop Frye has noted that Canada "has passed from a pre-national to a post-national phase without ever having become a nation (Frye cited in Lipset 1990: 6). The failure to agree on a uniform conception of Canada has beleaguered the country since its inception. Canada has never fully completed the first of Rokkan's two stages, penetration and standardisation. On the question of penetration, i.e. territorial control, Canada still faces the spectre of secession, fragmentation or even dismantling, as well as eventual absorption into a North American system, through NAFTA and through other very close ties with the US.[18] The threat of Quebec separation looms less starkly now than just a few years ago but it still exists. If such a movement were to re-emerge, it could rekindle several of the issues discussed in the mid-1990s. During the 1995 referendum, it appeared that there was no agreement as to what territory would make up an independent Quebec. This problem was compounded by pleas for partition from both inside and outside Quebec. Partitionists claimed that if Canada was divisible then it follows that Quebec likewise could be divided.[19] Second, in the case of Quebec separation, there may still not be any automatic assurance that the Rest-of-Canada would stay united. The Rest-of-Canada would likely have to be reconstituted. There are numerous regional and other tensions within Canada, which would likely make the process of reconstitution into a very complicated affair. However, in the last five years steps have been taken to establish a set of procedures for how a separation could come about. Among these steps are the Supreme Court's secession reference and the Federal Clarity Act – but even here Quebec separatist governments have disputed the findings and challenged the legitimacy of the Supreme Court to make such rulings.

Another prominent issue that has emerged in Canada is that of aboriginal self-government. Extensive aboriginal self-government – in territorial and jurisdictional terms – will not break up the country but will likely produce a far more complex conception of the location of sovereignty and the nature of citizenship. These issues arise out of the fact that Canada has never resolved the fundamental question as to where sovereignty is ultimately to be located.[20]

From these observations we may assert that in Canada it is still contested as to who should penetrate the territory, and how this should be done. The same applies to the standardisation stage. The Canadian debate has focused on how Canada deviates from successful attempts at forging unified nations and whether Canada is doomed to fail as a nation state. A veritable barrage of books has been written on the possible or even imminent failure of Canada.[21]

The above examples show that given their complex nature in territorial and communal terms, the EU and Canada are marked by particularly complex conceptions of identity, community and citizenship. Both entities are marked by a wide range of identities with complex and multi-faceted levels of attachment. At present, no one national identity can legitimately claim to be dominant in either case. For instance, in the EU, there is no single language, ethnic group or nation that can command majority support. There are fifteen national identities embedded in states, in a number of would-be nations, and in regions with well-developed regional identities. There is no clearly-defined European identity, although there have been numerous efforts to create one. But even these efforts are based on far more inclusive and universalist traits than those associated with national identity (Fossum 2001).

In Canada, although there is a clear majority of English-speakers, there are four sets of national identifications that are currently being promoted: a) rest-of-Canada Canadian nationalism (or Canada-without-Quebec nationalism), b) Quebecois nationalism, c) Aboriginal nationalism, and d) Canadian nationalism (Canada as it exists today). For Canada as a whole, language as a basis for identity is highly divisive, and has always been so. In addition, in recent years, as a result of large-scale immigration from all parts of the world and in particular from developing countries, and as a result of aboriginal quests for self-government, its cultural and ethnic composition have become far more complex and contested.

Perhaps it is more appropriate to label the EU and Canada 'post-national' rather than multinational. Both entities have supported a range of identities that are not based on and which may even challenge the link between state and nation.[22] Such identities may or may not have an explicit territorial reference – some may, for instance, be based on region or on gender. The entities also hold traits of what Charles Taylor has termed 'deep diversity'.[23] On Canada, Charles Taylor has observed that "(i)n a way, accommodating difference is what Canada is all about" (Taylor, 1993: 181).

It is also worth reiterating that with regard to participation, both entities have faced popular challenges to their initial executive-based and elitist manner of conduction the process of constitution making. They have responded to these challenges by opening up the processes. In the Canadian case, this helped create both a far more complex and unwieldy process and also a far more complex outcome (Charlottetown). In the EU the effects remain to be seen.

These examples suggest that neither Canada nor the EU have gone through some of the key stages in the process of state formation and nation building. This does not rule out that they may go through the stages in a different order. Whether they do or not, they may represent different conceptions of political community. They raise questions as to what polity-making entails in the contemporary world. Is it a more uncertain process than before, with little precise knowledge of both the nature and the direction of change? To use this strategy as a way to study how well the two entities comply with the standard tenets of the nation-state may not yield much reliable information, as the nation-state itself is transforming. Further, with regard to the question of nation-state transformation, we still do not know whether there is a uniform process at work. How then to capture the key features of the EU and Canada? The two last strategies may yield additional insights here.

**The Variation-finding Strategy**

The variation-finding strategy seeks to "establish a principle of variation in the character or intensity of a phenomenon having more than one form by examining systematic differences among instances" (Tilly 1984: 116). Barrington Moore used this strategy in his discussion of different forms of transitions to modern politics, i.e. to explain why some countries opted for capitalist democracy, fascism, socialism, and stalled democracy, respectively (Barrington Moore 1966, Tilly 1984). Moore's strategy was retrospective, in that it sought to trace the historical causes of different regime choices. Modernisation is the general phenomenon and regime form is the source of variation. A set of possible causal factors was identified and applied to the whole range of cases, to establish why this pattern emerged.

Patterns of variation could emerge through the establishment of different forms of organisation, such as supranational organisation, trans-national organisation, and novel types of international regimes. A retrospective approach would first seek to establish systematic similarities and differences among these and then search for the historical causes of the choice of different organisational forms. One relevant question could be to establish *why* it is that Western Europe, historically a state system, should now exhibit strong tendencies to depart from some of the core characteristics of this system, at the same time that the nation state template continues to be spread globally and adopted by other parts of the world. Canada also appears to be deviating from this template in important respects, whereas the U.S. appears to have had less of a tendency to do so. The patterns of polity change appear quite uneven. It may therefore be quite useful to search for relevant sources of variation, within certain given parameters, as permitted by this strategy.

One approach might be to use this strategy to examine whether the EU and Canada represent different cases of distinctly different forms of democratically sanctioned (or driven) departures from the standard tenets of the nation-state model. The EU has its roots in the state form and has been forged largely through interstate co-operation, and exhibits transformation of the nation-state form through the formation of an entity on top of established states, an entity with strong supranational characteristics. Insofar as it is novel, its novelty will be reflected in the institutions at the EU level, as well as at the member state level, as both differ from existing nation states. This would then be one case of departure from the nation-state. The EU has established democracy and the rule of law as guiding principles and it also requires that applicant states comply with these principles in order to become members. The EU also has very weak sanctioning abilities and relies on procedures that are subject to democratic sanction, albeit often deficient in relation to those we associate with democracy at the national level. The key point, however, is that insofar as the EU does comply with these criteria and insofar as it does represent the development of a new type of entity, it could be the first new type of polity that has emerged through peaceful and democratic means. Canada, on the other hand, may be a democratic departure from the nation-state model on the basis of *one* existing state (with several nations or would-be nations).[24] Canada is a democracy and has sought to abide by democratic procedures in its efforts at constitutional reconfiguration.

The variation-finding strategy helps establish whether these represent two different cases of democratic departures from the nation-state model, i.e. 'from within' a single state and 'from without', through the transformation of a system of states. However, to properly address this, the type of variation-finding strategy we need cannot merely be retrospective, as the two entities in their present state hardly constitute departures in a formal, principled sense. The comparison needs a certain prospective element. The prospective approach "begins with a particular historical condition and searches forward to the alternative outcomes of that condition, with a specification of the paths leading to the outcomes" (Tilly 1975: 14). Such an approach would be compatible with critical perspectives in International Relations, which "seek to identify the prospects for change in global politics – latent though they may be at present" (Linklater 1998: 22). This strategy then appears to have merit, with democracy as the common element, and regime form, as the source of variation.

The onus on the prospective element also shows up the obvious limitation in this strategy: it is not clear that either entity represents a clear-cut case of departure. The source of variation remains imprecise. Can the last strategy remedy this defect?

## The Encompassing Strategy

The fourth and last strategy, encompassing, "places different instances at various locations within the same system, on the way to explaining their characteristics as a function of their varying relationships to the system as a whole" (Tilly 1984: 83).

This strategy is premised on the presence of a large structure or process that the entities are located in relation to. One such large process could be globalisation. Globalisation has many carriers, and proceeds along a number of different dimensions. The first of two will be highlighted here. The first is the development of international and supranational legal norms, the second is the global spread of the capitalist mode of production, which is also entrenched in international and supranational legal norms. Before spelling these out, it is useful to spell out how globalisation contributes to the transformation of the state. David Held provides a broad-based assessment of how globalisation affects the state:

> first, the way processes of economic, political, legal and military interconnectedness are changing the state from above, as its 'regulatory' ability is challenged and reduced in some spheres; secondly, the way local groups, movements and nationalisms are questioning the nation-state from below as a representative and accountable power system; and thirdly, the way global interconnectedness creates chains of interlocking   political decisions and outcomes among states and their citizens, altering the nature and dynamics of national political systems themselves (Held 1993: 39).

These developments can be placed within the framework of the encompassing strategy, when the system of international and supranational law is thought of as the emerging structure, and the varied responses to this development as reflective of the entities' varying relationship to this system. Andrew Linklater's observation to the effect that "One result of globalisation and fragmentation is that new state structures which combine greater universalism with increased sensitivity to difference become possible in Europe and elsewhere in 'the pacified core..." (Linklater 1998: 8) is useful precisely because it brings forth the dynamic interaction between a uniform development and the varied responses to it that the entities take. As both the EU and Canada have been subject to the effects of globalisation, they both face stronger pressures for universalism and simultaneously for sensitivity to difference. As such, their vulnerability also makes them less imbued with the weaknesses of the nation-state as harbinger of democracy – elements such as the exclusion of non-nationals and intolerance of difference.

Below, in what follows, international developments are first mapped out, and then we will attempt to situate the EU and Canada within these developments. International law today represents a challenge to state sovereignty. Individuals and groups are recognised as legal subjects of international law, not only states. Further, the realm of international law is changing. It was earlier primarily focused on political and geopolitical matters but has become increasingly focussed on regulation of economic, social, communication and environmental matters. Concomitant with these developments is a change in the sources of international law. To a far greater extent than before the very sources of international law are international treaties or conventions, international custom and practice, and "the underlying principles of law recognized by 'civilized nations'" (Held et al. 2000: 63). One effect has been to generate an increased focus on the relation between the individual and their own government. Held et al. note that: "International law recognizes powers and constraints, and rights and duties, which have qualified the principle of state sovereignty in a number of important respects; sovereignty *per se* is no longer a straightforward guarantee of international legitimacy. Entrenched in certain legal instruments is the view that a legitimate state must be a democratic state that upholds certain common values" (Held et al. 2000: 65).

These legal developments have been particularly prominent in Europe, notably through the European Convention on Human Rights (ECHR of November 4, 1950) and European Law, where the two converge within the field of human rights. Here The ECHR "allows individual citizens to initiate proceedings against their own governments." What is especially unique here is that it is a European court which rules and binds the states, a court that is not part of the jurisdiction of the state. "Within this framework, states are no longer free to treat their own citizens as they think fit... The European Convention on Human Rights is most explicit in connecting democracy with state legitimacy, as is the statute of the Council of Europe, which makes a commitment to democracy a condition of membership" (Held et al. 2000: 68-9). These legal developments have contributed to the most explicit curtailments of state sovereignty occurring in Western Europe. This development is no doubt greatly reinforced and given added strength by the development of the EU as a supranational structure of governance. This development is endowed with further symbolic credibility by the Charter of Fundamental Rights of the European Union, which drew heavily on this emerging international system of rights (Tarschys and Menendez in Eriksen et al. 2003). This international system of rights was also important to the formation of the Canadian Charter. Alan Cairns notes that: "As the idea of entrenched rights became a powerful norm, countries without them could be seen as defying the spirit of the times. Writing in 1968, the Canadian legal scholar Maxwell Cohen asserted that 'Human rights became...within the past twenty years, an important piece of "debating" language ...part of the political dialogue, part of the debating experience of peoples in all parts of the world, even those in affluent societies'" (Cairns in Eriksen et al. 2003. Quotation cited in Cairns 1992, 28-29). Cairns goes on to note that international developments served to facilitate the developments of the Canadian Charter but the factors triggering this were domestic. The latter were also critical in the Canadian particular approach to accommodation of universalism and difference, as reflected in group-based rights and in the so-called notwithstanding clause, which permitted governments to opt out of some of the provisions of the Charter for renewable periods of 5 years.

International legal developments within the field of human rights strengthen the universalism element of each legal system. This contributes to the formation of more complex notions of legitimacy. At the same time they also aid in the development of group-based rights, hence helping to foster a different constellation of universalism – different than that which marks the states system. Consider a Canadian example: the pre-patriation constitutional system was based on two principles, namely parliamentary sovereignty at the federal and provincial level, and a second principle, the federal principle (which implies non-centralisation). In formal terms, the 1867 BNA Act gave the federal government a privileged position, but the initial British and consequent federal government preponderance in constitutional matters has been successfully challenged by provincial governments. The federal government's claim to prevalence has received scant support. The province of Quebec has long sought veto in constitutional matters and has traditionally conceived the process as bilateral, because Quebec separatists have conceived of Quebec as a nation on a par with the rest-of-Canada. This two-nation view of Canada has been challenged by the other provinces, which have argued that the federal principle entails provincial equality. No single province will have unique weight or importance in constitutional deliberations. Neither of these two principles – national and provincial equality – has been fully accepted. The patriation of the constitution in 1982, with the Charter of Rights and Freedoms, amplified the constitutional salience of a third principle of equality, that of equality of citizens,[25] or that of rights-based legitimation. This mode of legitimation, which is largely based on the notion of individual autonomy and popular sovereignty, challenges the notion of parliamentary sovereignty. Rights-based legitimation is premised on every citizen as a rights bearer who has a direct stake in the constitution because for the people to be truly sovereign, in normative terms, they have to consider themselves, and be considered as, the authors of the law (Habermas 1996). In Canada, then, three principles of equality vie for space: equality of nations, equality of provinces, and equality of citizens. Within this framework, the tension between universalism and difference plays itself out, and its accommodation is now both directly fed by and dependent on international developments.

The question of the legitimacy of the EU has become more similar to that of Canada. The EU is not only in the process of abandoning its initial indirect mode of legitimation – which was based on the parliamentary or popular (through referenda) sovereignty of each member state,[26] after Maastricht it has also sought to develop a more independent approach to legitimation which is particularly focussed on individual rights. Thus, although the question is more complex in the EU, there is a similar emerging tension between three principles of equality that resemble those that mark the present Canadian situation. The EU is seen as primarily based on the equality of member states, although this is challenged by two additional pleas for equality, that of equality of citizens and to a somewhat less extent that of equality of regions (nation-identifying ones as well as non-nation identifying ones).[27]

These principles speak to different ways of accommodating the tension between universalism and difference. The nation-state has provided one template for how this tension has played itself out, but its dominance may also serve to obfuscate the range of actual variation. An encompassing strategy may help tease this out and also yield added insights into how the important normative challenges that this tension encompasses can be handled.

**Conclusion**

In this chapter a number of reasons for why we might prefer to compare and contrast the EU with Canada, over comparing with the US are first listed. This is not to deny the usefulness of including the US. It is only to assert that there are as yet unexplored avenues that warrant further examination. To argue that two entities are comparable in some salient respects, is not akin to establishing what added insights such comparisons may yield. A more systematic examination of *how* entities might be compared is useful, in that it may help tease out the underlying patterns of similarity and difference, patterns that a simple juxtaposition will not easily reveal.

The chapter then went on to use Tilly's strategies of comparison, and discuss each of these in relation to Canada and the EU. The application of the strategies to the two entities would bring all the common factors listed initially into play, and would also force us to rank-order them in terms of salience. As such, the examination of how to compare is theoretically salient.

Whilst the individualising strategy is important, if this becomes the dominant strategy, we might end up losing touch with what are the truly unique features of the EU because we lose sight of what should be the point of reference. The universalising strategy has then the merit of helping us uncover the extent to which the EU does deviate from the usual process of state formation and nation building. Here the problem is that the stages can be reversed and also that there is no assurance that such a process will unfold in this way. What may appear as a similar line of development, could over time develop along a very different path and produce a very different type of political entity. To handle this problem, we need to keep alive the prospect that the entity in question may develop along a different path; hence we need to be cognisant of other paths and possible polities. To this end, it was argued that the two most useful strategies that were examined in relation to the EU and Canada are the variation-finding and the encompassing strategies. Both strategies are sensitive to the notion that the nation state and the nation state system are historical fixtures, which emerged in a particular set of historical circumstances, but they accept that the nation-state will be transformed if and when such fundamental conditions change. The strategies differ in that the variation-finding looks for different departures from the nation-state, whereas the encompassing looks at how the two cases respond to and develop novel responses to the moral universalism – cultural difference axis. The point in using these strategies is to strengthen the attention to what are truly unique aspects of the EU, through a more broad-based systematic assessment of similarities and differences. The point here is that no one or two strategies are better than any other – that cannot really be established *a priori*. If anything, the process of comparison is helped precisely when we use several and perhaps even combine strategies over time. One important challenge is to be clear on how we proceed in our comparative work, i.e. which strategy we are actually employing. Further, it would seem to be important to develop a clearer understanding of how the strategies can be used in conjunction with each other. Is there in the development of a political entity a particular strategy sequence? How useful would an explicit approach to the use of strategies be?


## Notes

1   Article 6(1), TEU, Official Journal C 340, 10.11.1997. European Parliament, Council and Commission "The Charter of Fundamental Rights of the European Union", Official Journal C364/8.18.12.2000.
2   Many analysts claim that it already has a material constitution. See Weiler 1995, 1999, Eriksen et al. 2003, forthcoming. Weiler has noted that the "condition of Europe ... is not, as is often implied, that of constitutionalism without a constitution, but of a constitution without constitutionalism. What Europe needs, thus, is not a constitution but an ethos and telos to justify, if they can, the constitutionalism it has already embraced" (Weiler, 1995: 220).
3   With regard to Canada this was a "conscious and habitual strategy of avoidance by which many of the 'big' questions were put aside or the response interminably delayed until some acceptable state of ripeness had blossomed... Basic constitutional issues were repeatedly shelved" (Cairns 1995: 103). On the EU pre-Maastricht, see for instance Weiler (1999).
4   This has frustrated many MEPs. Cf. EP Resolution of 17 May 1995, EP, Committee on Institutional Affairs CONF 4007/97. The EP has the right of assent only. MEPs claim that it was their efforts that led to the establishment of the Convention on the Future of Europe.
5   The Canadian federal parliament still has a more prominent role than its European counterpart, however.
6   D'Estaing, V. G. (2002) "Introductory Speech by president V. Giscard D'Estaing to the Convention on the future of Europe", SN1565/02.
7   There are opponents. See for instance the Contribution by Mr Jens-Peter Bonde, member of the Convention "The Convention about the Future of Europe", CONV 277/02, 01/10/2002, who argues for the need to develop two proposals.
8   They can be accessed from the Convention website. See http://european-convention.eu.int/
9   Barbier, Cecile (2002) "Results of the First Working Groups", Tomorrow Europe, December 2002, No. 11: 5.
10  http://european-convention.eu.int/bienvenue.asp?lang=EN
11  For more on these modes of legitimation see Fossum, 2000.
12  See Fossum 2002a for a comparison of the two charters, with special emphasis on the prospects for the EU Charter to spark a rights-based mobilisation in Europe.
13  Taken from Tilly 1984, 81.
14  See for instance Lipset's comparison of Canada and the U.S. (Lipset 1990).
15  See Fossum 2002b for one such assessment of Canada, and that also compares the EU and Canada.
16  Rokkan 1975 Rokkan's strategy is not universalising, as he acknowledges that entities can start with any one of these. Tilly labels Rokkan's strategy 'encompassing'.
17  It should be noted that the High Authority had a limited amount of taxing powers. See Article 49 in ECSC Treaty.
18  This has been a recurrent theme since the 1960s, at least. See for instance Grant 1966, Levitt 1970, Clarkson 1985, Fossum 1997.

19 The leader of the Reform Party, Preston Manning has noted that "if Canada is divisible, as long as the process employed respects the rule of law and the principle of democratic consent, then Quebec is divisible by the application of the same processes and the same principles." Remarks by Preston Manning, M.P.Leader of the Official Opposition, House of Commons – February 10, 1998, printed in Hansard.

20 For this point consult Cairns 1995 and Russell 1993. Russell notes that "the Canadian people may have become constitutionally sovereign without having constituted themselves a people. The Canadian people or peoples have not explicitly affirmed a common understanding of the political community they share" (235).

21 A small selection of titles of books and research reports would include: *The Secession of Quebec and the Future of Canada*; *Deconfederation: Canada Without Quebec*; *Must Canada Fail?*; *Secession: The Morality of Political Divorce from Fort Sumter to Lithuania and Quebec*; *One Country or Two? The Struggle for Quebec*; *Quebec-Canada: What is the Path Ahead?*; *The Collapse of Canada?*; *Dividing the House: Planning for a Canada without Quebec*; *Sovereign Injustice: Forcible Inclusion of the James Bay Crees and Cree Territory into a Sovereign Quebec*; *Tangled Web: Legal Aspects of Deconfederation*; *Breakup: The Coming End of Canada and the Stakes for America*; *Misconceiving Canada: The Struggle for National Unity Thinking about the Rest of Canada: Options for Canada without Quebec*; *'Cooler Heads Shall Prevail': Assessing the Costs and Consequences of Quebec Separation*; *Is Quebec Separatism Just?*; *Looking into the Abyss: The Need for a Plan C*; *La reve de la terre promise: Les couts de l'independance*; *Quebec-Canada: What is the Path Ahead?*; *Beyond Quebec: Taking Stock of Canada*; *Beyond the Impasse: toward reconciliation.*

22 For Canada see Cairns in Eriksen et al. forthcoming 2003 and Fossum 2001a, for the EU see Fossum, in Eriksen et al. 2003 and Fossum 2003.

23 To Taylor, deep diversity refers to a 'plurality of ways of belonging' to the Canadian federation and is open to multiple conceptions of citizenship which coexist within the same state (Taylor 1993).

24 Canada is often portrayed as a two-nation state. This has meant that there was no pre-existing agreement on a single Canadian nation, that could be defined along ethnic or linguistic lines and clearly sets Canada apart from its US counterpart. The key issue facing the American framers or 'Founding Fathers' was not to create one nation out of several, but rather what kind of government the nation should have. As Samuel Beer has observed, "(i)n the United States, nationalism is an indispensable support of federalism" (Beer, 1995: 225). Therefore, in the US, there was little problem in supporting diversity insofar as this would strengthen individual freedom: "the issue was to create a large country without destroying individual liberty and local initiative" (LaSelva 1996: xii). In Canada, since there was no pre-existing agreement on a single Canadian nation, the challenge was to establish a federal arrangement that could bridge the duality and foster an overarching sense of attachment to Canada. The importance of nationalism to the Canadian constitutional experience is revealed in the contrast between the Canadian term 'Founding Nations' as opposed to the American term 'Founding Fathers' (LaSelva 1996, Beer 1995).

25 For more comprehensive accounts of these 'three equalities' see Cairns (1991b: 77-100, 1995: 216-237), and Fossum (1994).

26 This notion of indirect legitimation entails that the EU's democratic legitimacy is to be based on the acknowledgement that the institutions at the EU-level are ultimately derived from the member-states, and as such are reflective of the interests and concerns of the member-states. In the draft entitled 'Report on The Functioning of the Treaty on European Union', it is observed that "(t)he Council is of course not subject to the control of the European Parliament, but it still seeks to ensure respect for the democratic functioning of the system, insofar as each of its members is politically responsible to the

national parliament before which he answers for the positions adopted at Union level" (Council of the European Union, 1995: 10). The EU is deemed to be democratic insofar as each member state is democratic, and insofar as the proposals are brought forth and sanctioned by each national parliament or by the populace if the parliament so deems. See also Beetham and Lord 1998a, 1998b, Wallace 1993 and Fossum 2000.

27  Powerful arguments can also be made that the nation state is an interregnum in Europe. See for instance Rokkan 1975, Fossum and Robinson 1999.

## References

Beer, S. (1995) "Federalism and the Nation State: What Can Be Learned from the American Experience?" in Knop, K., Ostry, S., Simeon, R. and Swinton, K. (eds) *Rethinking Federalism: Citizens, Markets, and Governments in a Changing World*, Vancouver: UBC Press.

Beetham, D. and C. Lord (1998a) "Legitimacy and the European Union", in Nentwich, M. and A. Weale, *Political Theory and the European Union*, London: Routledge.

Beetham, D. and C. Lord (1998b) *Legitimacy and the European Union*, London: Longman.

Bellamy, R. and D. Castiglione (1997) "Building the Union: The Nature of Sovereignty in the Political Architecture of Europe", *Law and Philosophy* 16: 421-45.

Bulmer, S.J. (1996) "The European Council and the Council of the European Union: Shapers of a European Confederation", *Publius* 26(4): 17-42.

de Burca, G. (1996) "The Quest for Legitimacy in the European Union", *The Modern Law Review*, 59:3, May 1996: 349-76.

Cairns, A.C. (1988) *Constitution, Government and Society in Canada*, Toronto: McClelland & Stewart.

Cairns, A.C. (1991a) *Disruptions: Constitutional Struggles from the Charter to Meech Lake*, Toronto: McClelland & Stewart.

Cairns, A.C. (1991b) "Constitutional Change and the Three Equalities", in Watts, D. and Brown, D.M. (eds) *Options for a New Canada*, Toronto: University of Toronto Press, 77-100.

Cairns, A.C. (1992) *Charter versus Federalism: The Dilemmas of Constitutional Reform*, Montreal & Kingston: McGill-Queen's University Press.

Cairns, A.C. (1995) *Reconfigurations: Canadian Citizenship and Constitutional Change*, Toronto: McClelland and Stewart Inc.

Cairns, A.C. (2003) "The Canadian Experience of a Charter of Rights", in Eriksen, E.O., Fossum, J.E. and A.J. Menéndez (eds) *The Chartering of Europe*, Baden-Baden: Nomos, pp. 93-111.

Canada, Department of Canadian Heritage (1999) *10th Annual Report on the Operation of the Canadian Multiculturalism Act*, Ottawa: Minister of Public Works and Government Services.

Castles, F. (1989) *The Comparative History of Public Policy*, Cambridge: Cambridge Polity Press.

Clarkson, S. (1985) *Canada and the Reagan Challenge*, Toronto: University of Toronto Press, 2nd ed.

Cook, C. (ed.) (1994) *Constitutional Predicament – Canada after the Referendum of 1992*, Montreal & Kingston: McGill-Queen's University Press.

Curtin, D. (1993) "The Constitutional Structure of the Union: A Europe of Bits and Pieces", *Common Market Law Review*, 30:17-69.

Curtin, D. (1997) *Postnational democracy: The European Union in search of a political philosophy*. The Hague: Kluwer Law.

Delanty, G. (1995) *Inventing Europe – Idea, Identity, Reality*, London: Macmillan.

Dehousse, R. "European Institutional Architecture after Amsterdam: Parliamentary System or Regulatory Structure?", EUI Working Paper RSC No 98/11. (http://www.iue.it/RSC7WP-Texts/98_11.html)

European Parliament (1995) *Resolution of 17 May 1995*, EP, Committee on Institutional Affairs CONF 4007/97.

Eriksen, E.O. (ed.) (1994) *Den politiske orden*, Bergen: TANO.

Eriksen, E.O. and J.E. Fossum (eds) (2000) *Democracy in the European Union – Integration through Deliberation?*, London: Routledge.

European Parliament, Intergovernmental Conference Task Force: "White Paper on the 1996 Intergovernmental Conference", Volume I, Luxembourg.

Fossum, J.E. (1994) "Nasjonalisme, føderalisme og konstitusjonalisme: Tre sentrale metaforer i kanadisk politikk", *Internasjonal Politikk*, 3, 363-390.

Fossum, J.E. (1998) "Executive Influence in the EU and Canada – A Brief Comparative Assessment", in Easingwood, P., Gross, K. and H. Lutz, *Informal Empire? Cultural Relations Between Canada, The United States and Europe*, published in Schriftenreihe des Zentrums fur Kanada Studien an der Universitat Trier, I&f Verlag, Kiel, Germany.

Fossum, J.E. and P.S. Robinson (1999), "A Phoenix Arises: The Social Reconstruction of Europe", *Policy, Society and Organisation* (Australia) 18.1-22.

Fossum, J.E. (2000) "Constitution-making in the European Union", in Eriksen, E.O. and Fossum, J.E. (eds), *Democracy in the European Union – Integration through Deliberation?*, London: Routledge.

Fossum, J.E. (2001) "Identity-politics in the European Union", *Journal of European Integration*, Vol.23, pp. 373-406.

Fossum, J.E. (2001) "Deep Diversity versus Constitutional Patriotism: Taylor, Habermas and the Canadian Constitutional Crisis", *Ethnicities*, Vol. 1, No.2, August, pp. 179-206.

Fossum, J.E. (2002a) "Charters and Constitution-Making. Comparing the Canadian Charter of Rights and Freedoms and the European Charter of Fundamental Rights", in Eriksen, E.O., Fossum, J.E. and A. Menendez (eds), *Constitution Making and Democratic Legitimacy*, ARENA Report No.5.

Fossum, J.E. (2002b) "The transformation of the nation-state: Why compare the EU and Canada?", ARENA Working Paper 28.

Fossum, J.E. "The European Union – In Search of an Identity", *European Journal of Political Theory*, Volume 2, No.3, 319-340.

Føllesdal, A. and P. Koslowski (eds) (1998) *Democracy and the European Union*, Berlin: Springer.

Giddens, A. (1990) *The Consequences of Modernity*, Cambridge: Polity Press.

Grant, G. (1965) *Lament for a Nation*, Toronto: McClelland and Stewart.

Habermas, J. (1993) "Struggles for recognition in constitutional states", *European Journal of Philosophy*, 1, 2: 128-155.

Habermas, J. (1994) "Struggles for Recognition in the Democratic Constitutional State", in Taylor, C. and Gutmann, A. (eds) *Multiculturalism: Examining the Politics of Recognition*, Princeton: Princeton University Press.

Habermas, J. (1995) *Diskurs, ratt och demokrati - Politisk-filosofiska texter i urval av Erik Oddvar Eriksen och Anders Molander*, Gøteborg: Daidalos.

Habermas, J. (1996) *Between Facts and Norms: Contributions to a Discourse Theory of Law and Democracy*, Cambridge, Mass.: The MIT Press.

Habermas, J. (1998) *The Inclusion of the Other – Studies in Political Theory*, Cambridge: Polity Press.

Habermas, J. (2001) *The Postnational Constellation: Political Essays*, Cambridge: Polity Press.

Held, D. (1993) "Democracy: From City-States to a Cosmopolitan Order?", in David Held (ed) *Prospects for Democracy: North, South, East, West*, Cambridge: Polity Press, pp. 13-52.

Held, D. (1995) *Democracy and the Global Order*, Cambridge: Polity Press.

Held, D., A. McGrew, D. Goldblatt and J. Perraton (2000) *Global Transformations*, Cambridge: Polity Press.

Honneth, A. (1995) *The Struggle for Recognition: the Moral Grammar of Social Conflicts*, Cambridge: Polity Press.

Howe, P. and P. Russell (2001) *Judicial Power and Canadian Democracy*, Montreal and Kingston: McGill-Queen's University Press.

Kagan, R. (2002) "Power and Weakness", *Policy Review*, No. 113, June-July: http://www.policyreview.org/JUN02/

Kymlicka, W. (1995) *Multicultural Citizenship. A Liberal Theory of Minority Rights*, Oxford: Clarendon.

Kymlicka, W. (1998) *Finding our way*, Oxford: Oxford University Press.

LaSelva, S.V. (1996) *The Moral Foundations of Canadian Federalism*, Montreal & Kingston: McGill-Queen's University Press.

Levitt, K. (1970) *Silent Surrender: The Multinational Corporation in Canada*. Toronto: Macmillan of Canada.

Linklater, A. (1996) "Citizenship and Sovereignty in the Post-Westphalian State", *European Journal of International Relations*, 2(1): 77-103.

Linklater, A. (1998) *The Transformation of Political Community*, Cambridge: Polity Press.

Lipset, S.M. (1990) *Continental Divide – The Values and Institutions of the United States and Canada*, New York: Routledge.

Macmillan, G. and Laureshen, N. (1990) "The Impact of Executive Decision-making in Federal and Quasi-federal Units: A Comparison of Canada and the European Community", Paper presented at the Annual Meeting of the Canadian Political Science Association, University of Victoria, May 27-29.

March, J.G. and J. P. Olsen (1989) *Rediscovering Institutions: The Organizational Basis of Politics*. New York: The Free Press.

March, J.G. and J.P. Olsen (1995) *Democratic Governance*, New York: The Free Press.

March, J.G. and J.P. Olsen (1998) "The institutional dynamics of international political orders", *International Organization* 52, 4: 943-969.

Marks, G., F.W. Scharpf, P.C. Schmitter and W. Streeck (1996) *Governance in theEuropean Union*, London: Sage.

Menéndez, A.J. (2003) "'Rights to Solidarity' – Balancing Solidarity and Economic Freedoms", in Eriksen, E.O., Fossum, J.E., and A.J. Menéndez (eds) *The Chartering of Europe*, Baden-Baden: Nomos, pp. 179-98.

Moore, Barrington (1967) *Social Origins of Dictatorship and Democracy: Lord and Peasant in the Making of the Modern World*, London: Penguin.

Morton, T. and R. Knopff (1999) *The Charter Revolution and the Court Party*, Peterborough, ON: Broadview Press.

Nickel, D. (1998) "The Amsterdam Treaty – a shift in the balance between the institutions!?", Harvard Law School, The Jean Monnet Chair, Working Papers 14/98. http://www.law.harvard.edu/programs/JeanMonnet/papers/98/98-14-C.html

Oakeshott, M. (1975) "The vocabulary of the modern European state", *Political Studies* 2-3: 319-341 and 4: 409-415.

Preuss, U.K. (1996) "Prospects of a Constitution for Europe", *Constellations*, Vol. 3 (no. 2): 209-224.

Rokkan, S. (1975) "Dimensions of state formation and nation building: a possible paradigm for research on variations within Europe", in Tilly, C. (ed) *The Formation of National States in Western Europe*, Princeton: Princeton University Press, pp. 562-600.

Ruggie, J.G. (1993) "Territoriality and beyond: problematizing modernity in international relations", *International Organization*, 47, 1: 139-74.

Russell, P.H. (1993) *Constitutional Odyssey: Can Canadians Become a Sovereign People?*, Toronto: University of Toronto Press, 2nd edition.

Sbragia, A. (ed) (1992) *Euro-Politics: Institutions and Policymaking in the "New" European Community*, Washington, D.C.: The Brookings Institution.

Scharpf, F. (1999) *Governing in Europe – Effective and Democratic?* Oxford: Oxford University Press.

Schmitter, P. (1992) "Representation and the Future Euro-polity", *Staatswissenschaft und Staatspraxis*, III(3): 379-405.

Schmitter, P. (1996) "Imagining the Future of the Euro-Polity with the Help of New Concepts", in Marks, G., Scharpf, F.W., Schmitter, P.C. and Streeck, W. (eds) *Governance in the European Union*, London: Sage, pp. 121-50.

Schmitter, P. (2000) *How to Democratize the European Union ... And Why Bother?*, Lanham: Rowman and Littlefield.

Smith, A.D. (1991) *National Identity*, London: Penguin.

Soysal, Y. (1994) *Limits of Citizenship – Migrants and Postnational Membership in Europe*, Chicago: University of Chicago Press.

Tarchys, D. (2003) "Goal Congestion – Multiple-Purpose Governance in the European Union", in Eriksen, E.O., Fossum, J.E. and A.J. Menéndez (eds) *The Chartering of Europe*, Baden-Baden: Nomos, pp. 161-78.

Taylor, C. (1985) *Human Agency and Language*, Cambridge: Cambridge University Press.

Taylor, C. (1986) *Philosophy and the Human Sciences*, Cambridge: Cambridge University Press.

Taylor, C. (1989) *Sources of the Self: The Making of the Modern Identity*, Cambridge, MA: Harvard University Press.

Taylor, C. (1993) *Reconciling the solitudes: essays on Canadian federalism and nationalism*, Montreal & Kingston: McGill-Queen's University Press.

Taylor, C. (1994) "The Politics of Recognition", in Taylor, C. and Gutmann, A. (eds) *Multiculturalism*, Princeton, N.J.: Princeton University Press.

Taylor, C. (1995) *Philosophical Arguments*, Cambridge, Mass.: Harvard University Press.

Tilly, C. (1975) (ed.) *The Formation of National States in Western Europe*, Princeton: Princeton University Press.

Tilly, C. (1984) *Big structures, large processes, huge comparisons*, New York: Russell Sage Foundation.

Wallace, H. (1993) "Deepening and Widening: Problems of Legitimacy for the EC", in S. Garcia (ed) *European Identity and the Search for Legitimacy*, London: Pinter, pp. 95-105.

Weale, A. and M. Nentwich (1998) (eds) *Political Theory and the European Union*, London: Routledge.

Weiler, J. (1995) "Does Europe Need a Constitution? Demos, Telos and the German Maastricht Decision", in *European Law Journal* 1(3): 219-58.

Weiler, J. (1999) *The Constitution of Europe, "Do the New Clothes Have an Emperor?" and other Essays on European Integration*, London: Cambridge University Press.

Chapter 3

# Toward a Canada-EU Partnership?

Donald Barry

## Introduction

Europe has long occupied a central place in Canada's foreign policy, not only as a region where major Canadian interests converge, but also as a counterweight to the country's highly imbalanced relationship with the United States. During the cold war years the North Atlantic Treaty Organization (NATO) was the principal link between Canada and Europe. As the cold war receded and European integration widened and deepened, the European Community (EC), known as the European Union (EU) since 1993, became an increasing focus of Canadian policy. This could be seen as early as 1976 when Canada and the EC concluded a "Contractual Link," which formalized economic consultation between them. In 1988 they established a "political dialogue" that gave Canada a link to the Community's developing European Political Cooperation (EPC) process on foreign policy. Two years later they signed a Transatlantic Declaration (TAD), which institutionalized high-level political contacts. This was followed in 1996 by the EU-Canada Political Declaration and Joint Action Plan to further cooperation on economic and trade matters, foreign policy and security, transatlantic issues, and new linkages, and in 1998 by the EU-Canada Trade Initiative (ECTI), created to advance the trade chapter of the Joint Action Plan.

NATO has been an important vehicle for enhancing Canada's defence. Moreover, the EU has long been the country's second largest trade and investment partner, although it trails the U.S. by a wide margin.[1] But the Canadian government's efforts to transform the alliance into a more broadly based "Atlantic Community" and promote North American and bilateral free trade with the EU have met with little success. As a middle power Canada lacks the political and economic weight of its U.S. and European partners whose interests dominate the transatlantic agenda. Current circumstances, though, may be more favourable to the development of closer Canada-EU relations. The establishment of the Joint Action Plan has broadened the range of contacts between Canada and the EU, creating new opportunities for cooperation. As well, growing business interest in the relationship may give new impetus to transatlantic trade liberalization. However, attitudes on both sides are a significant obstacle to efforts to deepen the relationship.

**The Atlantic Community**

"Canada," John Holmes once observed, "grew up in traction" (Holmes, 1976: 125). It was the product of a balancing act "between a declining but still imposing British hegemon and its rising North American challenger, the United States," in which it used its relationship with each as a counterbalance to the other (Sarty, 1993: 757). At the end of World War II Canada emerged as one of the strongest supporters of the creation of the United Nations (UN), which would ensure the participation of the United States and the United Kingdom in building a more durable world order and provide a forum in which Canada could manage its relations with those powers. When the cold war robbed the UN of its critical collective security function, Canada became the first country publicly to call for the creation of a North Atlantic security pact. The main purpose would be to link North America and Western Europe in a regional defence arrangement backed by American power. However, Canadian decision makers saw the pact as more than a military alliance. It would also serve as a means of building an Atlantic Community that would embrace economic cooperation. A broadly based alliance would constitute a "socio-economic alternative to communist ideology" and lessen the possibility that allied security cooperation would be impaired by quarrels over economic issues (Nossal, 1992: 84-85). Moreover, it would take the place of the "North Atlantic triangle," providing "a framework for conducting relations with Canada's most important partners where the disparity in power with the United States was diluted by the presence of the Europeans (Halstead, 1993: 153).[2]

After negotiations got under way Canada pressed for the inclusion of an article on non-military cooperation. Neither the Americans nor the Europeans showed any interest. They relented only when Ottawa threatened to reassess its participation if the provision were not adopted. The proposal became Article II of the 1949 NATO Treaty in which the members agreed to "contribute toward the further development of peaceful and friendly international relations by strengthening their free institutions, by bringing about a better understanding of the principles upon which these institutions are founded, and by promoting conditions of stability and well-being." They would also "seek to eliminate conflict in their international economic policies and will encourage economic collaboration between any or all of them." But Canadian efforts to breathe life into the article produced few results.

Despite its failure to institutionalize the Atlantic Community concept, Ottawa supported the integration of Western Europe as a means of reinforcing European security in NATO, while opposing a "dumbbell" or "two pillar" conception of the alliance that would subordinate Canada to the U.S. in a North American pillar (Pentland, 1991: 126). Ottawa looked to the General Agreement on Tariffs and Trade (GATT) as the principal instrument for managing its trade relations with the U.S. and Europe. Concerns about access to the EC market were, as Charles Pentland put it, "relatively muted." He adds, "The acceleration of internal tariff reductions, the inclusion of the new common external tariff in the successful Kennedy Round cuts in GATT, and the demand for imports and investment associated with rapid European economic growth, all meant that, except in the agricultural sector, the EC presented many opportunities for and few barriers to Canadian business. As long as this remained so, principled concerns about the fit between the CAP (Common Agricultural Policy) and the GATT or, more generally, the longer-term effects of regional blocs on the multilateral trading system, were likely to be of little practical consequence." Except for Prime Minister John Diefenbaker's government, Canadian decision makers "were content to seek trade access through multilateral channels, giving little consideration to a Community-oriented trade strategy as such" (Pentland, 1991: 126-127).[3]

## The Contractual Link

By the late 1960s concern about Canada's increasing trade and investment dependence on the U.S., together with the growing economic importance of the European Community and the likely economic impact of the U.K.'s pending entry into the EC, led Prime Minister Pierre Trudeau's government to focus its attention on Europe in a sustained way.[4] The government's 1970 review of external policy, Foreign Policy for Canadians, called for increased ties to Europe "to create a more healthy balance within the North Atlantic community and to reinforce Canadian independence" (SSEA, 1970: 14).

Canadian concerns took on a sense of urgency on August 15, 1971 when President Richard Nixon ended dollar-gold convertibility and placed a 10 per cent surcharge on all dutiable imports entering the U.S. in order to relieve persistent balance of payments problems. Ottawa, which had been exempted from similar actions in the past, sought relief from the measures, but its request was rejected. This led the government to make a fundamental reassessment of Canada's relations with the U.S. and gave impetus to the contemplated overture to Europe.

In the fall of 1971 Department of External Affairs officials presented a study to Cabinet, which identified three options for dealing with the U.S. These were: continuation of the status quo, closer integration, and a "long term strategy" to reduce dependence on the U.S. Cabinet chose the third alternative. The so-called "Third Option" consisted of internal measures to strengthen Canada's economy and culture, and diversification of external economic relations to counterbalance the country's relations with the U.S. The EC and Japan were identified as the most appropriate targets (SSEA, 1972).

Several obstacles stood in the way of closer Canada-EC relations. The first was the Community's inability to differentiate Canada's interests from those of the U.S. Contributing to this was the admitted "insubstantiality" of Canada's previous European policy. Although Ottawa had maintained relations with the EC since 1958, its principal links with Europe had been encompassed within NATO or pursued on a bilateral basis, especially with the U.K. and France. But by 1969 NATO appeared to be a diminished priority in Canadian policy, as demonstrated by the Trudeau government's decision to reduce Canada's troop strength in Europe. In addition, the U.K. was poised to join the EC, and relations with France were seriously strained as a result of President de Gaulle's support for Quebec independence. Also important was the structure of the GATT, which caused states to define their policies vis-à-vis major trading partners rather than smaller parties like Canada. Reinforcing this was the fact that Canada had worked closely with the U.S. in previous negotiating rounds.

The second obstacle was Washington's attitude toward any new Canada-EC arrangement. The source of Ottawa's concern was clear given Canada's highly imbalanced relationship with the U.S. and the likely effects of possible American retaliation. Similarly, the EC, which had been at odds with the U.S. over the Common Agricultural Policy, preferential agreements with third countries and Nixon's 1971 economic measures, did not want to aggravate its own strained relations with the Americans. U.S. officials had three preferences with respect to any Canada-EU arrangement: that it not be preferential, that it not be used as a vehicle for "ganging up" on the U.S., and that Canada not use any such arrangement to cut back on its trade with the U.S.

Finally, the European Commission, after it had become convinced of the utility of expanding the Community's relations with Canada, had to overcome the opposition of the U.K. and France. Both were reluctant to agree to any new relationship that could extend the Commission's powers beyond the traditional areas of commercial policy and foreign assistance contained in the Treaty of Rome at the expense of member states.

Canadian officials used several arguments to make the Community aware of Canada's distinctive interests. They contended that Canada and the EC shared an interest in maintaining a liberal international trading order, pointing to the dangers of a world composed of antagonistic trade blocs. Moreover, the complementarity of Canadian and EC economic structures offered opportunities to expand trade and enhance cooperation through joint ventures and European investment in Canada. A related selling point was Canada's importance as a stable long-term supplier of natural resources, especially energy, at a time of increasing international scarcity. Finally, Canadian officials argued that Europe, like Canada, had an interest in counterbalancing its relations with the U.S. so it, too, had a stake in Canada's independence.

While making the case for closer relations with the Community, Ottawa sought to avoid alienating the Americans. Diversification was not anti-American, nor did it imply that Canada would diminish existing ties with the U.S. As Marcel Cadieux, Canada's ambassador to the EC, put it, "The idea...is not to reduce in absolute terms our trade, our economic and financial relations with our good but powerful neighbour to the South but to increase simultaneously our relations both with the U.S.A. and with our other partners and thus achieve a different and better balance at a higher general level of exchanges (Quoted in Barry, 1980: 67-68). EC authorities were also mindful of American concerns. "We do not consider that the Community should be seen in crude terms as some sort of 'alternative' to Canada's links with the United States," said Commission Vice President Sir Christopher Soames, "But we do consider that Canada and the Community have their own particular and individual relationship to work out, and I hope that Canada would see the advantages in the development of a European dimension (quoted in Barry, 1980: 68).

Exploratory talks between Canada and the Community got under way in 1972 and continued intermittently during 1973. In April 1974 Ottawa presented a note to the European Commission, which called for formal discussions leading to the establishment of "a direct contractual link." This would include most favoured nation relations, a commitment to GATT principles, and provisions for consultation. Although the Commission considered the proposals too vague for serious discussion, they did provide an opportunity to seize the initiative. In a communication to the Council in September 1974 the Commission noted that Canada was the first industrialized country to seek a trade agreement with the Community. Since relations with developed states were more complex than those with third world countries, such an accord "would need to be of a new and different kind." The Commission asked for authorization to pursue a new form of cooperation agreement that would require the Council to take "a more dynamic view of Community competence than has been adopted hitherto" (Quoted in Pentland, 1977: 219).

Canada and the Commission made concerted efforts to respond to British and French concerns about the proposed agreement. Prime Minister Trudeau made three visits to Europe calling at EC headquarters and member state capitals. He stressed that the accord would not replace Canada's bilateral relations with member states and held out the possibility of increased European access to Canadian resources. Trudeau's interventions were reinforced by his government's decision to upgrade Canada's defence contribution by purchasing modern German Leopard tanks for its forces in Europe. This was done after Chancellor Helmut Schmidt emphasized that "Canada's desire for a contractual link was directly tied to its willingness to remain a loyal partner in NATO" (Rempel and Bleek, 2000: 87). For its part, the Commission stressed the importance of access to energy and raw materials, while attempting to ease concerns that the agreement would expand Community powers at member states' expense. The combined Canadian and Commission pressures eventually produced results. By June 1975 the principal features of the agreement, including the reciprocal extension of most favoured nation treatment, a commitment to foster economic cooperation, establishment of a joint economic cooperation committee, and an evolutionary clause to encompass future forms of cooperation had emerged. Meanwhile, Canadian and EU authorities continued to reassure the U.S. about the purpose of the agreement. Their assurances were acknowledged by Secretary of State Henry Kissinger who observed that Washington did "not object to a contractual relationship between Canada and Europe...as long as opposition to the United States does not become a cardinal principle for its own sake, which we do not believe is the case" (Quoted in Barry, 1980:69). Negotiations between Canada and the EC entered their final stage in March 1976 and were completed by the following June. The "Framework Agreement for Commercial and Economic Cooperation Between Canada and the European Communities" (Contractual Link) was signed by Canadian and Community representatives a month later.

As a political exercise the Contractual Link was a success. The Community's recognition of Canada as an actor in its own right helped bring the country out of the shadow of the U.S. and reinforced its sense of identity. However, as an economic exercise its impact was limited. Although the Department of External Affairs championed the initiative the departments of Finance, and Industry Trade and Commerce, which favoured a continuation of Canada's existing pragmatic approach toward the U.S., viewed it as risky. Community authorities also were skeptical that the agreement would produce major changes (Barry, 1980:68; Granatstein and Bothwell, 1990:161). More important, Canadian and European businesses preferred the familiarity of existing markets to exploring opportunities elsewhere. Thus, while the Contractual Link proved useful in reducing government impediments, it was not enough to alter the balance of Canada's trade with the U.S. and the EC. As a result the Third Option was abandoned.

Ottawa temporarily reversed itself after the 1979 energy crisis, attempting to use its resource wealth to achieve more arms-length relations with the U.S. In 1980 the Trudeau government adopted the National Energy Program aimed at Canadianizing the largely foreign-owned energy industry and tightened existing foreign investment requirements to scrutinize proposals from foreign investors more closely. These actions were combined with a strategy of "concentrated bilateralism" to diversify Canada's economic relations, the main targets being members of the Organization of Petroleum Exporting Countries and the newly industrializing states of the Third World (Nossal, 1984: 59-86). By the early 1980s a severe global recession, high interest rates and falling energy prices forced Ottawa to reassess its approach.

**Turning Toward the U.S.**

In 1982 the Trudeau government launched a major review of Canadian trade policy. Released the following year, it signaled the end of the diversification approach by proposing sectoral free trade with the U.S. (DEA, 1983). Follow-up discussions did not work out, but they did focus attention on the possibility of a comprehensive free trade accord. In 1985 Prime Minister Brian Mulroney, with strong support from the country's business community, sought free trade negotiations. President Ronald Reagan responded favourably. The talks got under way in 1986 and were completed the next year. The Canada-U.S. Free Trade Agreement (CUFTA) came into effect in 1989.

The conclusion of CUFTA did not mean that Canada had lost interest in Europe. Supporters of the agreement argued that it would force Canadian firms to become more productive in order to compete in the American market, thereby making them more competitive internationally. They also pointed out that even though exports to the EC had declined from 12 percent to 8 percent of Canada's overall foreign trade between 1976 and 1988, and sales to the US had increased from 68 percent to 72 percent during the same period, the Community remained Canada's second largest foreign market. Thus, when the EC approved the Single European Act, which would see the Community become a unified market by 1992, and codified the European Political Cooperation process that provided for consultation and cooperation on foreign policy, the Canadian government took steps to respond. It helped Canadian businesses take advantage of new trade and investment opportunities opened up by the single market program although, as Denis Stairs observed, this effort, which was part of a post-CUFTA trade strategy called "Going Global," had more to do with the search for economic opportunity than the pursuit of diversification (Stairs, 1999: 240-241). Ottawa also began a political dialogue with the Community that provided a  link to the European Political Cooperation (EPC) process.


**The Transatlantic Declarations**

These actions did not end Canada's efforts to expand relations with the EC. However, the immediate impetus for these efforts came from the U.S., which was coming to grips with the growing power and unity of Europe as the world moved from the cold war into the post-cold war era. Although Washington was in regular communication with Brussels it wanted a formal link to EPC to provide a means of making its views known before decisions were made (Potter, 1992: 7, 52). In a speech in May 1989, President George Bush signaled his government's interest in upgrading  relations with the EC by calling for a "new partnership" between the U.S. and the Community. Later that year Secretary of State James Baker proposed that the two sides "work together to achieve, whether in treaty or in some other form, a significantly strengthened set of institutional and consultative links" (Quoted in Henrikson, 1993: 167). U.S. and Community officials endorsed the project in December 1989. Bush and Commission president Jacques Delors held follow-up discussions in Washington in April 1990. Bush agreed to the Community's preference for a joint declaration rather than a treaty because the EC was still developing its foreign policy competence. Two months later the EC Council agreed to begin negotiations (Potter, 1992: 8-9).

For Canadian authorities the prospect of closer U.S.-EU links raised concerns that Canada would be relegated to the margins of the transatlantic relationship. Also, the fact that the U.S. and Mexico had begun discussing a possible free trade accord following the recent Canada-US Free Trade Agreement suggested a worrisome tendency toward bilateralism in American policy. If Washington reached a deal with the EC, Canada could find itself out in the cold (Henrikson, 1993: 178). Canada's interest in being included in any new transatlantic arrangement was supported by German foreign minister Hans-Dietrich Genscher. In a speech to the Canadian Parliament on April 5, 1990, Genscher repeated a suggestion he had made to Bush the previous day, that the U.S., Canada and the EC consider a transatlantic declaration "concerning the common challenges we face in the political, economic, technological, and ecological fields....in order to create a new basis of cooperation between the European Community and the two democracies in North America" (Quoted in Potter, 1992: 12).

Ottawa did not pursue Genscher's suggestion, although it did propose that the Canada-EC political dialogue be expanded to include regular meetings between the prime minister and the president of the European Council as well as increased official contacts (Clark, 1990). As Canadian officials saw it, the prospects for stable transatlantic relations depended on the effective management of economic issues. Since any U.S.-EC agreement would put the Americans in a favoured position and reduce Canada's already limited role in Europe, Ottawa should press for free trade with the Community on a Canada-EC or North American-EC basis. External Affairs minister Joe Clark took up the idea in a speech to the House of Commons in late May. He suggested that after the completion of the Uruguay Round of GATT negotiations, "the desirability of a formalized, open trading agreement between Canada and the European Community, perhaps including the United States – or indeed other members of the OECD" (Organization for Economic Cooperation and Development) might be examined (HC Debates, 1990: 12098). Neither the U.S. nor the EC showed interest. Moreover, in September Ottawa abandoned the idea when it decided to join the U.S. and Mexico in negotiating a North American free trade pact (see Barry, 1995).

When the Canadian government learned that the U.S. and the EC intended to proceed with a joint declaration it asked to be included. However, Washington contended that Canadian participation would weaken the effectiveness of the plan, which was aimed at formalizing bilateral contacts with the EC. It also argued that if Canada were included Mexico might want to join (Potter, 1992: 20-21). The reaction of Community states was mixed. Germany, the U.K., Spain and Portugal supported Canada. France and Italy, which held the presidency of the Council at the time and wanted the subject dealt with quickly, endorsed the U.S. stand. A compromise was reached when Canada agreed to a bilateral declaration similar to that being negotiated between the U.S. and the EC. The "Declaration on European Community-Canada Relations," was signed on November 22, 1990, a day before the signing of the "Declaration on European Community-United States Relations."[5]

The two declarations established a new political framework for the conduct of Canada-EC and U.S.-EC relations. They reaffirmed the importance of the values underlying the relationships and set out principles for partnership and common goals. The declarations committed the participants to cooperate in economic, scientific and cultural matters, and to meet emerging "transnational challenges," including terrorism, the drug trade, weapons proliferation, environmental problems, and large-scale migration and refugees.

The Canada-EC declaration, expanded the consultative mechanisms contained in the Contractual Link to include "regular" meetings between the prime minister and the presidents of the European Council and the Commission, bilateral meetings between the Secretary of State for External Affairs and the President of the Council of Ministers and the Commission, annual consultations at the official level, briefings for Canadian officials following EPC ministerial meetings, and closer dialogue between European and Canadian parliamentarians. The U.S.-EC declaration formalized "biennial" meetings between the American president and the presidents of the European Council and the Commission, similar discussions between the Secretary of State and EC foreign ministers, ad hoc consultations at the foreign minister level, briefings for American representatives following EPC ministerial meetings, and more dialogue between U.S. and EC legislators. An evolutionary clause, similar to that contained in the Contractual Link, allowed for new forms of cooperation as relations developed.

Taken together the declarations affirmed the importance of the North American-European relationship in the post war era. They also put Canada on an equal footing with the U.S. and the EC, thereby relieving Ottawa's concerns that Washington and Brussels would dominate the transatlantic dialogue. However, as Evan Potter has noted, "without the momentum of US-EC discussions it is unlikely that Canada would have been able to negotiate an agreement similar to the Transatlantic Declaration (TAD)" (Potter, 1992: 32).

## NAFTA-EU Free Trade?

Although the TADs broadened the scope of the North American-European Community dialogue they produced few results. Differing North American and European approaches toward security issues, shown in their responses to the Gulf war and the conflict in the former Yugoslavia, made common action more difficult than in the past. Economic tensions, which had been muted during the cold war, also increased, the most notable example being the clash between the U.S. and the Community over agriculture that delayed completion of the Uruguay Round of GATT negotiations until late 1993. Underlying these developments was the intensification of European cooperation and an emerging regionalism in the Americas. The EC was preoccupied with the completion of the single market project and launch of the Maastricht Treaty. Canada, the United States and Mexico were moving toward a North American Free Trade Agreement (NAFTA), which was seen as the first step toward the negotiation of a Free Trade Area of the Americas by 2005. This was matched by a plan to achieve free in the Asia Pacific region by 2010 for industrialized members and 2020 for developing economies.

These developments created concern on both sides of the Atlantic that the common interests that had joined North America and Europe during the cold war were eroding and that the two sides were drifting apart. Roy MacLaren, Minister for International Trade in Prime Minister Jean Chrétien's government, shared this concern. As he saw it, in an era in which strategic imperatives were giving way to economic demands, the only effective way to strengthen relations between North America and Europe was through the creation of a "comprehensive economic and trade partnership." In a speech in late October 1994 he asked, "Is it time to give serious consideration to a deeper Canada-EU trade framework, in turn paving the way for a more ambitious EU-North America link in the future" (MacLaren, 1994)? MacLaren won the support of the Prime Minister, who told the French Senate in a speech in December that the time had come to "consider a global trade liberalization agreement" between NAFTA and the EU (Quoted in Calgary Herald, 1994). In a follow-up letter to European Commission vice-president Sir Leon Brittan, MacLaren stressed the importance Canada attached to the transatlantic relationship and raised the subject of a NAFTA-EU accord (Confidential source).

The Commission, which was preparing to strengthen the EU's political and economic relations with Mexico along the lines of a recent overture toward MERCOSUR (the Southern Cone Common Market consisting of Argentina, Brazil, Paraguay and Uruguay) expressed interest in a North American-EU agreement as did several member states, including the U.K., Germany, Sweden, the Netherlands and Spain, which would assume the presidency of the Council during the second half of 1995 (Europe, 1995; Inside U.S. Trade, 1995; Gordon, 1996: 74; SSCFA, 1996). German foreign minister Klaus Kinkel put the issue in perspective in April 1995, observing that although the U.S. was actively pursuing NAFTA enlargement and trade liberalization in Asia Pacific, "there is no trans-Atlantic equivalent to this." He proposed that, "After the successful completion of the Uruguay Round the creation of a Trans-Atlantic Free Trade Area (TAFTA) should be seriously envisaged" (quoted in Gordon, 1996: 74).

The following month MacLaren visited London, Paris, Bonn and Geneva to assess interest in the project. In a speech in London he called transatlantic free trade "the next logical step" in the "crucial process of linking together potentially exclusionary blocs." He suggested that the pact include the gradual elimination of customs duties and non-tariff barriers, a commitment by the EU to begin separate bilateral negotiations with Canada, the U.S. and Mexico (because NAFTA was not a customs union), and that it be consistent with the objectives of the World Trade Organization (WTO), which had replaced the GATT following the conclusion Uruguay Round. To speed up progress the minister proposed that an "Eminent Persons Group" composed of respected persons from both sides of the Atlantic, be formed to draw up a detailed action program. The group would submit its first report in June 1996, in time for a summit of North American and European leaders (MacLaren, 1995). But by this time Canadian relations with the EU had deteriorated as a result of the "Turbot War" that saw Canada seize a Spanish fishing vessel in international waters off the Grand Banks (See Barry, 1998). Perhaps not surprisingly then, when the invitation to renew the transatlantic relationship was extended, Canada was not included.

Although Washington was interested in upgrading its relations with the EU, it did not share Canadian and European enthusiasm for free trade. Free trade had become a divisive issue in the U.S. following the conclusion of NAFTA, which had attracted substantial opposition led by labour and environmental groups. Deepening divisions in Congress over the place of labour and environmental standards in trade pacts prevented President Bill Clinton's administration from securing "fast track" authority to negotiate trade agreements that would not be subject to legislative amendment. In a speech in Madrid early in June, Secretary of State Warren Christopher skirted the free trade issue in signaling the administration's willingness to negotiate a new relationship. At a subsequent meeting with Sir Leon Brittan he promised only to give it "serious study" (Quoted in Preeg, 1996: 110). Whatever possibility there was for a NAFTA-EU free trade agreement thus disappeared. Relations between the North American countries and the EU would proceed along three separate tracks.

*The Joint Action Plans*

At their meeting in Washington in mid-June 1995, U.S. and EU leaders instructed senior officials to present recommendations to the next summit that would be held in Madrid in December of that year. The issue of free trade was raised in the officials' discussions. However, French opposition and the reluctance of the Americans to launch any new trade initiative in an election year put the issue on indefinite hold. Instead the group began preparing two documents: a statement of principles underlying the relationship and a joint action plan outlining steps to liberalize trade (Preeg, 1996: 110; Eurcom, 1995). The Canadian government pressed for trilateralization of the negotiation, but Spain, still smarting from the Turbot War, used its position to exclude Ottawa from the talks (Barry, 1998: 278; SSCFA, 1996: 117-118). In October MacLaren visited Germany, the U.K., Sweden and Spain to make Canada's case. He made little headway, although a German-Canadian working group was formed to develop a plan to strengthen Canada-EU economic relations (DFAIT, 1995).

At the Madrid summit President Clinton, Commission President Jacques Santer and Spanish Prime Minister Filipe Gonzales signed a "New Transatlantic Agenda and Joint U.S.-EU Action Plan." The Agenda reaffirmed the importance of the transatlantic relationship, and set out overall goals (peace and stability and development, global issues, expansion of trade, and transatlantic bridge building) and issues to be given special attention. The Action Plan identified more than 150 issues on which the two sides agreed to work together bilaterally and in multilateral fora. Among these was the creation of a "New Transatlantic Marketplace" to reduce barriers to the flow of goods services and capital, which would include a joint study of ways to encourage trade and reduce or eliminate tariff and non-tariff barriers (Del Eurcom, 1995). Encouragement was also given to the recently created Transatlantic Business Dialogue that brought together U.S. and European business leaders to develop recommendations for removing obstacles to trade and investment (See Cowles, 1996).

In January 1996 the German-Canadian working group sent its report to the Commission and the new Italian presidency. The report, which included many of the items contained in the U.S.-EU agreement, recommended a study to identify ways of facilitating trade "on a trilateral (Canada, USA., EU) basis wherever a trilateral basis is appropriate and offers reasonable opportunities for achieving substantial results" (Quoted in SSCFA, 1996: 123). On February 28 the Commission submitted its own proposals, many of which overlapped with those in the German-Canadian report. But the Commission's document, using the language of the U.S.-EU Action Plan, recommended only "a joint study on ways of facilitating trade in goods and services and further reducing or eliminating tariff and non-tariff barriers" (Eurcom, 1996).

The Council of Ministers approved the Commission's recommendations on March 25, 1996, although Spain insisted that negotiators be bound by the wishes of individual states. Canadian and EU officials wanted to complete the negotiations in time for signing at the next Canada-EU summit in Rome at the end of June. However, the talks reached an impasse over a Canadian proposal for cooperation to oppose the extraterritorial application of national laws such as the Helms-Burton Act, which seeks to punish foreign businesses using property in Cuba that was confiscated from American citizens by the Castro government. Spain and other member states supported the proposal, but they insisted that it also apply to Canada's Coastal Fisheries Protection Act that gave Ottawa the authority to arrest foreign vessels on the high seas. The deadlock was not broken until December 1996 when the agreement was finally signed at a Canada-EU summit meeting in Ottawa (Drohan, 1996a, 1996b, 1996c; Evans 1996; EU, 1996).

The "Joint Political Declaration on Canada-EU Relations and the Joint Canada-EU Action Plan," like its U.S.-EU counterpart, contained a political statement on the overall relationship and a broad agenda for action on trade and economic issues, foreign policy and security, global issues, and transatlantic links. A noteworthy departure was that, in addition to undertaking a joint study on ways of facilitating trade, Canada and the EU would "consider with the United States, on a case by case basis, trilateralization...for subjects contained in the new Transatlantic Market Place" (DFAIT, 1996). They also agreed to support the establishment of a Canada-EU business dialogue to provide advice on trade and investment matters.

Seven months later, in July 1997, the EU and Mexico concluded two agreements: an "Economic Partnership, Political Coordination and Cooperation Agreement," and an "Interim Agreement on Trade and Trade Related Matters," that institutionalized their political dialogue and laid the basis for formal free trade talks. The pacts were signed in December of that year (EU, 1997).

**The New Transatlantic Market Place**

Canadian authorities continued to press for a NAFTA-EU free trade deal. In a speech in London in October 1997, Chrétien called for the establishment of a

"Trans-Atlantic Free Trade Zone." He also expressed interest in concluding a free trade agreement with the European Free Trade Association (EFTA) in the expectation that this would draw Canadian and European businesses closer, and give impetus to the overture to the EU (Chrétien, 1997). The EFTA countries (Iceland, Norway, Liechtenstein and Switzerland) responded favourably.[6] But there was no reaction from the U.S., Mexico or the EU.

Although Washington and Brussels were not interested in a NAFTA-EU free trade deal they were prepared to consider liberalizing trade with each other. At their summit meeting in Washington in December 1997, the two sides decided to explore the prospects for a bilateral accord (See Pelkmans, 1998). The initiative was the brainchild of Sir Leon Brittan, who believed that strengthening the U.S.-EU relationship required a "grand political project" that would move the two sides beyond their traditional gradualist approach. This would also allow them to take a leadership role in the next round of multilateral trade negotiations (Europe, 1998a). The Clinton administration, which had recently lost a bid to renew its fast track negotiating authority, was "cautiously receptive" to the overture (Dinan, 1999: 544).

The issue was not raised at a Canada-EU ministerial meeting in Ottawa on January 16, 1998, the day after a similar gathering in Washington. In a speech delivered to an Ottawa audience Brittan noted that, "While Transatlantic relations have a clear trilateral dimension, there are also distinct bilateral interests that should be dealt with separately. In saying this I do not imply that our relations with the US will always be given higher emphasis. Indeed there are areas, as for example our basic philosophical approach to some trade and economic issues, in which the EU may have more common ground with Canada" (Brittan, 1998). When queried he replied that a Canada-EU free trade pact would not be practicable because it would lead to a similar demand from the U.S., and this would encourage a bilateral rather than a multilateral approach to trade (Cook, 1998).

Press reports revealing the existence of the U.S.-EU discussions surfaced early in February, raising the inevitable questions about Canada's participation. A spokesman for the EU delegation in Ottawa responded that, "Parties on both sides of the Atlantic seem to have the opinion that it is more difficult to come to a conclusion when you have three parties instead of two" (Cook, 1998). As the statement made clear, neither the U.S. nor the EU was willing to broaden the talks – as leading powers they first wanted a deal of their own. In addition, American officials were concerned that if Canada were included it would align itself with the EU against the U.S., or try to play the two sides off against each other. For its part, the EU, given its limited trade with Canada, had little incentive to bring it into the discussions; nor was it about to do anything that would make it more difficult for the Americans to negotiate.

Brittan's proposal for a "New Transatlantic Market Place," (NTM) won the approval of the Commission on March 11, 1998, shortly after that body endorsed a request for authority to begin free trade discussions with Mexico (Reuters, 1998a). The proposal, which was carefully crafted to exclude the sensitive issues of agriculture and culture, contained four main elements: free trade in services by the year 2000; elimination of industrial tariffs by 2010; reduction of technical barriers to trade; and liberalization of government procurement, intellectual property and investment regulations (Eurcom, 1998). It was to be taken up at the U.S.-EU summit meeting in London in May.

The French government was opposed, ostensibly because the project would undermine multilateral trade liberalization. More likely, Paris feared that agriculture and culture, both of which were troublesome issues for France, would be targeted by U.S. negotiators. That fear gained credibility when American officials said that both sectors would have to be included (Reuters, 1998b; Europe, 1998b). At a press conference on April 17, President Jacques Chirac sharply criticized the NTM proposal, describing it as "a personal initiative by Sir Leon Brittan who...went off to negotiate a free trade area between the United States and Europe, without a mandate." In a veiled reference to Brittan's role in fashioning a compromise deal on agriculture during the final stages of the Uruguay Round, he called the Commission vice-president "a repeat offender, having already done the same thing with Blair House, an event which has not left what can be called a good memory....Naturally, this point will not be on the summit agenda" (Quoted in Europe, 1998c). Chirac's position put France at odds with Germany and the U.K., both of which initially supported the proposal. But by the time the issue was discussed in the Council on April 27, positions had shifted. Luxembourg, Finland, Sweden, Denmark, Portugal and Greece favoured the initiative. The Netherlands, Belgium, Germany, Italy and Spain joined France in opposing it. The Council settled on a compromise that would upgrade relations with the U.S. by building upon the 1995 Joint Action Plan. It also insisted that the long-standing dispute with the U.S. over the Helms-Burton and Iran-Libya sanctions laws be resolved before any action could be taken. The following month the member states, including France, gave their approval to a directive authorizing the Commission to negotiate a free trade pact with Mexico (Europe, 1998d, 1998e, 1998f).

*The TEP and the ECTI*

Concerned about the prospect of new U.S.-EU advances and the likely launch of EU-Mexico free trade talks, Chrétien pressed Canada's case for more broadly based discussions when he met with Prime Minister Tony Blair in London on May 14, 1998, as the U.K. held the presidency of the EU at the time. Blair reportedly indicated that he understood Canada's position and held out the prospect of progress on the Canada-EU front after discussions with the Americans were completed (Drohan, 1998; Chrétien, 1998). Resolution of the Helms-Burton and Iran-Libya sanctions dispute allowed the EU and the U.S. to announce a new "Transatlantic Economic Partnership" agreement (TEP) at their summit meeting on May 18.[7] The TEP, which was intended to give sharper focus to the Joint Action Plan, would see the two sides join forces to improve market access for goods, services and agricultural products, and promote multilateral trade liberalization (U.S. Mission, 1998).

Following the U.S.-EU summit, Canadian officials drafted a paper identifying areas where Canada and the EU could advance their bilateral and multilateral agendas. The paper, which was presented to the Commission in October, received a favourable response from the EU. The two sides announced the launch of an "EU-Canada Trade Initiative" (ECTI) at their summit meeting in Ottawa in December 1998. Similar to the TEP, the ECTI was designed to further joint action on multilateral trade issues and enhance bilateral cooperation in such areas as mutual recognition, services, government procurement, intellectual property rights, competition, cultural cooperation and business contacts. The American and Canadian positions seemed to be coming together at this point, but as Denis Stairs noted, "this convergence was more, perhaps, because Euro-American aspirations had receded than because Euro-Canadian aspirations had gained ground" (Stairs, 1999: 246).

In June 1999, even as Canada was renewing its call for a NAFTA-EU free trade accord, the EU was preparing to launch trade liberalization talks with MERCOSUR and Chile (Cook, 1999; Bellos, 1999).[8] And in November of that year the EU and Mexico reached agreement on a free trade pact that will completely liberalize their trade in industrial goods by 2007 and agricultural products by 2010. Other provisions covered services, government procurement, investment, competition, intellectual property and dispute settlement. This was described by EU trade commissioner Pascal Lamy as "the most ambitious free-trade agreement the EU has ever negotiated," it was also the first transatlantic free trade accord (Quoted in Europe, 1999).[9]

Ottawa kept up its pressure for free trade, but shifted the focus from a NAFTA-EU to a bilateral deal. At the Canada-EU summit meeting in December 1999, Lamy told Canadian officials that although the EU preferred agreements with developing countries and some member states might object, he would consider a strong business case for an agreement. Subsequently, Canadian and Commission officials agreed to survey the attitudes of their respective business communities. The Department of Foreign Affairs and International Trade also undertook a study to determine the effects of tariff elimination on Canada-EU trade. The study was completed in March 2001 and presented to Lamy by Pierre Pettigrew, Canada's Minister of International Trade, at the next summit in Stockholm three months later. It concluded that eliminating tariffs would increase Canadian trade with the EU by 11.2 to 15.6 per cent depending on whether agricultural and processed food products were included. The EU's exports to Canada would grow by more than 34 per cent, whether or not agri-food products were part of the agreement. Canadian and European Commission representatives met in November 2001 to review the report. Commission officials said that they would carry out their own analysis of the effects of tariff and non-tariff barriers on Canada-EU trade. The two sides agreed to work together with a view to launching a joint study (HC Subcommittee, 2001; Scoffield, 1999; DFAIT, 2001a, 2001b).

At the Canada-EU summit in Toledo, Spain in May 2002, Canadian and EU leaders directed their officials to prepare a report on how to advance the trade agenda in time for the next meeting in Ottawa in December of that year. The Canadian government's view was that the analysis should include the possibility of a free trade agreement, but the European Commission remained lukewarm (Chrétien, 2002; Laghi, 2002).

The Canadian survey of business views of exporting to the EU was released in November. Eighty-seven per cent of respondents in all export sectors favoured free trade. Sixty-two per cent expected their exports to increase, 53 per cent said they would step up their marketing efforts in the EU, and 35 per cent reported they would be more likely to establish a permanent presence there under a free trade regime (Ipsos-Reid, 2002). The survey of European businesses, completed the following month, reported that although free trade was not identified as "a key objective....A large part of the Industry associations interviewed consider favourably the perspective of an FTA between the EU and Canada" (Dehousse et.al., 2002: 7,73). But Pascal Lamy, apparently unconvinced of the merits of a bilateral free trade agreement, argued that market access issues should first be addressed in the Doha Round of multilateral trade negotiations (Chase, 2002). At their summit meeting in December Canadian and EU authorities settled for a less ambitious commitment to design a "a new type of...bilateral trade and investment enhancement agreement."[10] Special emphasis would be placed on regulatory cooperation, which had been identified as a priority by Canadian and European businesses. They also agreed to undertake a full-scale review of the relationship with a view to strengthening ties (DFAIT, 2002).

**Conclusion**

The Canadian government's post war efforts to promote closer linkages with Europe demonstrate the limitations on Canada's ability to pursue its agenda in a setting dominated by major powers. Ottawa's early attempts to use Canadian participation in NATO to strengthen economic ties to Western Europe were not successful because they lacked the support of Canada's American and European partners. More recent efforts to promote free trade with the EU have met a similar fate.

Although Canada and the EU have a long-standing relationship it remains under-exploited. Canada's policy toward the EU has not been consistent, while the EU's preoccupation with the U.S. has tended to relegate relations with Canada to the background. Yet, the two sides have reason to intensify their cooperation. "Canadian and European values and interests are more alike than those between Europe and the United States," says Evan Potter, and their domestic and foreign policies frequently converge (Potter, 1999: 254). But Canada's linkages with the U.S. are growing. The more Canada integrates with the U.S. the less visible it becomes elsewhere. Thus, relations with Europe have a special significance. To the extent that the EU values Canada as an alternative North American voice it is in its interest to reinforce the connection.[11] However, it is clear that the EU is more important to Canada than Canada is to the EU. Consequently, in most cases the initiative will have to come from the Canadian side.

Canada's unequal but close relations with the U.S. and the EU can leave Canada vulnerable when their policies diverge, but offer opportunities for Ottawa to align with the EU in opposing damaging American policies or to act as an interlocutor between Washington and Brussels.[12] For example, Canada joined the EU in mounting a successful challenge in the WTO against the "Byrd Amendment," which allowed the American government to distribute funds collected from countervailing and anti-dumping duties to affected domestic producers. And German Chancellor Gerhard Schroeder, admitting that EU countries were in an awkward position to challenge a massive farm aid bill signed by President Bush in May 2002, called on the Canadian government to take the lead in pressing for an end to market-distorting subsidies (McCarthy, 2002b). It is not surprising, though, that Canadian and EU policies do not always coincide. For instance, Canada, a leading supporter of the International Criminal Court, parted company with the EU in opposing the UN Security Council's decision in July 2002 to give U.S. peacekeepers a temporary exemption from prosecution by the court after Washington threatened to veto the extension of the organization's peacekeeping mission in Bosnia unless the Council granted them immunity from the court's jurisdiction (Ibbitson, 2002; EU, 2002).[13]

Some observers argue that the EU's consensual approach to decision making is a serious obstacle to closer Canada-EU relations in that the EU can be held hostage in disputes over other issues involving individual member states. "In such cases," says Potter, "a problem with one member country automatically translates into a problem with the entire Union" (Potter, 1999: 218). For example, the U.K. blocked approval of the 1981 Canada-EC Long Term Fisheries Agreement for several months pending progress on a common fisheries policy (Barry, 1985). And, as we have seen, Spain held up the conclusion of the Canada-EU Political Declaration and Joint Action Plan to express displeasure over Canada's actions in the Turbot War. But the Contractual Link example shows how the Community overcame internal differences when an important issue of cooperation with Canada was at stake. Moreover, although the fisheries agreement and Turbot War issues hindered cooperation in the short run, they did not have lasting consequences for the relationship.[14]

Canada-EU cooperation has expanded dramatically since the conclusion of the Joint Action Plan in 1996. The bilateral agenda now extends well beyond commercial policy to include such issues as peace building and conflict prevention, land mines, small arms, organized crime, drug trafficking, law enforcement, immigration and border control, health and employment, information technology, and northern cooperation. The two sides have also concluded sectoral agreements covering scientific and technological cooperation, education and training, customs cooperation, humane trapping, mutual recognition, veterinary standards, nuclear research and development, competition policy, and wine and spirits. And in December 2002 Canada agreed to participate in the European Union Police Mission in Bosnia and Herzegovina, the first such operation to take place under the European Security and Defence Policy (DFAIT, 2002). Drawing these elements together in the form of a "Partnership Agreement" would raise the profile of the relationship and send a valuable signal of the importance both parties attach to their relations.

Still, trade remains at the heart of the Canada-EU relationship. Although Canadian and EU tariff structures are generally low, Canada and Western Europe both belong to large preferential trading blocs as a result of which neither enjoys the same advantages in the other's market. More troublesome are a variety of food safety, labeling, regulatory, procurement and registration requirements that hamper bilateral trade. Canada and the EU have concluded sectoral agreements to deal with individual problems, but it is unlikely that much more progress can be made in the absence of a comprehensive trade accord. As one Canadian official put it, "We have picked all the low fruit from the tree". To be sure, such issues as agricultural subsidies, food safety and environmental concerns would be best addressed in a multilateral trade negotiation. But as Pierre Lortie, then President of Bombardier Transportation, put it in an address in 2002, the multilateral option would not convey "any particular benefit to the EU-Canada trade relationship in the present decade. Canada would still remain one of the few countries worldwide with no preferential access to the EU market. Tariffs would continue to apply to goods traded between out two economies. Specific non-tariff barriers that have given rise to trade disputes between Canada and the EU would remain unresolved" (Lortie, 2002).

Although enthusiasm for free trade is high in some quarters in others it is tepid at best. Canadian trade officials are interested in greater economic cooperation, but they argue that Canada should focus its efforts on the WTO and the United States where it matters most, rather than on the EU, which accounts for a limited share of Canada's trade (SSCFA, 1999: 45). Many European Commission officials take a similar view. They see Canada as a prosperous but small market and are skeptical of the value of devoting hard-pressed resources to a free trade negotiation that would yield modest gains.[15] Until recently these attitudes were not offset by pressures from the Canadian and European business sectors. Unlike the U.S.-EU relationship, which included a major input from the business through the Transatlantic Business Dialogue, Canada-EU relations were largely a government-to-government affair.

However, there are signs that business interest in the Canada-EU relationship is increasing. The Canada-Europe Round Table for Business, created in 1999 to represent the views of Canadian and European businesses to decision makers in Ottawa and Brussels, is on record as favouring a free trade accord. This view is supported by the Department of Foreign Affairs and International Trade's tariff elimination study, which shows that free trade would yield measurable benefits, and the department's subsequent business survey, which shows that there is widespread support for such a project. The EU's survey also indicates support for free trade.[16] A 2001 House of Commons committee report on Canada-EU economic relations adds that an agreement would "alter the dynamics" of the relationship, making progress in dealing with trade barriers more likely (HC Subcommittee, 2001: 26). "The mere fact that the two governments are prepared to engage in trade negotiations," Pierre Lortie observes, "would provide an important impetus to the business community, signaling that the transatlantic trade relationship is a priority in both economic and political terms" (Lortie, 2002). In such areas as competition policy, culture and services, a bilateral agreement could set the stage for advances at the multilateral level. With its trade relations with Canada firmly established in the NAFTA framework, the U.S. is not likely to object. Indeed, a Canada-EU agreement could stimulate American interest in a transatlantic accord. Finally, it could serve as a catalyst for broader cooperation between Ottawa and Brussels.

The Canadian government should continue to make its case for free trade to the European Commission, and work with supportive member states like the U.K. and Germany, and the business community in order to keep the issue before the EU.[17] To ease concerns, free trade could be established as a long-term goal. However, Ottawa should not attempt to expand its security ties to Europe in the expectation that this will yield trade dividends. Although the EU would welcome increased contributions it insists that defence and economic relations are separate matters. Consequently, Ottawa should not let its interest in better trade relations lead it to increase its defence contributions beyond what it considers necessary for its own security reasons.[18]

## Notes

This chapter builds upon an article, "Canada's Elusive European Counterweight," which appeared in the Canadian Studies Journal (Taiwan), IV (2001), 104-136. I would like to thank Duane Bratt, Osvaldo Crocci, and Hon. Roy MacLaren for their helpful comments on an earlier draft.

1   In 2000 the U.S. accounted for 87 percent of Canada's total exports, up from 68 percent in 1976; and 64 percent of Canadian imports, compared to 69 percent 24 years earlier. Canada's exports to the EU declined from 12 to 5 percent, while imports from the EU increased from 9 to 10 percent of the country's overall imports during the same period. Canada's share of EU imports dropped from 2.7 to 1.7 percent, but the country's portion of EU exports remained steady at 2 percent. In contrast, the Canada-EU investment relationship has grown steadily. The EU accounts for about 19 percent of Canadian direct investment abroad, while 27 percent of foreign investment in Canada originates in the EU (compared to 64  percent in the U.S.).

2   In the fall of 1947 Canada experienced a serious balance of payments crisis caused by increased imports from the U.S. and declining exports to the war-weakened British market. This led Prime Minister Mackenzie King to authorize free trade negotiations with the U.S. at the end of 1947. Canadian and American officials reached agreement

on a tentative accord in March 1948.   However, King brought the talks to a halt, suggesting instead that the concept of economic cooperation be included in the proposed North Atlantic security pact, which was the subject of   secret   talks   in   Washington. King's change of heart reflected his growing concern that a bilateral free trade agreement would revive long-standing Canadian fears of political annexation by the U.S. (See Hilliker and Barry, 1995: 33-35, 38-39, 75-78.)

3   Diefenbaker declared in 1957 that his government would divert 15 per cent of Canada's trade from the U.S. to the U.K. in order to offset Canada's increasing dependence on the American market.   Four years later he strongly opposed the British government's application for membership in the EC, which would have ended preferential access for Canadian agricultural exports to the U.K. The application was vetoed by France.

4   This section is largely based on Barry (1980) and Pentland (1977).

5   For the texts see Potter (1992).

6   Negotiations between Canada and the EFTA countries got under way in 1999, but have not been completed as of November 2003.  The main stumbling block is a 25 per cent tariff that Canada imposes on vessels imported from non-NAFTA countries. In the meantime, Mexico and the EFTA states began free trade discussions of their own, which culminated in an agreement in November, 2000.

7   The agreement removed the threat of U.S. retaliation against member state firms operating in Cuba, Iran and Libya in return for the EU's undertaking not to aid companies deemed to be doing business in those countries in contravention of American law. The agreement was subject to congressional approval.

8   In April 2002 the EU and Chile concluded an "Association Agreement," the closest kind of relationship a third party can have with the EU.  The accord includes free trade, a political dialogue and other forms of cooperation. As of November 2003   negotiations with MERCOSUR were continuing.

9   Until the European Commission was reorganized in the fall of 1999, responsibility for relations with the Americas was divided, with the U.S. and Canada, and Mexico and the other Latin American countries being handled by different commissioners.  Moreover, each set of relationships was and continues to be driven by different imperatives.  The EU's southern wing, led by Spain and Portugal, plays a leading role in developing the EU's policies toward Latin America.  Mexico, the members of MERCOSUR and Chile, for their part, look to the EU to balance and diversify their external relations.  Primarily the Mexico-EU free trade agreement was aimed at addressing the sharp decline in trade between the two sides after NAFTA came into effect in 1994. Negotiations between  the EU and Mexico did not pose the same problems for the EU as would free trade talks with Canada and the U.S. because agriculture and culture were not significant issues.  At the same time, the agreement with Mexico gave the EU an entrée into NAFTA.

10  The view that market access should be addressed exclusively in the WTO universally shared.   Bolstered by the passage of fast track authority (renamed trade promotion authority) by the U.S. Congress in August 2002, the Bush administration has concluded free trade pacts with Chile and Singapore and is currently negotiating with five Southern African states, Central America, and Australia.  The administration takes the view that such agreements will add momentum to rather than detract from the Doha Round.

11  Dan Middlemiss and Denis Stairs, however, claim that, "there is now increasing anecdotal and other evidence that in recent years the Europeans have come to assume that Canada is so fully integrated with the United States—economically and diplomatically as well as militarily—that it can no longer be regarded as a useful interlocutor, much less as an independent player" (Middlemiss and Stairs, 2002: 29-30).

12 To be sure, Canada sometimes joins the U.S. in opposing EU actions. For instance, it supported American efforts to press the EU to modify the Common Agricultural Policy during the Uruguay Round of GATT negotiations.

13 Subsequently the EU agreed not to hand over American soldiers or officials to the court on the understanding that the U.S. government will try any of its citizens suspected of war crimes (Edwards, 2002).

14 It is interesting to speculate whether Spain would have maintained its opposition to Canada had the U.S. agreed to participate in a NAFTA-EU free trade negotiation in 1995.

15 To put the matter in perspective, Canada's merchandise trade with the EU is more that twice the value of that between the EU and Mexico, with which the EU has a free trade accord.

16 The survey notes, however, that European industries' "perception about the negotiation of such an Agreement remains quite vague, in terms of impact and improvement of their access to the Canadian market" (Dehousse et.al., 2002: 7). This suggests that free trade proponents need to continue their efforts to heighten European firms' awareness of the merits of a pact.

17 On British and German attitudes see Toronto Star (2001) and McCarthy (2002a).

18 For an excellent discussion of Canada's role in European defence see SSCFA (2000).

## References

Barry, Donald. 1980. "The United States and the Development of the Canada-European Community Contractual Link Relationship," *American Review of Canadian Studies*, X, 1 (Spring): 63-74.

Barry, Donald. 1985. "The Canada-European Community Long Term Fisheries Agreement: Internal Politics and Fisheries Diplomacy," *Journal of European Integration*, IX, 1 (Fall): 5-28.

Barry, Donald. 1995. "The Road to NAFTA," in Donald Barry, ed. *Toward a North American Community? Canada, the United States and Mexico*, Boulder: Westview Press, 3-14.

Barry, Donald. 1998. "The Canada-European Union Turbot War: Internal Politics and Transatlantic Bargaining," *International Journal*, LIII, 2 (Spring): 253-284.

Bellos, Alex. 1999. "Link to Europe bypasses US," *Guardian Weekly*, July 1.

Brittan, Leon. 1998. "The EU and Canada: A Transatlantic partnership." Address to the International Seminar Europe Towards the Milennium: The Relevance to Canada, Ottawa, January 16.

*Calgary Herald*. 1994. "Quebec will remain, Chrétien tells French," December 2.

Chase, Steven. 2002. "EU pours cold water on idea of free-trade zone," *Globe and Mail*, December 20.

Chrétien, Jean. 1997. "Address to the Canada-United Kingdom Chamber of Commerce," October 23.

Chrétien, Jean. 1998. "Address to the Canadian Club of London," May 14.

Chrétien, Jean. 2002. "Address by Prime Minister Jean Chrétien to the Forum of the Economy," May 9.

Clark, Joe. 1990. "Canada and the New Europe," Humber College, May 26, Statements and Speeches (SS) 90/32.

Cook, Peter. 1998. "Canada on sidelines as EU, U.S. discuss free trade," *Globe and Mail*, February 3.

Cook, Peter. 1999. "Canada in new push for trade deal with EU," *Globe and Mail*, June 17.

Cowles, Maria Green. 1996. "The Transatlantic Business Dialogue: Business at the Negotiating Table," *The International Executive*, 38, 6 (November/December): 849-856.

Dehousse, Franklin, Katelyne Ghémar and Tosonka Iotsova. 2002. "Business survey on conditions of access to the Canadian market, Final Report," Brussels: Centre d'Etudes Economiques et Institutionelles-CEEI, 2 December.

Delegation of the European Commission, Washington, D.C. (Del Eurcom). 1995. The New Transatlantic Agenda and Joint EU-U.S. Action Plan, December 3.

Department of External Affairs (DEA). 1983. Trade Policy for the 1980s: A Discussion Paper, Ottawa: Minister of Supply and Services Canada.

Department of Foreign Affairs and International Trade (DFAIT). 1995. "MacLaren and Kinkel Form Working Group on Transatlantic Relations," News Release, No. 193, October 17.

Department of Foreign Affairs and International Trade (DFAIT). 1996. Joint Political Declaration on Canada-EU Relations and Joint EU-Canada Action Plan, December 17.

Department of Foreign Affairs and International Trade (DFAIT). 2001a. Canada-European Union Trade and Investment Relations: The Impact of Tariff Elimination, Trade and Economic Analysis Division, March.

Department of Foreign Affairs and International Trade (DFAIT). 2001b. "EU-Canada Trade Initiative Progress: Report to the EU-Canada Summit," December 18.

Department of Foreign Affairs and International Trade (DFAIT). 2002. "Joint Statement by Canada and the European Union-Ottawa," December 19.

Dinan, Desmond. 1999. Ever Closer Union: An Introduction to European Integration, 2nd ed., Boulder: Lynne Reinner, 544.

Drohan, Madelaine. 1996a. "Deal with Europe a top priority," *Globe and Mail*, January 2.

Drohan, Madelaine. 1996b. "Spain stymies Canada-EU accord," *Globe and Mail*, June 26.

Drohan, Madelaine. 1996c. "Chrétien expounds two views of laws," *Globe and Mail*, June 27.

Drohan, Madelaine. 1998. "Canada seeks part in EU trade talks," *Globe and Mail*, May 15.

Edwards, Stephen. 2002. "Canada, U.S. in war court standoff," *National Post*, October 1.

Europe. 1995. "EU/Spanish Presidency: Spain will prepare an update of the Transatlantic Declaration-summit with ASEAN in 1995 or 1996?" No. 6405, January 25.

Europe. 1998a. "EU/United States: Sir Leon Brittan launches his Transatlantic Common Market Project—initial exchanges of views by Commission on Wednesday in view of deliberations on 11 March," No. 7171, March 2/3.

Europe. 1998b. "EU/United states: France rejects transatlantic free trade project and Washington calls for agriculture and audiovisual to be included," No. 7179, March 13.

Europe. 1998c. "EU/United States: Mr. Chirac is highly critical of the European Commission's initiative for a New Transatlantic Marketplace," No. 7203, April 18.

Europe. 1998d. "EU/United States: Council admits that the New Transatlantic Marketplace cannot be discussed at the Euro-American Summit—closer ties must be based on the Transatlantic Agenda," No. 7209, April 27/28.

Europe. 1998e. "EU/United States: Differences over 'New Transatlantic Marketplace' confirmed in Council conclusions, differences over Helms-Burton Act should be ironed out before 18 May summit," No. 7210, April 29.

Europe. 1998f. "Dropping of the Brittan Plan for a New Transatlantic Marketplace puts EU/United States relations back on the track of logic and mutual interest and significant results have already been obtained, but divergences continue especially American pressure on European agriculture," No. 7228, May 25/26.

Europe. 1999. "EU/Mexico: Conclusion of negotiations over the agreement that will create a bilateral free-trade area in 2007 (Industry) and 2010 (Agriculture)," No. 7601, November 26.

European Commission (Eurcom). 1995. "Progress Report on EU/U.S. Relations," No. 7, December.

European Commission (Eurcom). 1996. "Communication from the Commission to the Council on EU-Canada Relations," February 28.

European Commission (Eurcom). 1998. "Communication from the Commission to the Council, the European Parliament and the Economic and Social Committee, 'The New Transatlantic Marketplace'," March 11.

European Union (EU). 1996. "Europe and Canada Sign Historic New Agreement," News Release, December 18.

European Union (EU). 1997. Press Release, No. 12891, December 8.

European Union (EU). 2002. "Declaration by the Presidency of the European Union on the UN Security Council's unanimous decisions concerning Bosnia-Herzegovina /International Criminal Court," News Release, July 13.

Evans, Margaret. 1996. "EU ministers agree on Canada plan," *Globe and Mail*, March 26.

Gordon, Bernard K. 1996. "Trade Blocked," *The National Interest*, 45 (Fall): 71-79.

Granatstein, J.L. and Robert Bothwell. 1990. *Pirouette: Pierre Trudeau and Canadian Foreign Policy*, Toronto: University of Toronto Press.

Halstead, John. 1993. "Atlantic Community or Continental Drift," *Journal of European Integration*, XVI, 2-3 (Winter/Spring): 151-164.

Henrikson, Alan. 1993. "The New Atlanticism: Western Partnership for Global Leadership," *Journal of European Integration*, SVI, 2-3 (Winter/Spring): 165-191.

Hilliker, John and Donald Barry. 1995. *Canada's Department of External Affairs: Coming of Age, 1946-1968*, Montreal and Kingston: McGill-Queen's University Press.

Holmes, John W. 1976. *Canada: A Middle-aged Power*, Toronto: McClelland and Stewart.

House of Commons Debates (HC Debates). 1990: 12098, May 31.

House of Commons, Subcommittee on International Trade, Trade Disputes and Investment, Standing Committee on Foreign Affairs and International Trade (HC Subcommittee). 2001. Crossing the Atlantic: Expanding the Economic Relationship Between Canada and Europe, June.

Ibbitson, John. 2002. "Canada condemns world court compromise," *Globe and Mail*, July 13.

*Inside U.S. Trade*. 1995. "Europe Examining Closer Trade, Investment Ties with Mexico, NAFTA," January 27.

IPSOS-Reid Corporation (IPSOS-Reid). 2002. Survey of Canadian Business Attitudes Toward EU Trade and Investment Business, for DFAIT, July.

Laghi, Brian. 2002. "EU trade initiative proves tough sell for PM," *Globe and Mail*, May 10.

Lortie, Pierre. 2002. "The Case for a Free Trade Area Between Canada and the European Union," Canada-EU Summit High Level Business Forum, Toledo, Spain, May 8.

MacLaren, Roy. 1994. "Speech to the Canada-EU Colloquium," Toronto, SS 94/67, October 28.

MacLaren, Roy. 1995. "Address to the Royal Institute of International Affairs," London, England, SS 95/32, May 22.

McCarthy, Shawn. 2002a. "Chrétien extols access to U.S. market," *Globe and Mail*, February 20.

McCarthy, Shawn. 2002b. "Schroeder urges PM to speak against subsidies," *Globe and Mail*, June 25.

Middlemiss, Danford W. and Denis Stairs. 2002. "The Canadian Forces and the Doctrine of Interoperability: The Issues," *Policy Matters*, 3, 7 (June).

Nossal, Kim Richard. 1984. "Doctrine and Canadian Foreign Policy: The Evolution of Bilateralism as a Policy Idea," in Guy Gosselin, ed., *La Politique Etronjère du Canada: Approches Bilatérale et Régimale*,Québec: Universitée Laval, 59-86.

Nossal, Kim Richard. 1992. "A European Nation? The Life and Times of Atlanticism in Canada," in John English and Norman Hillmer, eds., *Making a Difference? Canada's Foreign Policy in a Changing World Order*, Toronto: Lester Publishing Limited, 79-102.

Pelkmans, Jacques. 1998. "Atlantic Economic Cooperation: The Limits of Plurilateralism," Centre for European Policy Studies, Working Document No. 122, September.

Pentland, Charles C. 1977. "Linkage Politics: Canada's Contract and the Development of the European Community's External Relations," *International Journal*, XXXII, 2 (Spring): 207-231.

Pentland, Charles C. 1991. "Europe 1992 and the Canadian Response," in Fen Osler Hampson and Christopher J. Maule, eds., *Canada Among Nations 1990-91: After the Cold War*, Ottawa: Carleton University Press, 125-144.

Potter, Evan H. 1992. "Canadian Foreign Policy-Making and the European Community— Canada Transatlantic Declaration: Leadership or Fellowship?" External Affairs and International Trade Canada, Policy Planning Staff Paper No. 92/6.

Potter, Evan H. 1999. *Transatlantic Partners: Canadian Approaches to the European Union*, Montreal and Kingston: McGill-Queen's University Press.

Preeg, Ernest H. 1996. "Policy Forum: Transatlantic Free Trade," *Washington Quarterly*, 19, 2 (Spring): 105-112.

Rempel, Roy and Wilhem Bleck, "Defence and Economic Linkages in Canadain-German Relations, 1969-1982," *Canadian Foreign Policy*, 7, 3 (Spring): 81-98.

Reuters. 1998a. EU Briefing, 3/4/98.

Reuters. 1998b. News Report, March 12.

Sarty, Leigh. 1993. "Sunset Boulevard Revisited? Canadian Internationalism After the Cold War," *International Journal*, SLVIII, 4 (Autumn): 749-777.

Scoffield, Heather. 1999. "Europe rejects free-trade deal with Canada," *Globe and Mail*, December 17.

Secretary of State for External Affairs (SSEA). 1970. Foreign Policy for Canadians: Europe, Ottawa: Queen's Printer.

Secretary of State for External Affairs (SSEA).1972. "Canada-U.S. Relations: Options for the Future," *International Perspectives* (Autumn).

Stairs, Denis. 1999. "The Pursuit of Economic Architecture by Diplomatic Means: The Case of Canada in Europe," in Donald Barry and Ronald C. Keith, eds., *Regionalism, Multilateralism, and the Politics of Global Trade*, Vancouver: University of British Columbia Press, 228-252.

Standing Senate Committee on Foreign Affairs (SSCFA). 1996. *European Integration: The Implications for Canada*, July.

Standing Senate Committee on Foreign Affairs (SSCFA). 1999. *Europe Revisited: Consequences of Increased European Integration for Canada*, November.

Standing Senate Committee on Foreign Affairs (SSCFA). 2000. *The New NATO and the Evolution of Peacekeeping: Implications for Canada*, April.

*Toronto Star*. 2001. "Blair asks Canada to bridge transatlantic gap," February 22.

U.S. Mission to the European Union (U.S. Mission). 1998. *The Transatlantic Economic Partnership*, May 18.

# PART II

# GOVERNING THE EU: WHAT CAN THE EU LEARN FROM CANADA?

Chapter 4

# Governing EMU Democratically: Some Lessons from Neofunctionalism and Fiscal Federalism

Amy Verdun[1]

## Introduction

The process of creating an Economic and Monetary Union (EMU) in the European Community carries with it an inherent problem of democratic accountability. The reason for this problem lies in the asymmetric[2] development of 'economic' and 'monetary' integration in the European Union (EU). Monetary policies have become centralized and placed in the hands of a politically independent European Central Bank, whose only mandate is to maintain price stability. On the other hand, Member States remain largely responsible for economic policies as no new European institution is envisaged to implement economic policies.[3] Since the introduction of the euro, it is therefore more difficult for individual Member States to ensure the right 'policy mix' of economic and monetary policies (Johnson 1994). In the event that one Member State suffers disproportionately from a shock hitting its economy, it may well discover that the use of merely national policy instruments will not be adequate for tackling the crisis. The Member State can no longer use monetary policy – it may not even seek to influence the European System of Central Banks (ESCB), let alone persuade it to change its policies for the better of the Member State-in-need. Furthermore, there is no common economic authority to be of assistance. Hence, the Member State will be confronted with, what will be referred to in this chapter as, 'the democratic deficit of EMU': there is no European political authority which can be held responsible for the course of either the overall economic policies conducted in the EU, or the European monetary policy.[4] At the same time the Member State's national policy instruments have become less effective, among other things, as a result of European integration.

From a normative perspective one might wonder why the EU has not developed a proper institutional framework which would avoid this problem. Many scholars have pointed to the 'democratic deficit' of the EC/EU, referring to the lack of democratic control of either the European Parliament (EP) or national parliaments over the policy-making process in which the European Commission and the European Council are the key actors (Boyce 1993, Martin 1995, Williams, 1991). A very general definition of this democratic deficit has been provided by Williams:

> The democratic deficit is the gap between the powers transferred to the Community level and the control of the elected Parliament over them, a gap filled by national civil servants operating as European experts or as members of regulation and management committees, and to some extent by organized lobbies, mainly representing business (Williams 1991: 162).

As a result some stress the need for the European Parliament to operate as does a national European continental 'second chamber' or British 'House of Commons'. Advocates of strengthening the EP are concerned about the fact that the European Commission as a policy initiator cannot adequately be democratically controlled. By the same token, the nature of the European Council of Ministers, a body consisting of national ministers, is difficult to control, as national parliaments can only deal with their own national minister. Lisa Martin (1995) suggests that many of these problems of representation and accountability need to be addressed at the national level.

Some authors have moved away from the power dichotomy between Council and Commission on the one hand, and EP on the other, and have emphasized that the issue of transparency and secrecy as well as the technocratic and elitist mode of policy-making in the EU – often referred to as the Monnet method of integration – have aggravated the problem of the democratic deficit (cf. Featherstone 1994, Chryssochoou 1995, 2001, Lodge 1994, Verdun and Stavridis 2001). The present chapter builds on the latter analysis, in that it assumes that the democratic deficit of EMU is a logical consequence of the earlier technocratic and elitist integration process, which in the case of EMU has led to an asymmetric process of economic and monetary integration.

This chapter is of course not the first to emphasise the problem of a democratic deficit linked to EMU. Two legal scholars, Francis Snyder (1994) and Christian Joerges (1994), have each also pointed out the democratic problems related to the different institutional arrangements in the Maastricht Treaty regarding 'economic' and 'monetary' policy-making in the EU. Furthermore, Dyson et al. (1995a) also recognize an inherent democratic deficit problem in the EMU process, for two reasons. First, they see a problem emerging because of what they call, the 'insularity' of the EMU process, i.e. a minor role played by interest groups and business elites compared to the one played by national governments in the 1991 Intergovernmental Conference negotiations on EMU. Second, the democratic deficit emerges if further development towards political union to flank EMU lags behind. They see the latter as a problem mainly because the ECB is independent and no provisions are made for linkage with fiscal responsibilities (Dyson et al. 1995a: 35 – for an opposing view see Jones 2002[5]).

To understand why the creation of EMU may give rise to a democratic deficit, it is necessary to look into the EU's history of economic and monetary integration. Even after understanding the origins of the status quo, questions about its future course also still remain relevant. Which political authority will be responsible for the end result when no European political body accompanies EMU? Is it necessary to change the role of European economic policy-making in EMU? In order to understand the democratic deficit of EMU, this chapter examines the particular nature of governance of the economic and monetary policies in the EU.[6] The chapter also examines whether the EU can proceed on the road it has embarked on, or whether it needs to consider a change of direction. To analyse the latter, the chapter looks at possible problems of political responsibility and policy instruments in the event of a country-specific shock occurring in the post-EMU environment.

In order to address these questions the remaining part of this chapter is organised as follows. The next section reviews some useful theoretical concepts developed by the neofunctionalists. Section three looks into the history of European economic and monetary integration in order to identify the mechanisms behind the integration process, and the historical development of asymmetry in integration in the two policy areas. The fourth section discusses the nature of economic and monetary governance in the EU. Section five reviews three scenarios for public finance in the EU and examines what lessons can be learnt from fiscal federalism. Finally, section six draws some conclusions.

## The Neofunctionalist Notion of Spill-over

Since the signing of the Treaty of Rome in 1958, economic and monetary integration have been a leading force in the European integration process. Long before the Single European Act (SEA) was planned, these policies were already at the core of the process. This chapter examines to what extent the elitist and technocratic mode of integration (also known as the 'Monnet method') forms the basis of the democratic deficit. Hence, it examines in some detail the neofunctionalist school of thought developed by Ernst B. Haas in the 1950s and 1960s and re-examines some of his conceptual tools of analysis for understanding the nature of economic and monetary integration.

Central to Haas' early work was the concept of 'spill-over' (Haas 1958, 1964). His assumptions were that political actors would start to shift their policy-making to the supranational level. At this level policies could be conducted more efficiently, as issues would become 'depolitized', and a common ideology would be shared. Policies which would enhance the welfare of the country would be the first to be transferred to the higher level, and hence support the process of regional integration.

Haas distinguished four areas where spill-over would have an effect (Haas 1968: 313). Integration of one policy area would give rise to the integration of other policy areas; this spill-over will here be referred to as 'sectoral spill-over'. Policy areas which could enlarge the common welfare were the first to be integrated, and gradually other policy areas would be affected by sectoral spill-over. As more policies would be conducted at the central level, political actors would feel the need to control this new level of policy-making, and shift their political loyalty to the supranational level; this is 'political spill-over'. Haas' assumption was that integration would be initiated by transnational non-governmental bureaucrats, technocrats, and experts, who would start cooperating together to achieve 'common goals'. Behind this mechanism lay a belief that these actors could coordinate their policy objective more easily since they would have common goals, and would not be restricted by ideological differences or by national politics. This process of transnational cooperation by national experts in order to obtain common objectives will be referred to in this chapter as 'cooperative spill-over'. Finally, in Haas' view, the integration process would appeal to countries who were not yet participating in the integration process, and they would want to become a member of the Community as well; this is 'geographical spill-over' (Haas 1968: ch. 8).[7] Because economic and monetary policies would likely be the first to be integrated, since they would be the most likely to enhance the common welfare, then it would make sense for policies to be decided by experts cooperating in a transnational or intergovernmental setting. Political authority over these policies could gradually move to the European level. Also, the greater economic area would attract other countries. These four types of spill-over (sectoral, political, cooperative and geographical) still seem to be useful for understanding the nature of economic and monetary governance in the EU, and the subsequent democratic deficit of EMU. This vision of integration also has its obvious limits, as pointed out by many scholars.

The criticism of the neofunctionalist approach voiced by inter alia the realists and the intergovernmentalists, focuses on three issues. First, they stressed the need to remain focused on the nation state and to consider the national governments as the primary actors; second, the need to take the external (international) circumstances into account when explaining integration; third, the need to reject the hypothesis that the integration process would have any inherent drive which would push integration forward (Hoffmann 1966, 1983, Keohane and Nye 1975, Taylor 1983, Webb 1983).[8] Hoffmann's classic 1966 article stressed that spill-over could happen with regard to welfare politics (economic and social politics) referred to as 'low politics', but would be unlikely ever to take place in the area of foreign policy or defence, i.e. 'high politics'. In a later article (Hoffmann 1983), he explained that the contents of 'high' and 'low' politics depended on many more factors than just the nature of the policy area: "'high' versus 'low' politics...can be misleading if it suggests that foreign policy and defence are always and exclusively 'high', which is not the case, and economic and social policies are 'low', which is certainly false, especially in periods of economic crisis." (Hoffmann 1983: 29 emphasis added).

In order to examine the nature of governance of economic and monetary integration and the democratic deficit inherent in this process, let us now turn to at the mechanisms of economic and monetary integration as they occurred during the long process that eventually led to the creation of EMU.

## Europe's Road to Economic and Monetary Integration

The Treaty of Rome did not envisage any integration of economic or monetary policies. It stressed the need for coordination, but merely as a voluntary act of member states. Since the Common Agricultural Policy (CAP) had become very successful in the 1960s, but had depended on stable currencies, the weak US dollar towards the end of that decade posed a large problem to the EC member states, as it undermined exchange rate stability. As a result, a complicated system of 'green currencies' was introduced in order to compensate farmers for currency fluctuations. In addition, when in mid 1968 the first phase of the customs union was completed well ahead of schedule, the time seemed ripe for the creation of an Economic and Monetary Union (EMU). This objective was formally launched in December 1969 at the European Council Summit in The Hague.

An ad-hoc group of monetary and financial experts (the Werner Group) was set up to study the route to EMU. The group consisted of high ranking officials representing each of the six member states, most of whom were chairmen of EEC financial committees. The group was chaired by the Luxembourg Prime Minister and Finance Minister, Pierre Werner. The Group managed to publish their report within the year (Werner Report, 1970), and the Council accepted its proposal with some amendments in March 1971.[9] The plan consisted of a parallel road to economic and monetary integration. EMU was to be created in three stages and completed in 1980. For both 'economic' and 'monetary' union a new institution was envisaged. The role of the 'Centre for Decision of Economic Policy' (CDEP) was to guide the Member States' economic policy. This meant that national economic policies would have to be coordinated on the basis of medium-term objectives, and that the broad outlines of macroeconomic policy and the general orientation of national budgets would be decided at the Community level (Werner Report, 1970; see also Kruse, 1980). The Werner Report also voiced the need for some degree of harmonisation of indirect taxes, and for adjusting tax regimes to ensure the free movement of capital. The monetary authority would conduct monetary policies and be responsible for the single currency. At the European level a consulting role was envisaged for the social partners.[10]

The underlying problem of the Werner Report had been a sharp difference of opinion between the West German, the Dutch, and the Italian officials ('the economists') on the one hand, and the French, the Belgian, and the Luxembourg delegation ('the monetarists')[11] on the other. The fundamental disagreement was whether economic convergence would be a necessary precondition for monetary integration or whether monetary integration would bring about economic convergence. The 'economists' favoured the first scenario and additionally stressed the need for more political integration (transfer of policy-making to the supranational level) before monetary integration. By contrast, the 'monetarists' – more hesitant of supranational policy-making – wanted to go ahead with locking exchange rates and claimed that economic convergence, and eventually political integration, would be its result.

The rest is history. Unfortunate international circumstances – the 1973 oil crisis, the end of the Bretton Woods system, high inflation – and diverging policy responses to these changed circumstances, made it impossible to maintain the subtle balance between the two camps. Efforts during the course of the 1970s to relaunch the EMU plan failed. The only meagre European monetary success was the participation of a small number of EEC and EFTA countries in the so-called 'snake', a European exchange rate mechanism. However, as many countries – notably, Britain, Italy, and especially France – failed to keep their currencies in the Snake, it was not a real EEC success.

When, in 1979, France indicated it wanted to join the European exchange rate mechanism, a new attempt was made at relaunching European monetary integration by establishing the European Monetary System (EMS) (Ludlow, 1982). This time the plan was less ambitious, and the primary aim was creating a zone of increasing monetary stability in the EEC. Again the international conditions were unfavourable. In 1979/1980 a second oil crisis occurred, and in 1982/3 a deep recession hit Europe. To make things worse, the international debt crisis emerged. But this time, the EMS did not collapse. What were the reasons for its surprising endurance?

When the EMS became operational in March 1979 the world stood at the crossroads of a new era in exchange rate policy collaboration. It coincided with a gradual change in conviction about the relationship between economic and monetary policies. During the 1970s monetary authorities, national governments, and economists across the globe had come to the conclusion that a trade-off between inflation and unemployment did not exist. At the same time new governments were elected in the United States and in the United Kingdom.[12] They told their central banks to target money supply in order to reduce inflation – a policy already pursued in West Germany and Japan. When in 1983 the French government abandoned its radical Keynesian policies overnight, it, too, started to pursue restrictive policies (Hall 1986). Eventually, Italy, Belgium, and Luxembourg also followed suit. During the 1980s the EC member states started to treat the D-Mark as an anchor-currency, and they closely monitored their monetary policies to those conducted in West Germany. On the whole the focus of government policies started to move away from 'dirigisme' to 'laissez-faire'; in other words, from welfare state policies towards neoliberal policies (cf. Rhodes 1995). What happened during those years was what often is referred to as 'the decline of the Keynesian state' or 'end of Keynesianism'. This decline led to a search for new policies and institutions to support these new policies (Marks et al. 1996).

The EC member states had also come to realise that Japan, and the Pacific Basin in general, were producing high quality products which were perceived as posing a serious threat to Europe's economic capacity (Keohane and Hoffmann 1991, Ruigrok and Van Tulder 1995). At the same time the EC member state monetary authorities and EC businesses were increasingly frustrated by a fluctuating dollar. Moreover, the large growth of financial services, capital mobility, and transactions in the 1980s contributed to a reduction of independent policy effectiveness of individual member states. These factors together gave rise to the launching of the Single European Act (SEA) which embodied the plan to create the internal market by late 1992 (Moravcsik 1991). In the fine print of the SEA a clause was incorporated to create EMU. The largest opposition to EMU had, until then, come from Margaret Thatcher, the British Prime Minister at the time. But, as the creation of the internal market nicely fit into her neo-liberal agenda she did not oppose the EMU clause. So, the Hannover Summit of June 1988 called for a study of how to achieve EMU.

As had happened before with the Werner Plan, a group of financial experts were asked to draft a blueprint for EMU. This time the group consisted of central bank presidents and a small number of independent experts, chaired by the Commission President Jacques Delors.[13] Again, its report was drafted in a matter of months, and was unanimously accepted by the committee.[14] The Delors Report, published in April 1989, in many ways resembled the Werner Report in that it suggested a parallel strategy to EMU. Again 'economic' and 'monetary' union were identified as separate processes.[15] Economic union was described as consisting of the single market, competition policy, regional and structural policies, and macroeconomic policy coordination. Monetary union would constitute a currency area in which currencies are irrevocably fixed and convertible (ideally a single currency) and the complete liberalisation of capital transactions and full integration of financial markets (Delors Report 1989: 18-20).

In contrast to what had been envisaged in the Werner Report, however, the Delors Report did not prescribe the need to create a European economic authority, nor did it want to institutionalise the dialogue between social partners at the European level. Regarding macro-economic policies and budgetary policies the report stressed the need to reduce "binding rules", i.e. "upper limits on budgetary deficits of individual member countries" (Delors Report 1989: 24). Further tax harmonisation was considered unnecessary; the report was counting on the decision to double the structural funds between 1988 and 1993 to be adequate in dealing with structural adjustment (Delors Report 1989: 22). On the whole the Delors Report appeared to be relying on market forces for desirable policy outcomes.

On the monetary side, the report did voice the need for a new community institution, the European System of Central Banks (ESCB). The bottom line of the section in the Report on the monetary union was to institutionalize the policies which the Member States had been pursuing during the 1980s: to combat inflation was considered the primary policy objective. In order to safeguard this objective, the Delors Report stressed the need for the ESCB to be politically independent. In other words, the Delors Report has institutionalised policy decisions on the monetary side but relied on market forces for coordination in the field of economic policy-making (see also Johnson 1994).

The recommendations of the Delors Report were incorporated without major changes in the Treaty on European Union (better known as the Maastricht Treaty).[16] The only amendments were that the Treaty specified a timetable for the creation of EMU and it incorporated criteria for excessive deficits and other criteria[17] – known as the convergence criteria – which Member States needed to fulfil in order to be eligible to join the third stage of EMU. On the institutional side, the ESCB was incorporated in the Treaty as the Delors Report had envisaged it, with only a minor alteration; a predecessor of the European Central Bank would be set up to manage the transition to the third stage. This so-called European Monetary Institute (EMI) would become operational once the Treaty had been ratified. During the Intergovernmental Conferences in 1990 the French government had submitted proposals which called for a new 'economic government' to flank the ESCB, but these proposals were not adopted by member states (Italianer 1993, Thiel 1995).

After EMU had been incorporated in the Treaty there were still a number of issues not settled. Following an initiative by Theo Waigel, the then German Finance Minister, a so-called 'Stability Pact' was created that stipulated the rules and regulations after EMU would enter stage 3 (see Crowley 2002, Heipertz and Verdun 2004). The rules envisaged would ensure that Member States once in EMU would continue to respect ceilings on budgetary deficits. The Stability and Growth Pact (as it was formally named when it was adopted in Amsterdam in 1997) envisaged a procedure with possible sanctions if Member States did not comply with the limits on budgetary deficits. The so-called Excessive Deficit Procedure (EDP) which is part of the SGP is an elaborate process in which member states and the European Commission exchange budgetary plans and figures showing actual performance. If they fail to meet the target they have a few years to make corrections before possible sanctions would be initiated. A few member states received an "early warning" for having an excessive deficit. By November 2003 however the German and French governments suspended the sanctions section of the SGP. This behaviour effectively violated the SGP rules and brought the EU member states into disarray as it is not clear what this violation of the rules will imply for the regime of macroeconomic policy-making in the EU.

## The Nature of Economic and Monetary Governance in the EU

What does this history of EMU tell us about the nature of governance in the EU? Let us now return to the four neofunctionalist concepts of spill-over mentioned in section two. Do these concepts describe these processes adequately?

The process of economic and monetary integration in the Community indeed seems to reveal itself as a gradual, technocratic and institutional process. Successful economic and monetary integration appear not to have been 'invented' on an ad hoc basis, but rather to have resulted from earlier Member State policy choices or successes with other integration goals. In this manner, the CAP gave rise to the first EMU plan. The fact that the Werner Plan failed was due to differences in opinion about the way to obtain EMU and its final aim. In the 1970s, the existence of the snake contributed to the creation of the EMS. The EMS, in turn, developed successfully once the member states made inflation convergence their primary objective. Next, the internal market became a feasible objective when member states embarked on neo-liberal policies and thus searched for a European strategy to respond to the international challenge. The relaunching of EMU then again became possible because its first stage contained the institutionalization of earlier policy decisions (EMS, the internal market, and capital liberalisation), and it would lead to institutionalising the price stability objective, using a step-by-step technocratic transfer of monetary policy sovereignty to a European System of Central Banks (ESCB). Hence, regarding both economic and monetary policy-making, convergence had taken place as for a large part, 'integration' implied institutionalization. This description of economic and monetary integration in the EC/EU discloses the neofunctionalist mechanism of 'sectoral spill-over', i.e. the success of the EMS enables the creation of the internal market, which then facilitates the launching of EMU.

'Cooperative spill-over', is illustrated by the way the various national technocrats and government officials cooperated. The speed with which they drafted reports, and the fact that these reports were accepted unanimously, are an indication of this type of spill-over. As was mentioned above, both the Werner Report and the Delors Report were drafted by monetary experts. In both the Werner Group and the Delors Committee every member state was represented, and the group members had much experience with transnational 'committee' negotiations. In the case of the Werner Group, most group members were chairmen of EEC economic or financial committees, whereas most members of the Delors Committee were central bank presidents. These officials settled their issues relatively quickly and managed to bring forward a workable blueprint. It would also seem that the idea of the transnational experts having aimed at a 'common goal' could be considered an adequate description of cooperative spill-over.[18] Again, it appears that the mechanism of cooperative spill-over was at work here.

Thirdly, though not dealt with in this chapter thus far, it is perhaps worth noting here that the process of economic and monetary integration may well have led to the enlargement of the Community (geographical spill-over). Denmark, Ireland, and the UK joined the EC in 1973, after the first stage of the customs union had been completed, and when the EMU plan was still a feasible objective. Greece became a member of the EC in 1981, two years after the EMS had been created (even though the Greek drachma remained outside it). Portugal and Spain joined in 1986, the year following the signing of the SEA. Finally, in 1994, after the Treaty of Rome had been revised and incorporated into the Maastricht Treaty, Austria, Finland, and Sweden joined the EU. They had to underwrite the whole acquis communautaire, and were not granted the right to have an opt-out, as had been arranged for Denmark and the United Kingdom.[19] Countries outside the EC/EU have been attracted rather than scared off by deepened integration. The Enlargement of the EU with ten new Member States in May 2004 is another clear example of this attractiveness.[20] The fact that so far no country, with the exception of Greenland, has ever stepped out of the EC/EU also shows that the European integration process may trigger geographical spill-over, or at least, it does not seem to pose an obstruction to other countries willing to apply for membership.

The history of economic and monetary integration in the EC/EU, however, provides little evidence for the last spill-over mechanism identified above as 'political spill-over'. The success of the integration process would cause, according to Haas, the political actors in Member States to gain supranational control over these processes, which would manifest itself in a shift of political loyalty to the European level. In Haas' view technocrats would be the first to operate at the supranational level (at first without political control), but the desire of supranational control would soon thereafter move the political process to this level. The history of EMU suggests that only the first part of the mechanism has taken place (consensus and transnational/intergovernmental cooperation of technocrats and governments), whereas the transfer of political control over the process to the European level has not occurred. This is where a democratic deficit has emerged, i.e. there is no political authority at the European level responsible for the outcome of economic and monetary policies.

The nature of economic and monetary governance in Europe, therefore, exists of two different policy-making regimes. The monetary regime is the result of Member States sharing a policy objective, namely, to aim for price stability – an objective which only recently has become generally accepted among member state governments, and which should not be endangered by political pressure – hence a de-politization of monetary policy has taken place. The assumption that this objective can only be guaranteed when the new European monetary authority is politically independent is the latest development in de facto policy consensus. The successful transfer of sovereignty over monetary policy to the European level was a result of years of de facto coordination, in the framework of the EMS, i.e. aiming policies at price stability and exchange rate stability (Gros and Thygesen 1998). Moreover, for most countries this policy implied following German monetary policies. Thus, the factual room for manoeuvre over monetary policy-making had decreased, leaving the 'costs' of EMU (i.e. loss of policy autonomy) to be perceived as small (Verdun 2000).

On the economic side the major development of European integration has been the establishment of the internal market. But apart from rules guaranteeing the freedom of movement of goods, services, capital, and persons, there seems to be very limited consensus about the conduct of other macro-economic policies, such as fiscal policies, cyclical policies, public finance, and other policies which can be used for stabilisation, allocation, and redistribution (such as social, regional and labour market policies). It has often been suggested that the development of economic integration in the Community has been relatively successful in abolishing rules which obstruct integration (negative integration), but has not been able to construct European policies to take their place (positive integration). However, as the European Union is not based on a European 'demos', or a European common identity, it has been widely held undesirable to transfer economic sovereignty to the European level. Thus, it has been decided that economic governance will remain at the national level, even if the increasing interdependence, induced by the European integration process and the internationalization of national economies, strongly restricts the choice of national economic policies as diverging policies increasingly prove to be unsustainable. Thus, the EU Member States are confronted with having to make national policy choices under difficult circumstances: they have fewer policy instruments, those that remain are less powerful, the conduct of the 'wrong' type of policies can be more damaging than ever, and there is no European (economic) authority to turn to if they cannot manage their economic problems on their own. Since the creation of EMU in 1999 the EU Member States have been governed in part by the ECB (monetary policy) in part by ad-hoc coordination of economic policies following the so-called "Broad Economic Policy Guidelines" (BEPG) and the SGP (see also Hodson and Maher 2001). As was mentioned above, even those rules seem not to hold. One should either move forward and be more proactive in coordination or let things be and possibly lack a credible commitment to coordination.

## Three Scenarios for Public Finance in the EU

Thus far, this chapter has argued that the European economic and monetary policies have been developed by monetary authorities following a pragmatic, technocratic, elitist road to integration. Progress was reached only on those policies where consensus could be reached, and about which all member states could at least see the benefits. The result has been what we referred to above as an asymmetric development of economic and monetary policy integration. What does this asymmetric EMU, where economic or fiscal integration lags behind monetary integration, imply for the healthy conduct of economic and monetary policies? What proposals and progress have been made in the field of public finance and fiscal harmonisation in the Community? What are the options at present, and why are the opponents of change so concerned? Yet, what happens if in the final stage of EMU a country specific shock occurs?

Proposals to harmonise taxation and introduce an 'economic' authority in the EEC have been around, notably in the Werner Report, but have never been close to realisation. In 1977 the first report examining the role of public finance in the EEC was published – the MacDougall Report. It was written by a group of 'independent' economists on request of the Commission of the EEC. By studying the role public finance in existing federations (e.g. the Federal Republic of Germany and the United States), it drew conclusions about the usefulness of a larger role of public finance in the EEC. Its conclusions were that a larger role for public finance could contribute to reducing the disparities in per capita income, regional disparities, and could play a role in cushioning short-term and cyclical fluctuations. It stressed that the diversity in per capita income across the EEC were at least as unequal between the nine members of the Community, as they are on average between the various regions of the eight countries studied in the report (Commission of the EC 1977: 12). However, as it was recognised that little support existed for extending the EC budget, the report's conclusions were that the Community's budget needed to be expanded by a mere 2 to 2.5 percent of Community GDP in the short run, and eventually account for 5 to 7 percent if a monetary union were to be created. It noted that "an essential characteristic would be that the supply of social and welfare services would nearly all remain at the national level. Such an arrangement could provide sufficient geographical equalisation of productivity, living standards and cushioning of temporary fluctuations to support a monetary union" (Commission of the EC 1977).

In retrospect, the MacDougall report was well ahead of its time. When published, the EMS had not even been set up, let alone a plan for EMU in the Community. Moreover, lack of support for further transfer of funding to the Community level (the European Regional and Development Fund had only just been established in 1975) made it impossible to look more carefully into its analytical findings concerning uneven development of economic and monetary integration. The 'eurosclerosis' of the early 1980s meant that the findings of the report never gave rise to policy initiatives until later that decade.

A start was made with the gradual harmonisation of indirect taxation during the preparations which led to the creation of the internal market.[21] In 1987 the Padoa-Schioppa Report was published which stressed the need to look closer at the Community's role in achieving an equitable distribution of the gains in economic welfare throughout the Community, as well as ensuring high levels of actual growth (Padoa-Schioppa Report 1987: 6). It warned against serious regional imbalances in the course of market liberalisation.

As was stated above, the Delors Report (1989) was very cautious in the sphere of EC budgetary and fiscal policies. It considered the planned extension of the Community budget between 1988 and 1993 to be sufficient, and indicated no further need for increasing European funds. It took the Commission until 1991 to embark on a new major study on public finance, 'Stable Money – Sound Finances' (Commission 1993a, 1993b). The study was completed in early 1992 but only published in 1993, as the Commission President Jacques Delors had put an embargo on its publication[22] due to the difficulties surrounding the Danish and French referendums on the ratification of the Maastricht Treaty and subsequent problems with the EMS that year (see Andrews 1995, Cameron 1993, Sandholtz 1996). As will be discussed below, when it came out in 1993 it had very cautious recommendations.

This brief history of Community public finance therefore shows very limited consensus about the need for extending the fiscal role of the Community or even harmonisation of taxes. This can well be understood from a point of view of the absence of an authority monitoring these policies at the EC/EU level, but also from member states' interest to determine the levels of taxation at the national level. It has been argued that the institutionalisation of monetary policy at the European level, without a similar development in the area of fiscal policy, creates a paradox. On the one hand, the member states need to coordinate fiscal policies to secure monetary union, whereas on the other hand, given the absence of a fiscal authority and a federal budget, it remains an important policy instrument for national adjustment. Furthermore, tax harmonisation has also been resisted as taxes prove to be only one of many factors which determine the cost of products, the location of firms, and the revenue of governments. Nevertheless, as monetary policies have been transferred to the European level, does this not have implications for the member states' policy mix of monetary and fiscal policies?

Let us now turn to three possible ways of conducting national macro-economic policies within an internal market and monetary union. The first scenario is the one put forward in 'Stable Money – Sound Finances' (Commission 1993a, 1993b) which favours a minimalist role for community public finance. The second is the alternative at the other extreme, suggesting the introduction of a much larger Community budget, known as fiscal federalism. The third is an intermediary solution, namely, to expand the budget of the European Union to cope with country specific shocks.

## A Minimalist Solution

General consensus in the European Union at present is to leave the Community budget unchanged – even with EMU having started and with enlargement occurring in 2004. The arguments supporting this view have been clearly elaborated in 'Stable Money – Sound Finances', a report drafted by 'independent economists' and by the officials of DG II, which was funded by the Commission.[23] The report was written on request of the Commission, who had "asked a group of independent economists to examine the role of Community public finance in the perspective of economic and monetary union" (European Commission 1993a: v).[24]

The report warned against greater centralisation of public finance, and supported instead that the EU budget would be increased very marginally over a period of 10 to 15 years to a maximum of 2 percent of Community GDP, arguing that this would be an adequate size for stabilization under EMU (European Commission 1993a: 6). Even with such a small Community budget, according to the report, the adjustment mechanism would be able to correct the normal macro-economic cycles. It did, however, argue that there was a case for having a Community role in the event of a country-specific shock. But it stressed that "inexpensive and effective mechanisms, explicitly designed for stabilization, could be operated at EC level for assisting member states hit by adverse economic developments" (European Commission 1993a: 1). By 'inexpensive', the report meant 0.2 percent of Community GDP. It is doubtful whether such a small figure would be effective. Surely 0.2 percent of Community GDP would not have adequately tackled a major country-specific shock, such as German re-unification.[25]

## Fiscal Federalism

Other academic scholars, however, have pointed to the fact that simple sectoral and structural fluctuations may prove to be similar in size and nature to a country specific shock. The theory of Optimal Currency Areas (OCAs) states that to have a single currency in a particular economic area requires either full economic integration in that area or high correlation of shocks. According to the OCA theory the desirability of using a common monetary policy would depend in turn on the costs and benefits of the loss of the option to devalue/revalue the exchange rate (McKinnon 1963, for a more recent discussion of the OCA theories and EMU see Crowley 2001). Even when a single currency is introduced in an economic area that fulfilled the criteria of the OCA, the absence of individual currencies which can be de- or revalued may still frustrate economic adjustment. The classic example often cited was the case of Massachussetts, where industry declined. That case showed that, due to the developments in global markets, this particular state would have benefited from a devaluation had there been a Massachusetts' dollar. However, as the state was part of a federation, the shock did not hit the state as badly as it could have, due to its membership of the USA federation. Fiscal transfers on aggregate benefited Massachusetts, as the decline in industry implied that on the whole the state contributed less in federal taxes to the federal budget, whereas it received more money from the federal state, in the form of unemployment benefits (Eichengreen 1990, 1993, Sachs and Sala-i-Martín 1989).[26]

The case of fiscal federalism in Canada should also be of great interest to Europeans. Fiscal federalism in Canada was influenced by the war experience and the creation of the welfare state. In certain sense it helped create a sense of Canadian political nationhood that could be mobilised in pursuit of Canadian policy goals (Lazar 2000: 4). Canadian fiscal federalism was most "centralised" in the mid 1980s, but since then there has been a trend to decentralise more public spending to the provincial level. The stabilization function in Canada is shared between the provincial and the federal level (Norrie and Wilson 2000). The Canadian case is also an example of how one can have a system that can be changed if the constituents are unhappy with the status quo (Banting, Brown and Courchene 1994) – certainly having a responsive system could be attractive to many EU member states.

More recently, authors have once again examined the prospect for fiscal federalism for the EU in light of the start of EMU. Authors such as Ackrill (2003) found that "despite much advice to the contrary, EMU has started without the EU having the means to undertake economic stabilisation across the euro area." (Ackrill, 2003 p.1). He finds that without stabilisation one needs to rely on flexibility in national fiscal systems. In order to be successful, convergence would need to be obtained first, but Ackrill does not address the issue as to what the effects would be if the coordination or the flexibility is lacking (which seems to be the case at the moment).

So what would be a more radical solution for Europe? The comparison with Canada and the United States has already been hinted at as offering a possible scenario for the distant future: a federal budget in the European Union similar to those in mature federations (Biehl and Winter 1990). An economic government would have to be installed to monitor these tax revenues.[27] This budget need not be very large, i.e. it could be less than twenty percent. Existing federations do not have budgets as high as the national budgets of the individual member state governments at present. This European Public Finance Union (PFU), as Biehl has named it, would include "those aspects of integration that are closely linked with taxation and spending" (Biehl 1994: 140; see also Pelkmans 1991: 89-90). However, as the EU is far from introducing a European income tax, or a European corporate tax, the EU could settle for a second best scenario whereby a two-stage progressive surcharge to the existing national income and corporation taxes could be introduced (Biehl 1994: 152). Theoretically, this gradual process and the earlier mentioned relatively low level of federal budgets should be some sign of relief for those who fear that a federal budget would imply higher European taxes on the whole. However, the European business representatives, in fact, are more afraid of "a European tax being levied on top of national taxes, whereby the national taxes would not be proportionately reduced".[28]

At present there is very little support for such radical change. The introduction of a federal authority with a federal budget, as advocated by fiscal federalists, lacks widespread governmental and public support as many dread the idea of moving towards a federal state.

## An EMU Support Fund

One compromise could be to augment the present European Community budget by raising funds for the type of shocks which can be expected now that EMU is fully operational. It would then have to be monitored by a European institution, would either be a new institution or one of the existing ones such as the Ecofin Council or the European Council. There would have to be rules that would ensure that member states meet certain criteria or objectives (i.e. meet the principles of securing low budgetary deficits). This fund could be called upon if meeting the rules of coordination (SGP) ended up being too costly for the economy. By including such a fund the EU would be offering a "carrot" rather than merely the "sticks" which we saw in the sanction mechanism of the SGP. A member state that finds its national policies inadequate in dealing with a particular economic difficulty could apply for European funding from the 'EMU Support Fund'. The fund would operate like a cohesion fund, with two important differences. Unlike the present cohesion fund where only the poorest countries can request funding for projects, funding from the 'EMU Support Fund' may be requested by all countries participating in EMU whose national economic instruments are failing to deal with a country-specific shock and/or a severe shock in any particular industrial sector. Hence, the introduction of the 'EMU Support Fund' would not make it necessary to introduce a full-scale economic government right away (as would be necessary in the case of fiscal federalism referred to above). Rather, by extending the institutional framework of European funds, the incremental process of integration of policies, institutions and competencies can be maintained. Moreover, if an economic or financial disaster should hit the domestic economy of an EMU member, other EMU countries are likely to be affected as well. For example, if the disaster causes excessive borrowing by the national government of the country initially hit by the shock, interest rates throughout the EMU-zone could possibly rise. Moreover, the country specific shock may well result in reduced imports from or exports to its trading partners. Thus, in order to provide stability in EMU, the introduction of an 'EMU Support Fund' could well benefit the other EMU participants.

## Conclusion

The nature of the progress of economic and monetary integration has engendered a further dimension to the problem of democratic accountability in the EU, which builds on the democratic problems identified by various political scientists and scholars of European integration. This chapter has defined the democratic deficit of EMU as the absence of a European political authority over aggregate European economic policies and a European single monetary policy. This chapter also shows that the democratic deficit of EMU is inherent to the nature of governance of the economic and monetary policies in the EU. It results from the technocratic history of economic and monetary policy-making, from maintaining the two separate categories, i.e. 'economic' and 'monetary' policy-making, and from a different nature of integration with regard to both areas of policy-making. With regard to economic policy-making mainly negative integration has been achieved, whereas regarding monetary policy-making positive integration has been achieved. Hence, the democratic deficit is a result of the fact that the independent conduct of monetary policies has become centralised, that is, has become institutionalized at the European level, while macro-economic policies remain decentralised at the member state level.

The economic and monetary integration process in the EU has closely followed three of the four neofunctionalist mechanisms of spill-over, that is, sectoral spill-over, co-operative spill-over, and geographical spill-over. In particular the concept of 'co-operative spill-over' is useful for understanding the role of transnational experts in the process of economic and monetary integration. Even the 1993 Report on public finance, 'Stable Money – Sound Finances', was set up as an expert 'non-political' study. However, the fact that Haas's fourth spill-over mechanism, political spill-over, has not taken place under EMU suggests that a lack of democratic accountability will be the result.

The chapter also suggested that the conduct of monetary policies (determining the level of inflation and exchange rates) have followed the logic of 'low politics' – even though it is clear that some dimensions of monetary policy (take for example the transfer of seigniorage, that is, the right to print money and the income generated from it) are sensitive, 'high politics', issues. Economic policies, on the other hand, excluding the policies which facilitated the creation of the internal market, have remained largely sensitive issues, and thus need to be categorised as 'high politics'.

As a result of continuing European integration and economic interdependence, the room for manoeuvre for member states to conduct diverging policies is very limited. This chapter reviewed three possible scenarios of public finance in the EU. It has examined the introduction of a 'federal' or 'economic' government with a 'federal budget', but has indicated that, though it may well in the future reduce the democratic deficit, it is unlikely to do so at present because it lacks political support. From the fiscal federalism literature and a short discussion of the systems in Canada and the USA it can be concluded that the EMU project would perhaps be based on firmer ground if a greater role for European transfers were introduced. But again, there is very little support for a larger redistributive federal governing role at the European level. Hence, this chapter suggests that the best way forward in the short run would be to introduce an 'EMU Support Fund', which would provide resources for tackling country specific shocks. It would serve as a temporary pragmatic solution to problems which may occur under an EMU which lacks a political authority to flank the ECB and which lacks a system of fiscal federal transfers.

## Notes

1 Earlier versions of this chapter were presented at the workshop 'The Transformation of Governance in the European Union', at the 24th Annual ECPR Workshops in Oslo, Norway, 29 March – 3 April 1996 and at the First Conference of the European Community Studies Association Canada, St Catherines 31 May-1 June 1996. This research forms part of the author's larger project on European economic and monetary integration. The author is grateful for having been granted a European Union Human Capital and Mobility Fellowship which enabled this research. The author would like to thank Thomas Christiansen, William Coleman, Thomas Diez, Beate Kohler-Koch, Brigid Laffan, Georges Pagoulatos, Alberta Sbragia, Albert Weale and the ECPR and ECSA-Canada workshop participants for useful comments on an earlier draft. The usual disclaimer applies.

2 The term 'asymmetric' is used here to indicate the difference in development of 'monetary' versus 'economic' integration. See for a discussion of the historic and institutional 'asymmetric' development of EMU Verdun (1996) and (2000a).

3 The absence of an economic authority flanking a currency issuing authority is a novelty in modern economic history (cf. Dyson, 1994). Mature federations such as Australia,

Austria, Canada, the Federal Republic of Germany, India, New Zealand, Switzerland and the USA, have both institutions. An example closest to the European monetary union may be the former Belgian-Luxembourg monetary union, which lasted for more than seven decades until 1999. It consisted of a small state, and a very tiny, very wealthy state respectively. Moreover, the Belgium/Luxembourg franc was for many years de facto pegged to the German national currency (the Deutschmark). Their monetary policies were coordinated accordingly.

4   See for a further elaboration on the 'democratic deficit of the EMU', Verdun (1998) and Verdun and Christiansen (2001).

5   Trade unionists, such as Bill Morris (1998) have made the link to outcome, and argue that EMU is bad for employment.

6   The concept of 'governance' has received considerable attention in the past ten years, see for example Bulmer (1994) Jachtenfuchs (1995, 2001), Jachtenfuchs and Kohler-Koch (1995), Kohler-Koch (1996), Kohler-Koch and Eising (1999), Rosenau (1992) and Scharpf (1994).

7   Though Haas identified four areas where the spill-over mechanism operates he only explicitly labelled one of the four categories, i.e. 'geographical spill-over'. The labels of the other categories have been introduced by scholars discussing the neofunctionalist thought, who usually identify only three categories of spill-over, i.e. 'sectoral', 'political', and 'geographical' spill-over (George 1991, Tranholm-Mikkelsen 1991, and Corbey 1993). In this chapter the choice is made to accept Haas' original four distinct areas, and add the category of 'co-operative spill-over'. This distinction is necessary to differentiate between the transfer of political loyalty and desire for political control at the supranational level on the one hand and the technocratic transnational policy cooperation on the other  hand.

8   Recently authors have also voiced renewed support for the neofunctionalist mode of thought, see inter alia Burley and Mattli (1993), Corbey (1993, 1995), Cornett and Caporaso (1992), Sandholtz and Zysman (1989), Stone Sweet and Sandholtz (1998), and Tranholm-Mikkelsen (1991). Good reviews of neofunctionalism and intergovernmentalism are provided in Rosamond (1996, 2003).

9   Some of the forceful statements had been watered down in order to leave room for interpretation at a later date.

10   See for a good discussion of role of the experts in creating the Werner Report, Rosenthal (1975). See for a general analysis of the rise and fall of the first EMU plan Dyson (1994); Kruse (1980) and Tsoukalis (1977).

11   The 'monetarists' in this context should not be confused with the followers of the doctrine of Milton Friedman.

12   Although the UK government decided that the British pound sterling would stay out of the Exchange Rate Mechanism (ERM) of the EMS it, nevertheless, considered low inflation to be its primary monetary objective. In 1985 the Bank of England abandoned domestic indicators in favour of the West German D-Mark, after discovering that targeting domestic nominal indicators failed to produce low inflation.

13   The process of monetary integration has in many ways been influenced by the role of experts. Elsewhere I have argued that the Delors committee could be considered an epistemic community as defined by Peter Haas (1992), see Verdun (1999).

14   Even the governor of the Bank of England, Sir Robin Leigh-Pemberton, considered the report a feasible blueprint for EMU, though he considered the question of whether to embark on such a project to be a purely *political* decision.

15   The economic union has been treated differently in the Delors Report than had been done in the Werner Report. The recent report identified a smaller role for the economic

union than its predecessor did. See for an analysis of the role of 'economic union' in the creation of EMU, Pelkmans (1991).

16  See for a discussion about the differences between the Delors Report and the Maastricht Treaty, Artis (1992) and Italianer (1993).

17  The 'convergence criteria' refer to inflation rates, interest rates, exchange rate performance, budgetary deficits and public debts (Treaty on European Union, Art. 104 and Art. 109, and annexed protocols). Member States seeking to qualify for entry into EMU need to meet the criteria. For eleven Member States this judgment was made in 1998. Greece qualified a little later. With the expansion of the EU with ten new Member States in May 2004 there will be more decisions made based on the convergence criteria.

18  These findings are consistent with the conclusions of Sandholtz (1993), and Dyson et al. 1995a) and (1995b), even though these authors also elaborate other aspects of the EMU process, such as the domestic/European dichotomy, the intergovernmental bargaining of Member States, and the role of financial markets and globalisation.

19  The opt-outs of Denmark and the UK, however, do indicate that there is always the possibility of an integration 'spill-back', cf. Schmitter (1971).

20  The Norwegian referendums against EC entry in 1972 and against EU entry in 1993 and the Swiss vote against joining the European Economic Area also in 1993, are exceptions to this trend. However, it can be questioned whether these countries would have wanted to join the EU and EEA respectively, if the integration process would have been less advanced.

21  On 3 June 1991 and 27 July 1992 the Ecofin Council further developed the harmonisation of VAT rates.

22  DG II (Ecfin) official (1992), interview with the author.

23  The report was published in *European Economy*, no. 53, and background studies were published in a separate voluminous report 'The Economics of Community Public Finance' published in *European Economy*, no. 5.

24  The report was not quite as independent as it could have been, as officials of DG II (now DG EcFin) largely contributed to the report. Even the chairman and the rapporteur were DG II (now DG Ecfin) officials.

25  Though this shock is unique in its scope and size, it is not unthinkable that an individual country may be hit severely by a country specific shock, or that some countries would be affected much more than others by a shock hitting all of the EU.

26  For a non-technical summary of the various arguments, see Taylor (1995).

27  As was mentioned above, the French government made proposals in 1991 to introduce such an economic government to flank the European central bank.

28  Official of the French employers' organization, CNPF. Interview with the author, November 1992.

## References

Ackrill, Robert (2003), 'Stabilisation in EMU: A Critical Review', in Baimbridge M. and P. Whyman (eds) (2003) *Fiscal Federalism and European Economic Integration*, New York and London: Routledge.

Andrews, David (1995), 'European Monetary Diplomacy and the Rolling Crisis of 1992-1993', in Rhodes, Carolyn and Mazey, Sonia (eds), *The State of the European Union. Building a European Polity?* Boulder: Lynne Rienner, pp. 159-76.

Artis, Michael J. (1992), 'The Maastricht Road to Monetary Union', *Journal of Common Market Studies* 30: 299-309.

Banting, Keith G., Douglas M. Brown and Thomas J. Courchene (eds) (1994) *The Future of Fiscal Federalism*, Kingston: School of Policy Studies.

Biehl, Dieter (1990), 'Deficiencies and Reform Possibilities of the EC Fiscal Constitution', in Crouch, Colin and Marquand, David (eds), *The Politics of 1992. Beyond the Single European Market*, Oxford and Cambridge: Basil Blackwell, pp. 85-99.

Biehl, Dieter (1994), 'The Public Finances of the Union', in Duff, Andrew, Pinder, John, and Pryce, Roy (eds), *Maastricht and Beyond. Building the European Union*, London and New York: Routledge, pp. 140-153.

Biehl, Dieter and Winter, Horst (1990), *Europa finanzieren – ein föderalistisches Modell*, with Weidenfeld, Werner; Fischer, Helmut and Stoll, Karin. Gütersloh: Bertelsmann.

Boyce, Brigitte (1993), 'The Democratic Deficit of the European Community', *Parliamentary Affairs*, 44(4): 458-77.

Bulmer, Simon J. (1994), 'The Governance of the European Union: A New Institutionalist Approach', *Journal of Public Policy*, 13(4): 351-80.

Burley, Anne-Marie and Mattli, Walter (1993), 'Europe Before the Court: A Political Theory of Legal Integration', *International Organization*, 47(1): 41-76.

Cameron, R. David (1992), 'The 1992 Initiative: Causes and Consequences', in Sbragia, Alberta (ed.) (1992), *Euro-Politics: Institutions and Policymaking in the 'New' European Community*. Washington DC: Brookings Institution. pp. 23-75.

Cameron, R. David (1993), 'British Exit, German Voice, French Loyalty: Defection, Domination, and Cooperation in the 1992-93 ERM Crisis', Paper presented at the Annual APSA meeting, Washington, DC, September.

Caporaso, James A. and Keeler, John T.S. (1995), 'The European Union and Regional Integration Theory', in Rhodes, Carolyn and Mazey, Sonia (eds), *The State of the European Union. Building a European Polity?* Boulder: Lynne Rienner, pp. 29-62.

Chryssochoou, Dimitris N. (1995), 'European Union and the Dynamics of Confederal Consociation: Problems and Prospects for a Democratic Future', *Journal of European Integration/Revue d'Integration Européenne*, 18 (2, 3): 279-306.

Chryssochoou, Dimitris N. (2001) 'The Nature of Democracy in the European Union and the Limits of Treaty Reform', *Current Politics and Economics of Europe*, Vol 10 (3): 245-264.

Commission of the EC (1977), Report of the Study Group on the Role of Public Finance in European Integration, vols 1 and 2 'MacDougall Report'. Brussels, Commission of the European Communities, Doc II/10/77, 2 volumes, April.

Corbey, Dorette (1993), *Stilstand is Vooruitgang. De Dialectiek van het Europese Integratieproces*, Assen and Maastricht: Van Gorcum.

Corbey, Dorette (1995), 'Dialectical Functionalism: Stagnation as a Booster of European Integration', *International Organization*, 49 (2): 253-84.

Cornett, Linda and Caporaso, James A. (1992), '"And Still it Moves!" State Interests and Social Forces in the European Community', in Rosenau, James N. and Czempiel, Ernst-Otto (eds), *Governance without Government: Order and Change in World Politics*, Cambridge: Cambridge University Press, pp. 219-49.

Cowles, Maria Green (1995), 'Setting the Agenda for a New Europe: The ERT and EC 1992', *Journal of Common Market Studies*, 33(4): 501-26.

Crowley, Patrick (2001) 'The Institutional Implications of EMU', *Journal of Common Market Studies*, 39(3): 385-404.

Crowley, Patrick (2002) 'The Stability and Growth Pact: Review, Alternatives and Legal Aspects', *Current Politics and Economics of Europe*, 11(3): 225-44.

De Grauwe, Paul (1992), *The Economics of Monetary Integration*, Oxford: Oxford University Press.

Delors Report (1989), Report on Economic and Monetary Union in the European Community (Committee for the Study of Economic and Monetary Union) Luxembourg: Office for Official Publications of the E.C.

Dyson, Kenneth (1994), *Elusive Union. The Process of Economic and Monetary Union in Europe*, London and New York: Longman.

Dyson, Kenneth and George Michalopoulos (1995a), 'Rescue or Transformation? The European State and the Politics of Economic and Monetary Union', paper prepared for the 23rd ECPR Workshop, Bordeaux, 27 April-2 May.

Dyson, Kenneth, Kevin Featherstone, and George Michalopoulos (1995b), 'Strapped to the Mast; EC Central Bankers between Global Financial Markets and Regional Integration', *Journal of European Public Policy*, 2(3): 465-87.

Eichengreen, Barry (1990), 'One Money for Europe: Lessons from the US Currency Union', *Economic Policy*, 10, April.

Eichengreen, Barry (1993), 'Is Europe an Optimum Currency Area', in Borner, Silvio and Grubel, Herbert (eds), *The European Community after 1992. Perspectives from the Outside*, London: Macmillan, pp. 138-61.

Featherstone, Kevin (1994), 'Jean Monnet and the "Democratic Deficit" in the European Union', *Journal of Common Market Studies*, 32(2): 149-70.

George, Stephen (1991), *Politics and Policy in the European Community*, 2nd edn. Oxford: Oxford University Press.

Gros, Daniel and Thygesen, Niels (1998), *European Monetary Integration*. 2nd edition, Harlow: Addison Wesley Longman.

Haas, Ernst B. (1968), *The Uniting of Europe. Political, Social and Economic Forces 1950-1957*, Stanford: Stanford University Press [1958].

Haas, Peter M. (1992), 'Introduction: Epistemic Communities and International Policy Co-ordination', *International Organization*, 46 (1): 1-35.

Hall, Peter A. (1986), *Governing the Economy. The Politics of State Intervention in Britain and France*, New York: Oxford University Press.

Heipertz, Martin and Amy Verdun (2004) 'The Dog That Would Never Bite? The Past and Future of the Stability and Growth Pact', *Journal of European Public Policy*, Vol. 11 No. 2.

Heipertz, Martin and Amy Verdun (2004) *Ruling Europe: Theory and Politics of the Stability and Growth Pact* (Max Planck Institute for the Study of Societies, Research Report, December 2003.

Hodson, Dermot and Imelda Maher (2001) 'The Open Method as a New Mode of Governance', *Journal of Common Market Studies*, 39(4): 719-46.

Hoffmann, Stanley, (1966), 'Obstinate or Obsolete? The Fate of the Nation-State and the Case of Western Europe', *Daedalus* 95(3): 862-916.

Hoffman, Stanley (1983), Reflections on the Nation-State in Western Europe Today', in Tsoukalis, Loukas (ed.) *The European Community: Past, Present and Future*. Oxford: Basil Blackwell, pp. 21-39.

Italianer, Alexander (1993), 'Mastering Maastricht: EMU Issues and How They Were Settled', in Greschmann, Klaus (ed.) *Economic and Monetary Union: Implications for National Policy-makers*, Maastricht: European Institute of Public Administration, pp. 51-115.

Jachtenfuchs, Markus (1995), 'Theoretical Perspectives on European Governance', Mannheim Working Papers no. 7.

Jachtenfuchs, Markus (2001) 'The Governance Approach to European Integration', *Journal of Common Market Studies*, 39(2): 245-64.

Jachtenfuchs, Markus and Beate Kohler-Koch (1995), 'The Transformation of Governance in the European Union', Paper presented at the Fourth Biennial European Community Studies Association Conference, Charleston, South Carolina, May 11-14.

Joerges, Christian (1994), 'European Economic Law, the Nation-State and the Maastricht Treaty', in Dehousse, R. (ed.), *Europe After Maastricht. An Ever Closer Union?*, München: Beck, pp. 29-62.

Johnson, Christopher (1994), 'Fiscal and Monetary Policy in Economic and Monetary Union', in Duff, Andrew, Pinder, John, and Pryce, Roy (eds), *Maastricht and Beyond. Building the European Union*, London and New York: Routledge, pp. 71-83.

Jones, Erik (2002), 'Macroeconomic Preferences and Europe's Democratic Deficit', in Amy Verdun (ed.) *The Euro: European Integration Theory and Economic and Monetary Union*, Lanham: Rowman and Littlefield, pp. 145-164.

Kenen, Peter (1969), 'The Theory of Optimum Currency Areas: an Eclectic View', in Mundell, R. and Swododa, A. (eds), *Monetary Problems of the International Economy*, Chicago: University of Chicago Press.

Keohane, Robert O., and Hoffmann, Stanley (eds) (1991), *The New European Community: Decisionmaking and Institutional Change*, Boulder, San Francisco and Oxford: Westview Press.

Keohane, Robert O. and Nye, J. (1975), 'International interdependence and integration', in Greenstein, F. and Polsby, N. (eds), *Handbook of Political Science*, Vol. 8 Addison-Wesley, Reading, Mass. pp. 363-414.

Kohler-Koch, Beate (1996), 'Catching up with change: the transformation of governance in the European Union', *Journal of European Public Policy*, 3(3): 359-80.

Kohler-Koch, Beate and Rainer Eising (eds) (1999) *The Transformation of Governance in the European Union*, London: Routledge.

Kruse, D.C. (1980), *Monetary Integration in Western Europe: EMU, EMS and Beyond*, London and Boston: Butterworths.

Lazar, Harvey (2000) 'In Search of a New Mission Statement for Canadian Fiscal Federalism', in Harvey Lazar (ed.) *Canada: The State of the Federation 1999/2000*, pp. 3-39.

Lodge, Juliet (1994), 'Transparency and Democratic Legitimacy', *Journal of Common Market Studies*, 32(3): 343-68.

Ludlow, Peter (1982), *The Making of the European Monetary System: A Case Study of the Politics of the European Community*. London: Butterworth Scientific.

Marks, Gary, Liesbet Hooghe and Kermit Blank (1996), 'European Integration from the 1980s', *Journal of Common Market Studies*, 34(3): 341-78.

Martin, Lisa (1995), 'Economic and Political Integration: Institutional Challenge and Response', unpublished paper, Harvard University, June.

Maurer, Andreas and Wolfgang Wessels (eds) (2001), *National Parliaments on their Ways to Europe: Losers or Latecomers?* Nomos: Baden-Baden.

McKinnon, R. (1963), 'Optimum Currency Areas', *American Economic Review*, 53.

Milward, Alan S. (1992), *The European Rescue of the Nation-State*, Berkeley: University of California Press.

Morris, Bill (1998), 'EMU and the Democratic Deficit', in Bernhard Moss and Jonathan Michie (eds) *The Single European Currency in National Perspective: A Community in Crisis?*, Houndmills: Macmillan, pp. 181-190.

Moravcsik, Andrew (1991), 'Negotiating the Single European Act: National Interests and Conventional Statecraft in the European Community', *International Organization*, 45: 19-56.

Moravcsik, Andrew (1993), 'Preferences and Power in the European Community: A Liberal Intergovernmentalist Approach', *Journal of Common Market Studies*, 31: 473-524.

Moravcsik, Andrew (1998), *The Choice for Europe: Social Purpose and State Power from Messina to Maastricht*, Ithaca: Cornell University Press.

Norrie, Kenneth and L.S. Wilson (2000), 'On Re-Balancing Canadian Fiscal Federalism', in Harvey Lazar (ed.) *Canada: The State of the Federation 1999/2000*, pp. 79-98.

Pelkmans, Jacques (1991), 'Towards Economic Union', in Ludlow, Peter (ed.) *Setting EC Priorities 1991-92*, CEPS, Brussels, October-November, pp. 39-100.

Padoa-Schioppa, Tommaso (1987), *Efficiency, Stability and Equity, A Strategy for the Evolution of the Economic System of the European Community 'Padoa-Schioppa Report'*, Oxford: Oxford University Press.

Rhodes, Martin (1995), '"Subversive liberalism": Market Integration, Globalisation and the European Welfare State', in *Journal of European Public Policy*, 2 (3): 384-406.

Rosamond, Ben (1995), 'Mapping the European Condition: The Theory of Integration and the Integration of Theory', *European Journal of International Relations*, 1 (3): 391-408.

Rosamond, Ben (2003), 'New Theories of European Integration', in Michelle Cini (ed.) *European Union Politics*, Oxford: Oxford University Press, pp. 109-130.

Rosenau, James N. (1992), 'Governance, Order, and Change in World Politics', in Rosenau, James N. and Czempiel, Ernst-Otto (eds), *Governance without Government: Order and Change in World Politics*, Cambridge: Cambridge University Press, pp. 1-29.

Rosenthal, Glenda, Goldstone (1975), *The Men Behind the Decisions: Cases in European Policy-Making*, Lexington, Mass., Toronto and London: Lexington Books, D.C. Heath.

Ruigrok, Winfried and Rob van Tulder (1995), *The Logic of International Restructuring*, London: Routledge.

Sachs, Jeffrey D. and Sala-i-Martín, Xavier D. (1989), 'Fiscal Federalism and Optimum Currency Areas: Evidence for Europe from the United States', Harvard University, reprinted in Canzoneri, M. Grilli, V. and Masson, P.R. (eds), *Establishing a Central Bank: Issues in Europe and Lessons from the US*, Cambridge: Cambridge: University Press, 1992.

Sandholtz, Wayne (1993), 'Choosing Union: Monetary Politics and Maastricht', *International Organization*, 47: 1-39.

Sandholtz, Wayne (1996), 'Money Troubles: Europe's Rough Road to Monetary Union', *Journal of European Public Policy*, 3(1), pp. 84-101.

Sandholtz, Wayne and Zysman, John (1989), '1992: Recasting the European Bargain', *World Politics*, 42: 95-128.

Scharpf, Fritz W. (1994), 'Community and Autonomy Multilevel Policymaking in the European Union', *Journal of European Public Policy*, 1: 219-42.

Schmitter, Philippe C. (1971), 'A Revised Theory of International Integration', in Lindberg, Leon N. and Scheingold, Stuart A. (eds), *Regional Integration: Theory and Research*, Cambridge, Ma.: Harvard University Press, pp. 232-64.

Snyder, Francis (1994), 'Monetary Union: A Metaphor for European Union?', in Dehousse, R. (ed.), *Europe After Maastricht. An Ever Closer Union?*, München: Beck, pp. 63-102.

Stone Sweet, Alec and Wayne Sandholtz (eds) (1998) *European Integration and Supranational Governance*, Oxford: Oxford University Press.

Taylor, Paul (1983), *The Limits of European Integration*, London and Canberra: Croom Helm.

Taylor, Christopher (1995), *EMU 2000? Prospects for European Monetary Union*, Chatham House Papers, London: Royal Institute of International Affairs.

Thiel, Elke (1995), 'The Shaping of the Framework for a Single Currency in the Course of the EMU Negotiations', Paper presented at the Fourth Biennial International ECSA Conference, Charleston, S.C., 11-14 May.

Tondl, Gabriele (2000), 'Fiscal Federalism and the Reality of the European Union Budget', in Colin Crouch (ed.) *After the Euro – Shaping Institutions for Governance in the Wake of European Monetary Union*, Oxford: Oxford University Press, pp. 227-56.

Tranholm-Mikkelsen, Jeppe (1991), 'Neofunctionalism: Obstinate or Obsolete? a reappraisal in the light of the new dynamism of the European Community', *Millennium* 20: 1-22.

Treaty on European Union (1992), CONF-UP-UEM 2002/92, Brussels: Office of the European Communities.

Tsoukalis, Loukas (1977), *The Politics and Economics of European Monetary Integration*, London: George Allen and Unwin.

Verdun, Amy (1996), 'An "Asymmetrical" EMU Economic and Monetary Union in the EU: Perceptions of Monetary Authorities and Social Partners', *Journal of European Integration /Revue d'Integration européenne*, 20 (1) Autumn, pp. 59-81.

Verdun, Amy (1998), 'The Institutional Design of EMU: A Democratic Deficit?' *Journal of Public Policy*, Vol 18(2): 107-132.

Verdun, Amy (1999), 'The Role of the Delors Committee in the Creation of EMU: An Epistemic Community?' *Journal of European Public Policy* 6(2): 308-28.

Verdun, Amy (2000), *European Responses to Globalization and Financial Market Integration: Percepetions of Economic and Monetary Union in Britain, France and Germany*, Houndmills: Palgrave Macmillan.

Verdun, Amy and Thomas Christiansen (2001), 'The Legitimacy of the Euro: an Inverted Process?' *Current Politics and Economics of Europe*, Vol 10 (3): 265-288.

Verdun, Amy and Stelios Stavridis (2001), 'Introduction: Democracy in the European Union', *Current Politics and Economics of Europe*, Vol 10 (3): 213-26.

Webb, Carole (1983), 'Theoretical Perspectives and Problems', in Wallace, Helen, Wallace, William and Webb, Carole (eds), *Policy-making in the European Communities* (2nd edn.), New York: Wiley pp. 1-42.

Werner Report (1970), 'Report to the Council and the Commission on the Realization by Stages of Economic and Monetary Union in the Community'. Council and Commission of the EC, Bulletin of the EC, Supplement 11, Doc 16.956/11/70, 8 October.

Williams, Shirley (1991), 'Sovereignty and Accountability in the European Community', in Keohane, Robert O. and Hoffmann, Stanley (eds), pp. 155-76.

Chapter 5

# Intergovernmental Relations in the European Union and Canada: The Place of Local Government

John B. Sutcliffe

## Introduction

As has been noted on many occasions, the European Union (EU) is a unique political organization in world affairs.[1] While the EU has "state-like" features that make it more than a traditional intergovernmental organization, it is not the political equivalent of a state – even a federal state such as Canada (Wallace, 1982). The EU member states are not the equivalent of the Canadian provinces, the EU's institutional structure does not replicate that of the Canadian federal government, and its legal system is not a parallel of the Canadian legal structure. This presents a problem for those interested in examining the European Union in a comparative context. For some scholars, such comparison is pointless because the process of integration is an example of traditional interstate relations and is unlikely to move much beyond a cooperative system dominated by the central governments of the participating states (for more on this debate, Hix, 1998; Hurrell and Menon, 1996).

It is not, however, necessary to accept the view that integration in Europe is creating a federal state, or state-like entity (Burgess, 1999), to argue that a comparative study has merit. The European Union, as it is currently constituted, does have characteristics that find their parallel in federal systems. Its policy-making process, while not an exact replica of any extant state, does have features that echo those found in federal states. The European Union, like Canada, is a multi-level polity where political activity takes place in a range of institutional and geographic settings. In both systems, moreover, different types of political decisions have different characteristics. Treaty revisions (or constitutional reform) are not the same as policy-making (which varies from policy sector to policy sector), which is also distinct from policy implementation (Peterson and Bomberg, 1999). No single actor, or set of actors, has a monopoly of political power in these settings and over these different types of political activity. Instead, decisions are made on the basis of bargaining among a range of different actors, located in different institutional settings at different geographic levels.

The purpose of this chapter is to examine the extent to which decision-making in both systems includes a place for local government. Specifically, the chapter examines relations between local government and the upper tier of government in both systems; that is, the involvement of Canadian local authorities in federal politics and the involvement of European local authorities in the European Union. There are, however, limits to this study resulting from the complexity of the multi-level polities being compared. A comprehensive study of the place of local government within the two polities requires an examination of the place of local authorities at the next territorial level of government (the member states in the EU and provinces in Canada), as well as the study of local government involvement in different policy areas and decision types over time. Local-provincial-federal relations vary in Canada across time, policy area, and across provinces. This is also the case in the European Union. For example, the structure, financing and political powers of local authorities fluctuate from province to province in Canada. This is even more evident in the European Union where the constitutional position of local government varies markedly from member state to member state (see Hooghe, 1996; Loughlin, 2001). The European Union contains federal states (such as Germany) where local governments are the responsibility of the state level governments all the way through to centralized states (such as Greece) where local governments barely exist. A number of studies point to the fact that local government engagement with the European Union is shaped by this variation in domestic position (see Klausen and Goldsmith, 1997).

As a result of this diversity, it is impossible to generalize about intergovernmental relations within Canada and the EU. Marked variations are evident across member states/provinces, policy areas, and time. This study reduces some of this complexity by focusing on particular territorial areas. In the Canadian case, the focus is on local government in Ontario. In the European Union, the focus is on local government in the United Kingdom. In both cases, the chapter provides an overview of the formal and informal involvement of local authorities from these areas in a range of policy areas and decision types at the federal/European Union levels. In both cases it is apparent that there is uncertainty about the current place of local government within these decision-making processes, and disagreement about local government's future role.

## The Formal Position of Local Government in Intergovernmental Relations

In both cases examined here, a purely formal reading of the constitutional position of local government would suggest that local authorities play only a very limited role in political activity at the Canadian federal and European Union levels respectively.

*Local Government in the European Union*

In the case of the European Union, the founding treaties made no mention of regional and local government, and nor did they provide a place for this level of government within the formal decision-making structures of the EU. Representatives of the central governments sign the treaties, and the elected representatives of the central governments, along with appointed national officials and European-level officials, dominate the key institutions.

The first formal change in this situation occurred with the signing and ratification of the Maastricht Treaty in the early 1990s. One provision of this treaty was the creation a Committee of the Regions, to be composed of representatives from regional and local bodies (Warleigh, 1999).[2] This marked the first treaty recognition that local authorities (along with regional governments) had a role to play in the European Union's decision-making structure. At the same time, the treaty also allowed for representatives from regional authorities to sit as a state's representative on the Council of Ministers.

The actual impact of these changes is limited, however. First, the Committee of the Regions is purely a consultative body. It may issue opinions but these opinions need not necessarily be incorporated into the positions adopted by the Commission, Council, or European Parliament. Scholars of the Committee of the Regions disagree over the question of whether it has the potential to evolve into a significant institution (see Christiansen, 1996; Jeffery, 2002). None, however, argue that the Committee is currently one of the major institutions in the European Union that is consistently able to influence treaty and policy development in the union. The key decisions remain the preserve of the Commission, the Council of Ministers, and, to an increasing degree, the European Parliament. It is also the case that while local and regional representatives may now sit on the Council of Ministers, they can do so only if authorized by their central government. Only a small number of states (Germany is one example) permit this to occur. Moreover, when they do sit on the Council of Ministers, they do so as representatives of their entire state and not as representatives of a single regional and local area. This provision in the treaties thus only marginally increases regional and local authorities' capacity to influence European Union decision-making (Hooghe and Marks, 2001: 83).

The formal status of local authorities within the European Union is therefore limited. At the same time, the European Union has no formal power to affect the structure and power of local authorities within member states, as this is the responsibility of the individual member states. The principle of subsidiarity, for example, does not apply to the local level of government. This principle was introduced first by the Single European Act, and has been further developed in the Treaties of Maastricht and Amsterdam. It suggests that the European Union should act only if that action is more effective than action by the member states and if the purposes of that action cannot be sufficiently achieved by member state action. It does not, however, give local authorities the power to claim that decisions should best be taken at the local level (see Lazer and Mayer-Schoenberger, 2001).

Decisions taken at the European Union level cannot, therefore, force member states to accept an enhanced role for local governments within their territory. The structure, financing, and powers of local government are questions decided at the member state level. In the case of Britain, the central government has traditionally been the level of government responsible for determining these issues. Prior to the devolution measures introduced by Tony Blair's Labour government, the central government in London had the capacity to legislate unilaterally to change the structure of local government, its financing, its policy competences and even to abolish entire local authorities. The most notable evidence of this central power occurred during the Conservative administrations of Margaret Thatcher and John Major (1979-1997). Although there is some debate as to whether the measures fully achieved the desired results (Marsh and Rhodes, 1992), there is no doubt that the central government introduced a range of measures that impacted directly on local authorities during this period. These measures included forcing local authorities to amend their working practices, and periodic revisions to the system of local government financing. They also included restructuring the territorial coverage of local government. In 1986 several metropolitan authorities (including the Greater London Council) were abolished as a result of central government legislation. This was followed in the 1990s by a broader review of local government structure. In Scotland, this review led to a two-tier system of local government being replaced in 1996 by a system of single-tier, unitary authorities (Midwinter, 1993). In England and Wales, a mixed system was introduced with unitary councils introduced in some areas, and the two-tier structure maintained in others. In both cases, the review of local government structure was initiated by the central government and not as a result of requests from the local level (see Sancton, 2000).

Devolution has complicated the situation to some degree. In 1999 the central government established a Scottish Parliament and Welsh Assembly following referendum results demonstrating support for such a development. In both cases the devolved Parliament/Assembly now has some responsibility for local government within its territory (Bogdanor, 1999; Keating, 2001). In Scotland, for example, it is now the Scottish Parliament, not the UK central government, which has the legislative capacity to amend the structure, financing and functional responsibilities of local government. In the case of Wales, the Assembly has executive control over local government, with legislative responsibility remaining in London. Devolution has thus changed the political context for local authorities in these territories. It has not, however, changed the fact that the constitutional position of local government is not secure. Local authorities are responsible to the next territorial level of government (either the UK central government, the Scottish Parliament, or Welsh Assembly), and crucial decisions regarding the place of local government in the political system can, and are, taken at that level even in the absence of support from local authority representatives.

This is important in the context of local authority engagement in politics at the European Union level. This engagement can clearly be affected by decisions taken in the domestic setting over which local authorities may have little or no control. For example, upper level government decisions to reduce the funding available to local authorities may reduce local authorities' capacity to monitor the EU policy-making process by hiring European officers or maintaining an office in Brussels. Equally, the extent of local authorities' interest in the EU policy process will be determined by their functional responsibility in the domestic setting, as determined by the next level of government. Finally, structural reorganization of local government will undoubtedly impact upon local authorities' capacities to participate in EU politics. One example of this was evident in the 1996 reorganization of local government in Scotland, which, as noted above, led to the introduction of single-tier unitary authorities. Part of this reorganization saw the disappearance of Strathclyde Regional Council, a local authority that had been at the forefront of local government efforts to participate in European Union policy-making (John, 1996: 133; Sutcliffe, 1997).

The formal position, therefore, indicates that British local authorities are not likely to be major participants in European Union policy-making, and that any participation that occurs is likely to be heavily influenced by the domestic constitutional setting.

## *Local Government in Canada*

An examination of the formal place of local government in Canadian politics finds many parallels with the position of British local authorities within the European Union. One major study of local government in Canada suggests that the dominant tendency has been to see local governments as "bit players" in Canadian politics (Graham et al, 1998: 1). Indeed, an initial study suggests that local authorities are not major participants in federal politics. An informal survey of some popular introductory texts to Canadian politics supports this impression. None devoted an entire chapter to local government, and many did not even contain a reference to local or municipal government in their index. A more formal study of the Canadian constitution also leads to the conclusion that local authorities have limited input in politics at the federal level (Keating, 1991).

Canadian local governments do not have a secure place within the Canadian constitutional structure, and indeed they receive only very limited attention in the constitution (Fowler and Siegel, 2002). Sections 91 and 92 of the Constitution outline the powers held by the federal government and provincial governments respectively. Section 92(8) gives provincial governments control over local government. As such, local governments are the creatures of the provinces. Provincial governments can create new local authorities, restructure existing authorities, amend the policy functions of local governments, and have a significant impact, through transfer payments, on the funding that local governments have at their disposal. The extent of this influence has been particularly evident in recent years. Provincial governments across Canada have, for example, legislated to amalgamate (or consolidate) local governments (see Sancton, 1996; 2000). One of the most notable examples of this was the creation, as of 1 January 1998, of the City of Toronto, the "mega-city", by the then Conservative Ontario Government. Similar amalgamated municipal governments have also been established in Ottawa, Hamilton and Sudbury, replacing two-tier structures, which contained multiple municipalities.[3] These amalgamations have occurred in the absence of demands from citizens or local authorities, and even in the face of local opposition (Sancton, 2000; 2002). Thus, the creation of the City of Toronto faced opposition in all the affected municipalities, as well as a court challenge. None of this affected the provincial government's capacity to force the change through. As Williams and Downey (1999) note, the Ontario government pursued a top-down approach to reforming the structure of local government and demonstrated only a limited concern for local government cooperation.

The constitutional structure thus places Canadian local authorities firmly within the control of the provinces. As such there is no place in the constitution for a formal institutional relationship between local authorities and the federal government. One effort to change this occurred in the 1970s with the creation of a federal Ministry of State for Urban Affairs (1971). Opposition from the provincial governments, however, limited the work of this ministry and ultimately lead to its abolition in 1978 (Tindal and Tindal, 2000: 229-33). Other efforts to change this formal situation have also been unsuccessful. Thus, the major municipalities have periodically argued they should have a formal place in the Canadian constitution (Graham et al, 1998).[4] A range of municipal actors made this argument at the time of the 1982 patriation of the constitution, with one of the most forceful expressions coming from the Federation of Canadian Municipalities' Task Force on Constitutional Reform (Tindal and Tindal, 2000: 243). A more recent example occurred in 2000 when the City of Toronto debated the possibility of becoming a "city state", and thus on separating itself from provincial control (Benzie, 2000). Neither of these efforts was successful. The efforts by municipalities to negotiate a place in the constitution have been blocked by the provinces, and the Ontario Government dismissed outright the notion of a referendum to create a "city state". Formally, the constitutional position of local authorities remains as it was in 1867.

Within Ontario, therefore, the provincial government is responsible for the structure, financing and policy responsibilities of local government. The structure of local government that has emerged over time from this provincial control is complicated with municipalities of radically different sizes existing within different structures throughout the province. In some areas of Ontario, a system of single-tier municipalities exists. These local authorities are responsible for all the services provided by local government in their area. The most notable example of this type of structure is the City of Toronto (referred to above), but this is by no means the only example. Others include separated cities such as London and Windsor, as well the amalgamated cities, such as Hamilton, that followed the creation of Toronto. The majority of Ontario citizens now live within this type of local authority structure. Elsewhere, there exist two-tier local government structures. In southern Ontario some municipalities exist within counties whereas elsewhere, other municipalities exist within regions. In both cases, the upper-tier authorities (county and region) are responsible for services (such as land use planning) that require some degree of coordination across a wider territory than that covered by the individual municipal governments. The difference between the two structures is that regions have a wider range of functional responsibility than do the counties (Tindal and Tindal, 2000: 193-201).

As well as determining the structure of local government in Ontario, the provincial government is also responsible for controlling what the municipalities do. These functions are determined by legislation, a key element of which is the provincial Municipal Act.[5] As noted by Graham et al., provincial legislation generally has tended to be restrictive and has set tight controls over local government action, restricting that action to functions narrowly outlined by statute (1998: 175). This situation has been supported by court rulings (Tindal and Tindal, 2000). The Ontario government has traditionally also played a significant part in determining the money that local governments have available to perform their assigned functions (Siegel, 2002). This has been evident in two ways. First, in terms of the conditional and unconditional grants that the province provides to local authorities, and secondly, through its control over local government capacity to borrow money.

Over the last decade, each of these areas of provincial control over local government has witnessed varying degrees of change. As noted above, restructuring of local government has been a dominant feature of the 1995-2003 Conservative provincial government's agenda. Alongside this, the provincial government has also sought to amend the functions performed by local authorities through a process known as "disentanglement" (Tindal and Tindal, 2000). The ostensible aim of this exercise has been to clarify the functions performed by each level of government in Ontario, and thus provide for greater efficiency and clearer lines of public accountability. Critics have argued that the exercise has been more aimed at "downloading" service responsibility onto municipal government without also providing them with the financial means to carry them out (Graham et al, 1998). Finally, the financing of local government has also changed. As David Siegel notes, there has been a reduction in provincial transfers to local authorities (that has occurred simultaneously with a reduction in federal transfers to the provinces), and a gradual shift from conditional to unconditional grants for those provincial transfers that remain (Siegel, 2002). Thus, local governments have been less constrained by provincial constraints on their expenditure, but at the same time have had to rely on their own resources (such as service fees) to compensate for an overall reduction in provincial transfers.

The relationship with the provincial government is thus clearly of first order importance to local government in Ontario. As will be examined below, this does not mean that local authorities have no interest in the actions of, or relationship with, the federal government. It does, however, indicate that this relationship will be affected by developments at the provincial level.

**The Informal Role of Local Government in Intergovernmental Relations**

In both the European Union and Canada, then, a reading of the formal constitutional situation suggests only a limited role for local authorities at the highest territorial level of politics. Even the weakest understanding of political activity suggests, however, that it is necessary to examine more than the formal situation, and that the reality of political practice often diverges from constitutional formality. To an extent, this is true with respect to local authorities in both the European Union and Canada.

*British Local Government in the European Union*

Although denied a formal place in the political structure of the European Union until 1993, and with only a limited consultative role thereafter, British local governments became interested in the European Union at a much earlier date. There were multiple reasons for this. First, local governments are often responsible for implementing policy decisions taken in the European Union. They have for this reason, at the very least, an interest in securing information about the EU's policy-making process, and need to be aware of the potential impact of EU legislation on their activities (Bongers, 1992; Goldsmith, 1997; John, 2000; Mazey and Mitchell, 1993). In addition, the local governments have an interest in the possibility of shaping EU legislation to the benefit of their region or municipality. Second, local governments are affected by major economic developments in the European Union. Single European Market measures, for example, have a significant impact on regional and local economies, particularly those in peripheral locations. Thirdly, and arguably most significantly, local governments have been attracted to the European Union by the prospect of securing funding for their area from the structural funds, the EU's main financial tool for promoting regional development.

In addition to the reasons why British local governments have sought to develop links to European Union policy-making, there are also a number of reasons why the European Commission has encouraged such local participation (Tömmell, 1998). Thus, the Commission maintains links with local authorities because these authorities provide the relatively small administration with information that is vital in the preparation of policy proposals. This information is important because, as noted above, local authorities are often the organizations that have responsibility for implementing policies agreed at the EU level. As such, these organizations are ideally placed to provide information about the way in which policy proposals may work in practice. In addition, it has been suggested that the Commission is keen to develop ties with local authorities because such actors provide a source of potential allies in confrontations between the Commission and member state governments. It was for this reason that the Commission was one of the champions (along with the German Länder) of the Committee of the Regions (Jeffery, 2002).

For these reasons, British local governments (as well as local authorities elsewhere in the European Union) have taken a variety of steps to increase their awareness of, and participation in, European Union policy-making (Hooghe, 1995). Virtually all British local governments have established internal procedures for collecting and distributing information on the European Union (John, 1996). A number of local governments have opened information offices in Brussels, either independently or in collaboration with other local authorities or actors (Jeffery, 1996). Strathclyde Regional Council (since abolished) was one of the first local authorities to open such an office. Finally, British local governments have entered into relationships with other local authorities aimed at sharing information, "best-practice" procedures, and producing coordinated lobbying approaches to European Union policy-making. These networks exist at an informal level; created by regularized contacts among local authorities (McAleavey and Mitchell, 1994). They also exist in formal organizational structures such as the Committee of the Regions.

The extent of this local government activity with respect to the European Union goes beyond what might be expected from the examination of the formal place of local government in the EU's decision-making structures. A key question, however, is whether it is important. As Charlie Jeffery has identified, the mere fact of local government interest in the European Union, and their efforts to participate in decisions at that level, does not mean that these efforts are guaranteed to be successful. Activity does not necessarily translate into influence (Jeffery, 2000). This issue has sparked a debate (see Jordan, 2001). On one side are those who argue that this local government activity is significant and indeed is a sign of a new type of politics within the European Union. This political activity involves actors at all territorial levels (European, national, regional and local), where decisions are the product of bargaining among actors at these different levels (Hooghe and Marks, 2001; Hooghe, 1996). In the words of Hooghe and Marks, "decision-making competencies are shared by actors at different levels rather than monopolized by national governments" (2001: 3). This perspective does not necessarily argue that the European Union is creating a new European order; a "Europe of the Regions" (Loughlin, 1996). It does, however, suggest that policy-making within the European Union area is not dominated by the central governments of the member states and that these governments have lost policy-making autonomy to actors below (at the regional and local levels) and above (at the EU level) (Keating, 1998).

Intergovernmental perspectives take a contrary position and thus suggest that local government engagement in the European Union is insignificant, or at least it is not universally significant across all member states. Thus, it is important only insofar as central governments allow it to be important, or is based on a pre-existing prominent position for regional or local authorities within the member states concerned. According to this perspective, the central governments still have the capacity to control local government participation in the European Union (Bache, 1998). Even in those policy areas where local governments have the greatest incentive to seek influence over policy-making, such as the structural funds, it is difficult to find evidence of local government influence (McAleavey, 1995). According to these intergovernmental perspectives, the European Union, for the most part, is a traditional intergovernmental organization. Local authority engagement in the EU is not evidence of a diminution of central governments' role in policy-making or of the transformation of governance towards a Europe of the Regions. According to this perspective, therefore, the limited nature of local governments' constitutional involvement in the European Union provides an accurate reflection of the place of local authorities in EU policy-making.

Evidence from the engagement of British local authorities in European Union policy-making does not totally support the views of either perspective. Through the 1980s and 1990s most British local authorities developed at least some capacity to monitor EU politics and to seek to have their views represented at that level. This has occurred most visibly through the opening of offices in Brussels. In general terms, British local authorities have been among the better organized to participate in EU politics (Goldsmith and Sperling, 1997). They have, for example, been at the forefront of many attempts to develop trans-national networks of local actors (McAleavey and Mitchell, 1994). The extent of this activity accords with those perspectives that posit an important role for local actors in the European Union. However, it is important to identify that not all British local authorities are interested in, and have become engaged in, European Union policy-making to the same extent. This has been identified by a number of studies of sub-national participation in the European Union. Peter John, for example, has developed a typology of local authorities with respect to their interest in the European Union, and the extent to which they have organized to operate at the European Union level (John, 1994). In this typology, some local authorities are "fully Europeanized" whereas others demonstrate only marginal interest in European issues. Likewise, a study by Goldsmith and Sperling points to variation in British local governments' approach to the European Union.

> Whilst a small minority of large local governments, such as Strathclyde, Birmingham, Glasgow and Manchester, or areas like South Yorkshire, have been particularly active, the majority are still somewhat inward looking. Most local authorities have small teams dealing with European matters, indeed often only a single person... (Goldsmith and Sperling, 1997: 118).

Thus, local authorities are not necessarily similar in the extent to which they are engaged at the European Union level. It is also the case that the extent of local authority engagement differs across policy area and, within policy areas, across different phases of the decision-making process. Thus, British local authorities, not surprisingly, have been particularly interested in those EU policy sectors that affect their domestic policy responsibilities and little interested in those that do not, hence demonstrating the extent to which the local-EU relationship is shaped by the domestic context (the local-national relationship). Local authorities, therefore, have demonstrated considerable interest in EU legislation is such areas as public procurement, the environment, transportation and regional development. As noted, this latter sector is one where local authorities have lobbied hard to influence the general contours of the policy field as well as specific funding decisions within the field.

Within the policy sectors in which British local authorities have an interest, it is also possible to point to variation. In this instance, the variation exists in terms of the stage of the policy-making cycle in which the local authorities seek to participate (Peterson and Bomberg, 1999: 10-28). As in any political system, there are different types of EU decision and different phases of decision-making. Periodic treaty revisions, for example, set the context for specific policy decisions in different sectors, which in turn have to be implemented at the national and local level. Each of these decision types may exhibit different characteristics and involve a slightly different range of interested actors.

The question of determining whether British local authorities can exert any influence over European Union policy-making is therefore a complicated one. It is complicated by the fact that not all local authorities are interested in exerting influence to the same extent, and by the fact that different policy fields and different stages of policy-making may provide different answers. It is also complicated by the methodological difficulty in determining influence over any political decision. The fact that an individual or other actor advocates a particular policy choice, and that choice is adopted, does not mean that the decision was taken because of the actor's influence. The decision may have occurred as a result of other actors' intervention, or because of other factors, and thus have little to do with the pressure exerted by the actor. Thus, even the fact that EU decisions emerge that are supported by local authorities, does not provide concrete evidence of local authority influence.

Definitive conclusions about the significance of British local authority participation in European Union decision-making are therefore difficult to make. It is, however, possible to state that British local authorities are not prominent actors and are not consistently involved in all aspects of EU policy-making (John, 2000: 890). There are, for example, certain types of decision where their role is very limited. This applies particularly to the treaty revisions that have become a more or less permanent part of EU politics in the last decade. In their study of the 1996 IGC, for example, John and McAteer argue that British local governments were not influential participants as indicated by the fact that the positions they advocated were not adopted in the Treaty of Amsterdam that followed the IGC (John and McAteer, 1998). In other types of policy decision, in different policy sectors, it is possible to suggest that British local authorities have exerted more influence alongside actors at the European level and from the national government. In the case of regional policy, for example, a number of studies indicate that local governments have been able to influence, if to a limited degree, the overall contours of the policy sector, and to a greater degree, specific decisions regarding the implementation of regional development funds (Hooghe and Marks, 2001).

Even in this sector, however, it should be noted that most scholars point to the continuing importance of the central government in shaping local government participation in this EU policy sector (Bache, 1998; Bache and Jones, 2000: 16).

There is, therefore, a place for British local governments in European Union policy-making. This is evident in the extent to which these authorities have used scarce resources to develop a capacity to monitor EU activity and lobby for desired policy outcomes at this level. The dominant actors continue to be central government representatives along with the representatives of the EU institutions,[6] with the position of British local authorities in many ways being closer to that of an "attentive public" than to that of principal participants in decision-making. Nevertheless, as "intergovernmental relations" perspectives would suggest (Rhodes, 1988) the different levels of government are involved in a mutually interdependent relationship where each level has resources that allow them to affect decision-making. Local governments are certainly the junior partners in this relationship. Nevertheless, in certain sectors, at certain times, and at certain decision-making levels, they are capable of exerting some influence over the final decisions.

Whether this limited degree of involvement and influence over decision-making increases in the future is also a matter of debate. One scenario is that the level of local participation in the EU may decline. Across the EU, there is evidence of regional and local actors taking less of an interest in the European Union than was the case in the 1980s and early 1990s, in part because of a reduction in the quantity of EU legislation being passed (see John, 2000). It is also the case that British local authorities are in the process of evaluating their EU activity (including, for example, their presence in Brussels) and many may decide to scale back the resources devoted to this activity. This possibility seems particularly likely in the event of a reduction in the structural funds devoted to the UK following a prospective EU enlargement to include East European states.

On the other hand, the situation is fluid, and there are at least reasons to suggest that a strengthened role for British local authorities in EU policy-making is possible. The 2001 re-election of the Labour government has, at least to some extent, revitalized local government in the UK (Travers, 2001), and this may be reflected in a more vigorous role for local government within the European Union. At a minimum, better relations with the national government may make it easier for local authorities to use domestic channels as a means of influencing EU policy.[7] In addition, the EU system of governance is once again in a period of transition. The Convention on the Future of Europe, which began deliberating in 2002, presented a Draft Constitutional Treaty for Europe in June 2003 (European Convention, 2003). This draft treaty may form the basis of a new constitutional treaty to be agreed by the member state governments in 2004. In a parallel process, the Commission has also been proposing reforms to EU decision-making. One consequence of this dual revision process may be an enhanced role for regional and local authorities within the European Union. The Commission, for example, continues to encourage formal and informal regional and local participation within the European Union. In 2001 the Commission produced a White Paper on European Governance (Commission, 2001), which indicated that regional and local authorities must be a central part of governance in the EU:

> At the EU level, the Commission should ensure that regional and local knowledge and conditions are taken into account when developing policy proposals. For this purpose, it should organize a systematic dialogue with European and national associations of regional and local government, while respecting national constitutional and administrative arrangements (Commission, 2001: 13).

Similarly, the Committee of the Regions and other local governments have called for an enhanced role for regional and local authorities to be incorporated in a new constitutional treaty (see Committee of the Regions, 2002). There is, however, no guarantee that these demands or proposals will lead to a dramatic change in the place of local authorities in EU policy-making. The Draft Constitutional Treaty has not proposed a substantial increase in the presence of regional and local authorities in EU policy-making (European Convention, 2003). It has not, for example, proposed a significant revision to the powers of the Committee of the Regions. In any case, there is no guarantee that the central governments will be able to reach agreement on a new treaty or, if they do, that it will closely follow the draft treaty.

## The Informal Role of Local Government in Canadian Federal Politics

As in the case of local authorities within European Union policy-making, the constitutional situation does not mean that there is no relationship (either individual or collective) between Canadian local governments and the federal government. Indeed, a number of scholars indicate that intergovernmental relations in Canada are considerably more complicated than the constitutional framework suggests (see Tindal and Tindal, 2000: 207).

As within the European Union, there are a number of factors that explain why this is the case. First, decisions taken at the federal level clearly impact on the work of local government and the areas over which they have responsibility. One example is the federal government's impact on municipal planning and the shape of the modern Canadian city. Decisions taken at the federal level since the Second World War helped to lead to an expansion of the suburbs and the development of an extensive local transportation infrastructure (Tindal and Tindal, 2000: 84-5; see also Magnusson, 1983). Environmental policy provides a second example. Here, as noted by Price (2002), municipalities' attempts to deal with environmental concerns within their territory have to account for decisions taken at the federal level (as well as at the local, provincial and international levels).

Perhaps the clearest example of federal involvement in policy areas that affect local government is provided by infrastructure. In this area, local governments have been eager to seek federal government involvement and specifically federal government funds to pay for infrastructure projects at the local level (see Andrew and Morrison, 2002). In the 1980s, for example, the municipalities developed a lobbying campaign, through the Federation of Canadian Municipalities, which called on the federal government for financial assistance for municipal infrastructure. The federal Liberal Party adopted this within its 1993 election campaign manifesto, and this in turn led to the Liberal Government establishing a Canada Infrastructure Works programme (Andrew and Morrison, 2002: 244; also Graham et al, 1998: 187). This programme pledged $2 billion from federal funds for infrastructure projects in local areas (Tindal and Tindal, 2000: 233).

In the current period there is also considerable evidence of local politicians demanding federal financial support for infrastructure projects. To varying degrees, this position has received support from within the Liberal government. At the 2002 FCM annual meeting, for example, the Industry Minister, Allan Rock, suggested that the federal government has a "moral obligation and an economic incentive" to step in and help urban centres solve growing problems of traffic gridlock, housing and poverty. The former Finance Minister, now Prime Minister, Paul Martin, also talked about a new financial deal for Canadian cities, without being specific about the details of such a new deal (see Lewingston, 2002: A15). [8]

In policy and financial terms, therefore, the federal-local relationship has changed somewhat from when Keating suggested that, "the federal level has no direct links with local governments and provides virtually no resources for them" (1991: 59). Of equal significance is the fact that federal decisions can affect local governments indirectly through their impact on provincial governments. Thus, many municipal politicians claim that they are facing a financial crisis, notwithstanding the federal contribution to local infrastructure projects (see FCM, 2002; but see also Coyne, 2002). A number of academic observers support this claim (Graham et al, 1998: 203; Tindal and Tindal, 2000). A major reason for this, it is argued, is the federal government's emphasis on deficit and debt reduction through the 1980s and 1990s. This priority led to a reduction in federal transfer payments to the provinces, which in turn, the provinces passed on to municipalities by reducing the size of provincial grants to local government (Siegel, 2002).

There are, then, a number of reasons why local governments in Ontario (and Canada generally) must be concerned about developments at the federal level, and thus why they have sought to develop a relationship with the federal government. As noted above, the existence of this relationship was given formal expression in the 1970s with the establishment by the Liberal government of the federal Ministry for Urban Affairs headed by a Minister of State for Urban Affairs in 1970s (Feldman and Milch, 1981; Tindal and Tindal, 2000). This development, however, failed in large part because of provincial government opposition to a perceived federal encroachment on their constitutional responsibilities. Nevertheless, a federal-local relationship continues to exist. There are indeed multiple points at which local government can seek to access the federal policy-making process, and at which federal and local policy-makers connect.

Local governments approach the federal government individually. There is obviously a greater possibility of this occurring for the large municipal authorities, such as Toronto, which are headed by high-profile politicians. This reflects the fact that not all municipal governments are equal at the provincial level. Dupré (1968) referred to this situation as one of "hyper-factionalized quasi-subordination", thus identifying that while provincial governments are clearly the senior partners in the local-provincial relationship, some municipalities are not completely dominated. The larger local governments in particular are capable of exercising influence at the provincial level (see Andrew, 1995).

> Municipalities also approach the federal government on a multilateral basis. This occurs both through the provincial-level municipal associations such as the Association of Municipalities of Ontario (AMO) and the Federation of Canadian Municipalities (Graham et al, 1998: 196). In addition, municipalities can seek to influence policy at the federal level by attempting to influence the policy positions adopted by their provincial government. Municipalities often, for example, seek to develop good working relations with the Members of the Provincial Assembly in their area and use this as a means of influencing debate at the provincial level (Graham et al., 1998: 195).

The opportunities for local engagement with political debate at the federal level are not mutually exclusive. It is frequently the case that local authorities will use all possible avenues to influence policy as it affects their municipality. One example of this (and of the interaction among the three levels of government) is the attempt by Windsor's City Government to secure financial assistance to facilitate cross-border traffic through the Windsor-Detroit border. This debate has involved local, provincial and federal politicians as well as interested parties at all three levels. In July/August 2002 the federal government budgeted $600 million for border infrastructure expenditure, a part of which will be spent on the Windsor/Detroit crossing.

While it is one thing to suggest that local authorities have a reason to be interested in federal politics, and that local politicians attempt to engage with their federal counterparts, it is quite another to suggest that local governments are capable of influencing federal policies. As in the case of local authorities within the European Union, local activity, and even consultation, does not equal political influence. Even when the federal government adopts policies that correspond with the demands of municipalities it is exceptionally difficult to demonstrate conclusively that this policy resulted from local influence. The federal government may well have adopted the policy for reasons unrelated to local pressure. In the case of the federal expenditure on border crossings, for example, there were factors other than local pressure that influenced the federal government's decision. These included pressure from the trucking and manufacturing industries to speed up border crossings, as well as an awareness of the general economic benefits to be gained from facilitating faster border crossings.

It is also possible that the senior level of government only pays attention to those local authorities that support the position it was intending to adopt in any case. One of the consequences of the multiplicity of local authorities, and local representative bodies, is that a diversity of local views exists on any issue. Even within Ontario, not all local governments support the same policy choices. There is, rather, variation depending, for example, upon the size of the local government, its geographic location, and demographic characteristics. Assessments of the FCM and AMO highlight the existence of this variation among municipal governments. They indicate that these bodies are often forced to adopt lowest-common-denominator positions as a result of divisions among their members (Tindal and Tindal, 2000: 241). The variation in views that exists within these municipal representative bodies therefore often serves to weaken the strength of their lobbying voice.

A federal-local government relationship, therefore, exists within the Canadian political system. As Fowler and Siegel (2002) indicate, almost every policy area in Canadian politics involves actors at every level of government, and policy outcomes are affected by action at all levels. Nevertheless, local government is very much the junior partner in this intergovernmental relationship. The relationship of primary importance to municipal government remains that with the provincial government, and the relationship with the federal government exists on an informal or quasi-formal basis.

Local government's future in this policy-making system is one that is subject to debate. One perspective is of a system of local government in crisis. Here it is claimed that local authorities lack money, at a time when the provinces are "downloading" more responsibilities on to them, and when the future looks to be one of ever increasing demands (infrastructure) on more limited municipal resources. In this view also, local authorities are not seen as legitimate partners by the provincial government. Their views are frequently ignored. This view is expressed by Tindal and Tindal, who argue that:

> there is still little indication that provinces are committed to genuine advance consultation with municipalities. The governing parties have their own agendas which they have been pursuing with marked determination, especially in provinces such as Alberta and Ontario. Municipalities and other local governments are being reformed to satisfy the fiscal and ideological objectives of these ruling parties, with little regard for the wishes of municipal associations or the feelings of local citizens (Tindal and Tindal, 2000: 253).

According to this perspective local government's place within the political system generally, and thus its relationship with the federal government, is one that is under threat.

On the other hand, a more positive perspective exists. According to this perspective it is possible to envisage a stronger more inclusive role for local government within the political system at both the provincial and federal levels. In the view of Fowler and Siegel for example, the process of "disentanglement" (referred to above), "involves an attempt to eliminate the confusion of shared authority by allocating responsibility for particular services unequivocally to one level of government. This promises to give local governments greater scope for action in areas that have been allocated to them" (2002: 9). Fowler and Siegel continue by arguing that the impact of disentanglement combined with the restructuring of local government "will likely result in a significant increase in the power of the municipal level of government" (2002: 14). Thus, although provincial governments are unlikely to allow municipalities to secure full constitutional status, there are grounds for believing that "local governments will gradually obtain a de facto status as real governing and policy-making bodies, which provincial governments would never allow them to attain de jure" (2002: 14).

In the case of local government in Ontario, some level of support exists for this argument in the shape of the new Municipal Act (2001) and the associated Memorandum of Understanding (Association of Municipalities of Ontario and the Province of Ontario, 2001). The memorandum indicates that the provincial government is "committed to cooperating with municipalities in considering new legislation or regulations with a municipal impact" (ibid: 2). These developments at least suggest that the provincial government is willing to give local government more policy-making discretion and a large say in the formation of provincial policies that affect it. This, in turn, has at least the possibility of giving local government a larger voice at the federal level.

**Conclusion**

In both the European Union and Canada local government's place at the senior level of policy-making is, to some extent, in a state of flux. In neither case do local authorities have a constitutionally secure place in the political processes at the European Union/federal levels.[9] In both cases, however, local governments are clearly affected by decisions made at these levels, if to differing degrees in different issue areas, and have made efforts to engage in policy-making. These efforts go beyond what could be expected from a formal reading of local government's place in the EU treaties and Canadian constitution. Nevertheless, in neither case are local authorities consistently included in policy-making at the senior level of government. Their engagement is heavily influenced by the next level of government (the provincial level in Canada, and the national government in the United Kingdom), and it is most often the case that their position is that of an "attentive public;" that is, interested in decision-making and affected by decisions taken without being able to exercise influence over these decisions.

The way in which this situation will evolve is open to question in both systems, but in neither case can it be expected that local governments will be given a radically different constitutional position in the near future.

**Notes**

1  Although the European Union only came into existence in 1993, this chapter follows the
   now conventional practice of using this title to refer to the earlier institutional structures
   of European integration.
2  The Maastricht Treaty left it to the member state governments to select their state's
   members of the Committee. These members did not necessarily have to be
   representatives of regional or local elected authorities. The Treaty of Nice  changes this
   somewhat. Member state governments will still select their state's representatives but
   these individuals must hold a regional or local electoral mandate or be accountable to an
   elected assembly.
3  In other provinces, megacities have also been formed – Montreal in Quebec and Halifax
   in Nova Scotia are notable examples.
4  For a recent example, see the Joint FCM/CAMA Task Force's Policy Statement on the
   Future Role of Municipal Government (June 2002) See /www.fcm.ca/.
5  The Ontario legislature passed a new Municipal Act in December 2001. This took effect
   on 1 January 2003.
6  There continues to be an academic debate regarding the importance of the EU
   institutions (such as the European Commission) in EU decision-making (see Moravcsik,
   1998; Hooghe and Marks, 2001). In Moravcsik's view, for example, the role of the
   Commission is simply that of 'agent' to the member state governments.
7  The Labour government's devolution program has, as yet, unclear implications for EU
   policy-making. The Scottish Parliament and Welsh Assembly may be able develop an
   active role within EU policy-making (although formally EU matters are reserved to the
   UK government). This, however, may lead to a reduced role for local authorities in these
   nations.
8  The 2002 annual FCM meeting, and Martin's speech, was overshadowed by Martin's
   subsequent resignation from cabinet. This resignation marked the formal opening of a
   leadership contest within the governing Liberal Party, which culminated in December
   2003 with Martin becoming Prime Minister of Canada. At the time of writing, the
   implications of Martin's leadership for local government are still unclear.
9  This constitutional status of local authorities varies from state to state. The situation in
   Switzerland, for example, is similar to that of Canada. Local governments are not
   mentioned in the constitution and are the responsibility of the cantons. The situation in
   New Zealand is similar to the United Kingdom. In both Germany and Denmark,
   however, local governments do have a formal place in the constitution and a guaranteed
   right to exist (see Hughes et al., 1998).

**References**

Andrew, C. 1995. 'Provincial-Municipal Relations; or Hyper-Fractionalized Quasi-
    Subordination Revisited', in J. Lightbody (ed.), *Canadian Metropolitics: Governing Our
    Cities*, Toronto: Copp Clark, pp. 137-160.
Andrew, C. and Morrison, J. 2002. 'Infrastructure', in E.P. Fowler and D. Siegel (eds),
    *Urban Policy Issues: Canadian Perspectives*, Oxford: Oxford University Press, pp. 237-
    252.
Association of Municipalities of Ontario and the Province of Ontario 2001. Memorandum of
    Understanding, Toronto: Government of Ontario.

Bache, I., 1998, *The Politics of European Union Regional Policy: Multi-Level Governance or Flexible Gatekeeping?*, Sheffield: Sheffield Academic Press.

Bache, I. and R. Jones 2000. 'Has EU Regional Policy Empowered the Regions? A Study of Spain and the United Kingdom', *Regional and Federal Studies*, 10, (3): 1-20.

Benzie, R. 2000. 'Harris' stinging letter propels vote on city-state', *National Post*, 12 May, p. A20.

Bogdanor, V. 1999. *Devolution in the United Kingdom*, Oxford: Oxford University Press.

Bongers, P. 1992. *Local Government in the Single European Market*, Harlow: Longman.

Burgess, M. 1999. *Federalism and the European Union: The Building of Europe*, 1950-2000, London: Routledge.

Christiansen, T. 1996. 'Second Thoughts on Europe's "Third Level": The European Union's Committee of the Regions', *Publius*, 26, (1): 93-116.

Commission of the European Communities 2001. European Governance: A White Paper, COM(2001) 428 final, Brussels.

Committee of the Regions, 2002. 'CoR members open the Convention's debate on Europe's cities and regions', Press Release COR/02/06026, 28 June.

Coyne, A. 2002. 'A new new deal for cities', *National Post*, 14 August, p. A15.

Dupré, J.S. 1968. *Intergovernmental Finance in Ontario: A Provincial-level Perspective*, Toronto: Ontario Commission on Taxation, Government of Ontario.

European Convention 2003. Draft Treaty Establishing a Constitution for Europe, Conv 850/03, Brussels, 18 July.

Federation of Canadian Municipalities (FCM) 2002. 'Cities need a new deal', Press Release, 23 May, www.fcm.ca/newfcm/Java/frame.htm.

Feldman, E.J. and J. Milch, 1981. 'Coordination or Control? The Life and Death of the Ministry of Urban Affairs', in L.D. Feldman (ed.), *Politics and Government of Urban Canada*, Toronto: Methuen.

Fowler, E.P. and D. Siegel 2002. 'Introduction: Urban Public Policy at the Turn of the Century', in E.P. Fowler and D. Siegel (eds), *Urban Policy Issues: Canadian Perspectives*, Oxford: Oxford University Press, pp. 1-16.

Goldsmith, M., 1997. 'British Local Government in the European Union', in J. Bradbury (ed.), *British Regionalism and Devolution: The Challenges of State Reform and European Integration*, London: Regional Studies Association, pp.215-234.

Goldsmith, M. and Sperling, E. 1997. 'Local Governments and the EU: The British Experience', in M. Goldsmith and K. Klausen (eds), *European Integration and Local Government*, Cheltenham: Edward Elgar, pp. 95-120.

Graham, K.A., Phillips, S.D. and Muslove, A.M. 1998. *Urban Governance in Canada: Representation, Resources, and Restructuring*, Toronto: Harcourt Brace.

Hix, S. 1998. 'Elections, Parties and Institutional Design: A Comparative Perspective on European Union Democracy', *West European Politics*, 21, (3): 19-52.

Hooghe, L. (ed.) 1996. *Cohesion Policy and European Integration: Building Multi-Level Governance*, Oxford: Oxford University Press.

Hooghe, L. 1995. 'Subnational Mobilization in the European Union', *West European Politics*, 18, (3): 175-198.

Hooghe, L. and Marks, G. 2001. *Multi-Level Governance and European Integration*, Lanham: Rowman & Littlefield.

Hughes, M., Clarke, M., Allen, H. and Hall, D. 1998. *The Constitutional Status of Local Government in Other Countries*, Edinburgh: The Scottish Office Central Research Unit.

Hurrell, and Menon, A. 1996. 'Politics Like Any Other? Comparative Politics, International Relations and the Study of the EU', *West European Politics*, 19, (2): 386-402.

Jeffery, C. 2002. 'Social and Regional Interests: ESC and Committee of the Regions', in J. Peterson and M. Shackleton (eds), *The Institutions of the European Union*, Oxford: Oxford University Press, pp. 326-346.

Jeffery, C. 2000. 'Subnational Mobilization and European Integration: Does it Make a Difference?', *Journal of Common Market Studies*, 38, (1): 1-23.

Jeffery, C. 1996. 'Regional Information Offices in Brussels and Multi-Level Governance in the EU: A UK-German Comparison', *Regional and Federal Studies*, 5, (3): 356-365.

John, P. 2000. 'The Europeanisation of Sub-national Government', *Urban Studies*, 37 (5-6): 877-894.

John, P. 1996. 'Europeanization in a Centralizing State: Multi-Level Governance in the UK', *Regional and Federal Studies*, 6, (2): 131-144.

John, P. 1994. 'What is the European Function?', *Local Government Policy Making*, 20, (5): 11-13.

John, P. and M. McAteer, 1998. 'Sub-national Institutions and the New European Governance: UK Local Authority Lobbying Strategies for the IGC', *Regional and Federal Studies*, 8, (3): 104-124.

Jordan, A. 2001. 'The European Union: An Evolving System of Multi-Level Governance...or Government?', *Policy and Politics*, 29, (2): 193-208.

Keating, M. 2001. 'Managing the Multinational State: Constitutional Settlement in the United Kingdom', in T.C. Salmon and M. Keating, *The Dynamics of Decentralization: Canadian Federalism and British Devolution*, Montreal: McGill-Queen's University Press, pp. 21-45.

Keating, M. 1998. *The New Regionalism in Western Europe: Territorial Restructuring and Political Change*, Aldershot: Edward Elgar.

Keating, M. 1991. *Comparative Urban Politics: Power and the City in the United States, Canada, Britain and France*, Aldershot: Edward Elgar.

Klausen, K.K. and Goldsmith, M. 1997. 'Conclusion: Local Government and the European Union', in M. Goldsmith and K. Klausen (eds), *European Integration and Local Government*, Cheltenham: Edward Elgar, pp. 237-254.

Lazer, D. and Mayer-Schoenberger, V. 2001. 'Blueprints for Change: Devolution and Subsidiarity in the United States and the European Union', in K. Nicolaidis and R. Howse (eds), *The Federal Vision: Legitimacy and Levels of Governance in the United States and the European Union*, Oxford: Oxford University Press, pp. 118-143.

Lewingston, J. 2002. 'Cities need funding options, Rock says', *Globe and Mail*, 3 June, p. A15.

Loughlin, J. (ed) 2001. *Subnational Democracy in the European Union: Challenges and Opportunities*, Oxford: Oxford University Press.

Loughlin, J., 1996, '"Europe of the Regions" and the Federalization of Europe', *Publius*, 26, (4) pp.141-162.

Magnusson, W. 1983. 'Introduction', in W. Magnusson and A. Sancton (eds.) *City Politics in Canada*, Toronto: University of Toronto Press.

Marsh, D. and Rhodes, R.A.W. (eds) 1992. *Implementing Thatcherite Policies: Audit of an Era*, Buckingham: Open University Press.

Mazey, S. and J. Mitchell 1993. 'Europe of the Regions: Territorial Interests and European Integration: The Scottish Experience', in S. Mazey and J. Richardson (eds.) *Lobbying in the European Community*, Oxford: Oxford University Press, pp. 95-121.

McAleavey, P. 1995. 'European Regional Development Fund Expenditure in the UK: From Additionality to Subtractionality', *European Urban and Regional Studies*, 2, (3): 249-253.

McAleavey, P. and J. Mitchell 1994. 'Industrial Regions and Lobbying in the Structural Fund Reform Process', *Journal of Common Market Studies*, 32, (2): 237-248.

Midwinter, A. 1993. 'Shaping Scotland's New Local Authorities', *Local Government Studies*, 19, (3): 351-367.

Moravcsik, A. 1998. *The Choice for Europe: Social Purpose and State Power from Messina to Maastricht*, Ithica, NY: Cornell University Press.

Peterson, J. and E. Bomberg 1999. *Decision-Making in the European Union*, New York: St. Martin's Press.

Price, T. 2002. 'Sustainable Cities', in E.P. Fowler and D. Siegel (eds), Urban Policy Issues: Canadian Perspectives, Oxford: Oxford University Press, pp. 139-154.

Rhodes, R.A.W. 1988. *Beyond Westminster and Whitehall*, London: Unwin.

Sancton, A. 2002. 'Metropolitan and Regional Governance', in E.P. Fowler and D. Siegel, *Urban Policy Issues: Canadian Perspectives*, Oxford: Oxford University Press, pp. 54-68

Sancton, A. 2000. *Merger Mania: The Assault on Local Government*, Montreal: McGill-Queen's University Press.

Sancton, A. 1996. 'Reducing Costs by Consolidating Municipalities: New Brunswick, Nova Scotia and Ontario', *Canadian Public Administration*, 39, (3): 267-289.

Siegel, D. 2002. 'Urban Finance at the Turn of the Century: Be Careful What You Wish For', in E.P. Fowler and D. Siegel (eds), Urban *Policy Issues: Canadian Perspectives*, Oxford: Oxford University Press, pp. 36-53.

Sutcliffe, J.B. 1997. 'Local Government in Scotland: Reorganization and the European Union', *Regional and Federal Studies*, 7, (2): 42-69.

Tindal, C.R. and Tindal, S.N. 2000. *Local Government in Canada*, 5th edition, Scarborough: Nelson.

Tömell, I. 1998. 'Transformation of Governance: The European Commission's Strategy for Creating a "Europe of the Regions"', *Regional and Federal Studies*, 8, (2): 52-80.

Travers, T. 2001. 'Local Government', in A. Seldon (ed.), *The Blair Effect: The Blair Government 1997-2001*, London: Little, Brown and Co., pp. 117-137.

Wallace, W. 1982. 'Europe as a Confederation: The Community and the Nation State', *Journal of Common Market Studies*, 21: 57-68.

Warleigh, A. 1999. *The Committee of the Regions: Institutionalising Multi-Level Governance*, London: Kogan Page.

Williams, R.J. and T.J. Downey 1999. 'Reforming Rural Ontario', *Canadian Public Administration*, 42, (2): 160-192.

# PART III

# POLICIES IN AN INTERGOVERNMENTAL CONTEXT: WHAT CAN CANADA AND NAFTA LEARN FROM THE EU?

Chapter 6

# Comparing the EU and NAFTA Environmental Policies: Comparative Institutional Analysis and Case Studies

Joseph F. Jozwiak, Jr. and Patrick M. Crowley

## Introduction

It is well known that the European Union (EU) and the North American Free Trade Agreement (NAFTA) have developed along distinctly different paths, the former now becoming an economic and monetary union, as well as incorporating some elements of political union, while the latter has largely maintained its status as a free trade area. One policy area though in both regional integration projects that has been incorporated in the Treaties establishing EU and NAFTA is environmental policy, albeit from radically different perspectives.

 With integration of the single market proceeding quickly from the SEA through Maastricht and Amsterdam, trade and economic development has been the primary focus in the EU. However, environmental considerations have also been important in the development of the EU, and the practice of integrating environmental concerns into nearly every aspect of EU public policy has been fostered by the Commission, supported by the European Court of Justice, and accepted by the European Council. The Commission's Environmental Directorate has spent the greater part of the last three decades expanding both the scope and depth of the EU's environmental policy at the supranational level. It has become adept at sensing trends developing at the member state level and encouraging their introduction at the supranational level. The simple fact that many issues related to the environment concern cross-border spillovers places the Commission in an institutionally favorable position to construct EU-wide solutions. Member states still play a vital role in the creation of the EU's environment policies, however. Furthermore, as the Commission applies the principle of subsidiarity to this policy area, member states play a critical role in transposing and implementing directives, as well as reporting back to the Commission as to how (in)effectively environmental standards are carried out at lower levels.

In the NAFTA context, environmental issues were only introduced when the Canadian-US Free Trade Agreement (CUFTA) was expanded to NAFTA by incorporating Mexico. The North American Agreement on Environmental Cooperation (NAAEC) was the product of these 1992 negotiations, and was largely the result of concerns that lower environmental standards or enforcement of standards in Mexico would result in a "race to the bottom" in terms of environmental quality in North America. Environmental issues were of such concern though that they were even placed in the preamble of the NAFTA, which implies that trade liberalization will only occur in the context of respect for the environment.[1] These supranational concerns were not limited to the environment though, as NAFTA also established the Washington, DC-based Labor Commission.

In theory, as Alesina, Angeloni and Schuknecht (2001) explore, there are good arguments why the environment needs to have a supranational, if not international, competency established. The involvement of the EU as regards EU-wide externalities therefore seems desirable, as is also the case for the NAFTA countries. In the EU, roughly 2-3 percent of legislation has been environmental, and roughly 6.2 percent of court activity between June 1997 and March 2001 was related to the environment.

This paper then seeks to compare the institutional arrangements, policy formulation and implementation of environmental policy from a continental comparativist perspective, and seeks to highlight both differences and similarities in the way in which environmental policies are monitored within the regional trading blocs. Scant research on the EU and NAFTA from a comparativist perspective has been undertaken to date (although Crowley (2002) and Clarkson (2000) are exceptions), and little comparativist work that has been done on environmental policy between the EU and NAFTA from an institutional perspective, with Stevis and Mumme as the notable exception (2000).

Section 2 takes a closer look at the institutional context in which environmental policy is found in both the EU and NAFTA, and seeks to formulate some objective criteria for comparing the two arrangements. Section 3 employs two case studies, one from the EU and one from NAFTA. Section 4 explores some theoretical considerations and presents an analytical framework for the comparison of the two approaches, while section 5 presents some tentative conclusions.


## Institutional Context

*The EU*

EU environmental policy-making occurs in an institutionally rich arena where the construction of policy is a complex and complicated process with actors from all levels seeking to influence policy (Wallace and Wallace, 2000; Zito, 2000).

Environmental policy is often the result of the EU responding to member state demands. These demands can range from member states who insist that their high environmental standards become the EU's norm, to others who have enacted a more basic level of protection, to a few who have simply done nothing and may be seeking EU assistance in removing these standards altogether. It is the Commission's task to bring these various national regulations to a degree of convergence so that these diverse national regulations do not detrimentally impact on the internal market (Nugent, 1995, 1997; Peters, 1994; Peterson, 1995). Typically, the Commission is forced to act because member states have complained to it about the actions of other member states. Also, the Council often asks for the Commission to move on a particular matter. In addition, in the environmental policy area the European Parliament (EP) is well known for encouraging the Commission to address problems with legislative proposals (Judge, 1993; Judge, Earnshaw and Cowan, 1994.). Therefore, in the EU, the responsibility for the creation and implementation of environmental policy is shared between the member states and the EU. It is generally the case that EU directives are minimum standards which must be attained by all member states. However, member states still maintain a degree of sovereignty of this area, and can enact higher standards provided these do not come into conflict with other aspects of EU policy, especially when higher environmental standards come to be seen as barriers to the free operation of the single market.

The Commission may move first, and often assumes the role of an agenda setter (McCormick, 2001; Pollack, 1997). Most of its powers in this role come from its ability to "manage" the policymaking process, either formally or informally. Initially, it informally manages the construction of environmental policy. The draft legislation is written inside of a particular section of the Environmental Directorate (DGXI). Even before the drafting process has begun, and certainly while it is underway, DGXI may hold several meetings at which representatives from environmental groups, business groups, national policy making authorities, and even members of other directorate generals with special interest in the proposal may be invited. During these meetings "invitees" may help write the initial drafts, or comment on the subsequent versions of the draft legislation. It is also at this point that the Commission may make use of data gathered and analyzed by the European Environment Agency (EEA).[2]

Once these rounds of meetings have taken place, and multiple versions of the proposal have been circulated through the policymaking community, the Commission may hold yet another series of meetings. In these meetings the Commission may seek to justify its position to groups that have difficulties with some, if not all, of the proposed directive. The Commission explains its position, suggests ways the directive might be implemented. It may also suggest that if more "cooperative" methods do not yield results, more regulatory measures could be enacted. All the drafting and meetings occur under the shadow of prospective voting blocs in both the Council and the EP. While the Commission has powers that allow it to mitigate the influence of the EP on any proposal, it takes the power of the Council to delay, or even block, its proposals more seriously.

Once the Commission is relatively satisfied with its proposal, it formally announces its proposal. It is at this point that the formal rules of policymaking become relatively important. As the sole initiator of policy, it is uniquely placed to influence the course and tenor of debate over its proposals. As a result of the changes to the treaty at Amsterdam, environmental policy now proceeds solely under the rules of co-decision. The Commission's proposals are first dealt with substantially at the EP's first reading. The Commission need not except EP amendments, although it usually takes them into consideration. It tries to incorporate as many of them as possible, especially those that support the position of the Commission. Accepted amendments are written in and then the proposal is sent to the Council.

Once in the hands of the Council, any proposal can undergo considerable revision, although a careful Commission usually has dealt with core Council concerns before this point. The proposal goes first through the Committee of Permanent Representatives (COREPER), where it is debated and revised by expert groups involved in technical analysis. The working group then sends its changes to the larger political group inside the Council, and often a proposal will move back and forth between the two levels of the Council several times (Hayes-Renshaw and Wallace, 1997). Once the Council has achieved its Common position, the directive returns to the Commission for more "fine tuning." Afterwards, the Commission sends the proposal back to the EP for its second reading. There are significant hurdles for resurrecting amendments rejected in the first reading, they must be approved by an absolute majority to be eligible for conciliation. If the Commission, however, ignores amendments that the Council does approve of, it can face some embarrassing moments. This seldom happens, though, as members from the Commission are in constant informal contact with both the EP and the Council. After this point the Commission is formally out of the policymaking process, as any disagreements between the EP and the Council are handled in conciliation (Earnshaw and Judge, 1996; Garman and Hilditch, 1998). But again, the Commission can play an informal broker role between the other institutions. Once conciliation is over, which involves last minute negotiations over a few points – sometimes major but more often than not relatively minor, the Council reaches it final position and sends the proposal back to the EP for a final vote. Although it is a rarity, the EP has the option of killing legislation at this point. For the most part, the difficult deals have already been made and the vote here is almost just a matter of protocol.

The implementation of legislation has been more difficult for the Commission, given the fact that it must rely on the member states to do this (Börzel, 2001). Laws are first transposed for national consumption, which is usually accompanied by a flurry of activity on the part of industry associations with regards to how it should be interpreted. In the case of the environment, Union legislation is usually the ceiling for action, especially for member states that do not have a significant history of environmental activity. Union legislation is often a floor, however, for those member states with more ambitious national programs. The Commission often engages in advisory meetings, where the policymaking community is again invited to participate in suggesting ways to get legislation into action. It may also meet with representatives of the various member state environmental agencies in order to reach some understanding as to the spirit of the legislation. Laws are usually written with generous phase-in periods, often extending years, as well as having interim targets through which the Commission can begin to measure the whether member states have been effective in their efforts to implement a directive.

If the Commission thinks that member states are lagging in their efforts, it has legal resources to encourage, or ensure, member state action. The first step in legal actions against a member state is a "letter of formal notice," a warning to member states that they must take their treaty obligations seriously. The next step is the issuance of a reasoned opinion, delivered when the Commission feels that a member state has done little to meet a directive's particular objective, and is generally seen as a precursor to legal action. The Legal Affairs division of the Commission plays a significant role in this process. Over the course of issuing reasoned opinions, the division has two main tasks. The first is to operate cooperatively, engaging member states in a dialogue on the directive. Here, the division offers legal opinions as to whether member states are meeting directive's guidelines, and in this task the division offers suggestions as to what might be an acceptable interpretation of any directive. The final task is to build cases against member states that have either ignored Commission entreaties to action, or have willfully subverted the implementation process by engaging in actions run counter to the Union's intentions. No member state wants to be brought before the ECJ, but there are times when non-compliance offer advantages, if only to forestall the costs of compliance as long as possible. The Commission uses its ability to bring suits against member states for failure to comply with legislation only as a last resort, as it recognizes that while this is a great sanctioning power, it also shows that member states can treat Union efforts with a degree of disdain. This position of relative weakness vis-à-vis member states is underscored by the fact that the Commission most often relies on national environmental non-governmental organizations, industry associations, or even other member states to file complaints with the Commission for it to realize that problems exist with implementation.

## NAFTA

### Institutions

The institutionally rich environment that comprises EU decision making at the supranational level is simply lacking in NAFTA. This is even more the case with regards to the environment. Whereas the environment appears prominently in the pre-amble to the NAFTA, Article 104 of the NAFTA makes plain that environment concerns should be subordinate to trade and economic concerns. As McKinney (2000) notes in the NAFTA there are essentially only three supranational institutions, but only one pertains to the environment. The Free Trade Commission (FTC) is the governing body of the NAFTA, and its annual meetings rotate between the countries, with occasional meetings held in conjunction with international meetings outside of North America. A more permanent NAFTA secretariat was supposed to be established in Mexico, and plans were made to locate it in Mexico City, but this body has yet to materialize. The second supranational body is the Commission for Labor Cooperation (CLC), whose origins can be found in the North American Agreement on Labor Cooperation (NAALC),a subsidiary agreement to the NAFTA. It is situated in Washington DC,[3] and its purpose is to promote cooperation on labor laws and standards in NAFTA. However, it has little ability to establish common labor standards or regulations lacks enforcement powers.

The Commission for Environmental Cooperation (CEC) is the NAFTA supranational institution charged with monitoring the implementation of environment legislation and following up on complaints over enforcement. The CEC is headquartered in Montreal, Quebec, Canada and comprises three different bodies: the Council, the Secretariat and a Joint Public Advisory Committee. The Council's main charge is the implementation of the North American Agreement on Environmental Cooperation (NAAEC). It is composed of cabinet-level representatives of the member countries, or their designate, and it is required to meet at least once a year in a public forum. The chair of the Council rotates amongst the members and it usually makes its makes decisions by unanimity. It can, however, make recommendations and encourage the upward harmonization of environmental standards and regulations. The secretariat has an executive director who serves a renewable three year term, which rotates among the countries. The Secretariat provides technical advice and expertise on environmental issues to the council and to the public, where appropriate. The Joint Public Advisory Committee consists of fifteen members, with an equal number chosen by each of the member countries. It meets concurrently with the Council. It reviews reports developed by the Secretariat and with the approval of two of the three Council members, it can receive a "factual record." Each country is also allowed to convene national advisory and governmental advisory committees, which can provide further input from civil society concerning the implementation of the NAAEC.

*Environmental Policy Oversight*

Within the NAAEC, Articles 13-15 detail the procedure for filing complaints by individuals and organizations against member countries, the so-called "citizen submission" process. The procedure provides for a Secretariat-led investigation into environmental issues concerning non-enforcement. Complainants must allege real harm and are required to have already used member country authorities in an effort to seek redress. In any complaint the member country has the right to respond to the complaint within 30 to 60 days. At this point if two of the three council members of the Secretariat agree, then a "factual record" is developed. This is then submitted to the member country which, in turn, has 45 days to comment on its accuracy. The Secretariat takes into account the member country comments, and if approved by two of the three council members, the factual record is made public within 60 days. In the citizen submission process no provisions exist for an arbitration panel or trade sanctions.

The complaint procedure for member countries is different from the citizen submission process. Under part V of the NAAEC, a member country can file a complaint about a persistent pattern of failure by another member country to enforce its environmental laws. The member country seeking redress must first file a complaint, which has to be reviewed by the complainant country through a consultative process. If consultations fail to provide a satisfactory resolution within 60 days, the Council is convened after 20 further days. If, after 60 days, the council has failed to resolve the problem, a five-member arbitral panel can be convened. The hearings take place in secret and the findings of the panel are then given to the countries concerned. After a 60 day response period, a final report is given to the countries concerned. The Council has 15 more days to consider the conclusions of the final report, and at this point it is published.

The purpose of the arbitral panels is to draw up an action plan agreeable to all parties involved in the complaint. If there is continued disagreement on the action plan, then the arbitral panel can be reconvened to decide whether the action plan is acceptable. If it decides it is not, the arbitral panel can impose a non-refundable monetary fine up to 0.007 percent of the total trade in goods between the countries concerned. This fine is then given to the CEC. It can be spent on environmental enforcement projects, or other related activities in the country that paid the fine, if approved by the Council. If the issue is also trade related, the case can be taken before an arbitral panel, where trade sanctions are also a possible enforcement mechanism. If for some reason the country in question refuses to pay the fine, an further procedure is initiated, which suspends NAFTA benefits (i.e. lower tariffs) sufficient to collect the fines imposed.[4] Any fine collected at this point goes only to the complainant country and not back to the CEC for spending in the accused country. While this environmental enforcement process appears to be tough, there are many opportunities for those countries accused of persistent infringement of their own laws to make amends and to remedy the situation. It is also noteworthy that, to date, no complaints under part V of the NAAEC have been made.

*Chapter 11 Issues*

Many of the issues that have arisen in NAFTA relating to the environment have not been settled through arbitral panels under the NAAEC, but rather directly under the NAFTA treaty Chapter 11 tribunal procedure. Chapter 11 establishes a system of binding arbitration for resolving any dispute between an investor from one NAFTA country and the government of another NAFTA country. Article 1139 defines an investment as "enterprises, equity or debt securities in enterprises, loans, dividends, real estate and contractual or other interests associated with capital commitments". Articles 1102 and 1103 establish non-discrimination between domestic and foreign investors and non-discrimination between investors from different countries, and Article 1105 establishes a minimum standard of treatment for foreign investors, as defined by international law.

The most controversial section of Chapter 11 concerns uncompensated expropriation (Article 1110). There may be no direct or indirect nationalization or expropriation or any "measure tantamount to nationalization or expropriation" of an investment by another country unless the expropriation is for a public purpose, on a non-discriminatory basis, in accordance with law, and on payment of compensation.[5] The article also includes the following:

> Nothing in this Chapter shall be construed to prevent a Party from adopting, maintaining or enforcing any measure otherwise consistent with this Chapter that it considers appropriate to ensure that investment activity in its territory is undertaken in a manner sensitive to environmental concerns (Article 1114(1)).

Thus in the Chapter 11 context, a strong non-discriminatory position is established and maintained between member countries. One reading of the clause suggests that no minimum environmental standards are set. At the same time, and much like the EU, as long as barriers to trade and investment are not created, the possibility exists that higher standards could also be enacted.

In terms of the process to initiate arbitration under Chapter 11, it is the complainant that submits a notice of intention to submit a claim to arbitration at least 90 days before the claim is submitted. Once the claim is submitted the complainant can request arbitration under one of three internationally-accepted procedures.[6] In the cases that have been before tribunals to date, there have been 2 members appointed by the countries concerned in the complaint, and one expert that has been appointed from outside of the NAFTA countries, usually from the EU. The place of arbitration is usually outside both of the countries involved in the complaint, typically in the third NAFTA member country.

*Comparing Institutional Structures*

The above serves to reinforce the very different frameworks used to create, pass, implement, monitor, and enforce environmental policies in both regional integration organizations. Table 6.1 below summarizes the main features of the institutional context in which environmental policy is found in both the EU and NAFTA. The fact that both regional integration agreements have recognized the externalities associated with environmental policy and have bodies that deal with environmental policy is not to imply that the two bodies have similar status in the regional agreements. The CEC is recognized as being under resourced and relatively powerless, whereas the EU Commission is recognized as a legitimate actor in the areas where it possesses policy competencies.

## Table 6.1 The Institutional Context for Environmental Policy

| Item | EU | NAFTA |
|---|---|---|
| **Supranational status of environmental policy** | Shared member state/supranational policy competency (Commission) | Member state policy competency |
| | DG-Environment integrates environmental policy into all areas of single market | CEC monitors and coordinates environmental policy, but with particular reference to trade concerns |
| **Construction of Policy** | Member state: legal specification cannot conflict with EU directives | Member state: autonomous in specification |
| | Supranational: member states, EP, and Commission usually suggests directives | Supranational: NAAEC encourages higher standards |
| **Policy harmonization/coordination** | Commission formally proposes Actual standards member state determined | Actual standards member state determined |
| | Minimum standards set by EU: harmonized/ *acquis communautaire* | Coordination in certain areas done by CEC (movement of hazardous materials) |
| **Monitoring/Reporting** | Reporting at member state and at supranational level (EEA) | Reporting at member state level |
| | Monitoring at member state/supranational level | Monitoring at member state/supranational level |
| **Enforcement** | Fines levied on corporations at member state level | Fines levied on corporations at member state level |
| | Supranational to member state enforcement: Commission able to warn member states | NAAEC article allows for intergovernmental enforcement |
| | ECJ has fining ability | CEC has only influence of a "factual record" |

**Backgrounders and Case Studies**

*Backgrounder – EU*

While the European Union has developed a series of principles that govern its environmental legislation, a similar set of principle exists only partially for NAFTA. The Union's environmental policy rests upon the following principles: the polluter pays principle, the source principle, the integration principle, the prevention principle, and the precautionary principle. NAFTA's environmental policy encompasses the polluter pays principle, but none of the others. In the EU's case the principle was in existence well before treaty incorporation, as originally set out in the 1st Environmental Action Program created by the Commission in 1975. The principle was based on charging polluters for the costs of environmental damage, charges which would encourage polluters to search for production processes that pollute less and that make more rational use of environmental resources, or to develop products that entail less waste. The principle was to be achieved through charges as well as the imposition of a set of minimum environmental standards.

The effectiveness of the principle rested on the ability of both the EU and the member states to implement it. Early Union efforts in the application of this principle included the Waste Oil Directive (75/439) and the European Court of Justice (ECJ)'s decision in the *Waste Oils* case (83/240). In the latter case, as it was used by many member states, the source principle had gained widespread acceptance in the EU. It simply suggested that environmental damage should be prevented at the source, by using "end of the pipe" technology to set emission standards. The source principle was unexpectedly extended when the ECJ applied it in the *Walloon Waste* case (C-2/90). The proximity principle governs the hazardous waste policy area, where the Commission has consistently supported the idea that wastes should be handled as close to the source as possible. As a consequence, shipments across the EU were limited as much as possible. The question before the ECJ was whether Walloonian measures restricting imports of foreign waste were discriminatory. The ECJ held that the Walloonian measures were not, arguing that the proximity principle meant that every region, municipal or other local authority must take measures to ensure that the reception, processing and removal of its own waste. Waste needed to be disposed of as close as possible to the source in order to limit transport. As such, waste movements of all types were to be restricted as much as possible. Such shipments would only be encouraged when it was not practical for member states to construct their own treatment centers, as for example for smaller member states such as Luxembourg or where the member state produced minimal amounts of hazardous waste, such as Ireland.

While there has been minimal effort to properly integrate environmental aspects into the economic aspects of NAFTA,[7] there have been considerable efforts to integrate environmental measures into all sectors of EU policy. Even so, these remain controversial, especially in conjunction with setting or maintaining high standards of protection. This debate came to a head during the discussions over the interpretation of language in the Maastricht Treaty, where fundamental objectives of the EU's environmental policy were laid out; specifically, the preservation and protection of the environment. The EU was also to promote measures at the international level to deal with regional or worldwide environmental problems, and the treaty explicitly called for a "high level" of environmental protection, although the exact meaning of "high" was never spelled out. The actual implementation of these standards, therefore, has to be examined on a case by case basis and cannot be ascertained directly from the treaty itself.

The EU professes to follow two other environmental principles, the prevention and precautionary principles. The first may be partially followed by the US (and by extension, NAFTA), the latter certainly not. The prevention principle was included in the Single European Act (SEA), which argued that prevention is better than cure; the "best environmental policy consists in preventing the creation of pollution or nuisances at the source, rather than subsequently trying to counteract the events" (Commission, $3^{rd}$ EAP, quoted in Jans, 1996). Placing the prevention principle in actual legislation, it suggests that there must be limits as to the amount of waste initially produced, that products be designed and produced to allow for easy recycling, and the support of products and practices that encourage re-use rather than recycling. For example, adherence to this principle would mean the end of one-way packaging. More expansive in scope is the EU's precautionary principle, a notion that is largely rejected by NAFTA member countries. The principle suggests that if there was a strong suspicion that an activity might cause environmental harm, a pro-active stance should be taken. If there is a perceived threat, then it is better to strictly regulate or even ban the activity before the environmental damage is done.

*EU Hazardous Waste Case Study*

Since the mid-1970s the Commission has introduced considerable legislation covering the handling of hazardous waste, limiting its handling, shipment and disposal. The first major efforts to restrict hazardous waste related to a particular industry, the titanium dioxide industry. The Commission wrote two pieces of legislation regulating the industry, forcing high recovery standards of pollutants. Following on from these successes, the Commission introduced legislation in 1974 that dealt with the broader aspect of the issue of hazardous waste. The first two directives, 75/439 on waste oils and 75/442 on waste, prevented the discharge of the untreated products into the environment and encouraged member states to prevent excess production of waste and encourage alternative schemes that could recover waste. The first directive on hazardous waste (78/319) was passed in the late 1970s, which encouraged member states to reduce the production of waste, and harmonized arrangements concerning the disposal of these wastes. In the 1980s several directives were passed, including directives on the management of on sewage sludge (86/278/EEC), as well as two directives dealing with the disposal of waste, including hazardous waste, from municipalities (89/369 and 89/462). It also passed a directive (84/631) that encouraged measures for the identification, tracking and control of trans-frontier shipments of hazardous waste. In conjunction with its cooperation in the Basle Accords, the EU passed a new directive on hazardous waste (91/689/EEC). In it the EU sought to create a system of labeling hazardous waste, as well as preventing its shipment to unsuspecting parties, usually less developed countries in Europe, or overseas.

While it is one thing to propose legislation and achieve its passage through the EU institutions, it is an entirely different thing to actually have the member states implement the legislation in the way intended by the Commission, and in a timely manner. This case is the first to employ provisions originally found in the in the Treaty of Maastricht, which enables the ECJ to impose fines on member states when it has failed to take the necessary action to comply with obligations under Community law.[8] Specifically, the case involved Greece's unwillingness to stop uncontrolled dumping at a site near the mouth of the Kouroupitos river, in the Chania region on the island of Crete. In 1987 the EU had first received complaints from local communities about uncontrolled dumping of industrial and hospital waste into a ravine near the mouth of the Kouroupitos. A US military base, located at Souda, also used the Kouroupitos site to dump toxic and hazardous waste. During the 1980s local officials reported that the materials would frequently self-combust, largely due to the large amount of organic matter in the site. These fires would burn uncontrolled for significant periods of time. It was also reported that hazardous materials continually leached into the sea, as the dump is situated about 200 meters from the water's edge. The Commission began its own investigations into the dump in 1988. Over the course of the next several years, the Commission issued several warnings to the Greek government. Finally, the Commission filed a formal complaint against Greece and forwarded its case to the ECJ.

In 1992 the ECJ ruled against Greece, ordering it to comply with the *acquis*. The Court ruled that Greece was not in compliance with Community legislation on hazardous waste (Directives 75/443/EEC and 78/319/EEC) by "failing to take the necessary measures to ensure that in the area of Chania waste and dangerous waste are disposed of without endangering human health and without harming the environment, and by failing to draw up for that area plans for the disposal of waste and toxic and dangerous waste..." ( ECJ, C-45/91). These directives were required to be met by January 1, 1981, according to the Accession Treaty signed by Greece. After the judgement the Commission spent considerable time trying to work with Greece in efforts to get the latter to comply with the 1992 ECJ judgement.

Over the course of the next three years, the Commission and Greece engaged in a series of warnings and responses concerning the waste site. On October 11, 1993, the Commission reminded the Greek authorities that the ECJ ruled against them and noted that little had been done to comply with the judgment. On August 24, 1994, the Greek government informed the Commission that efforts toward compliance were being undertaken, specifically that local waste management officials had received preliminary approval for two landfill sites at Kopinadi and Vardia, and that studies assessing the environmental impact of the sites were being prepared. A significant part of the delay was the result of resistance from the local populace. They filed numerous complaints and initiated several legal briefs expressing their opposition to the proposed location of the new facilities, which would be situated closer to populated areas. Greek Environmental Minister Costas Laliotis noted that opposition to the new sites was longstanding and hostile, and complained that "Every time I move to solve the crisis, they bring out the guns and brandish black flags" (*Time Europe*, July 17, 2000). The Greek government expected that these assessments would be completed by year end, which would allow local officials to make final decisions on the construction, operation, supervision and restoration of a suitable waste site.

Beyond this letter setting out the preliminary steps toward compliance, the Commission received no other information. As a result, the Commission decided to start procedures under Article 171(2) of the Treaty, and on September 21, 1995, it gave two months to explain its failure to comply. On December 14, 1995, Greece belatedly informed the Commission that local officials had selected a waste disposal site and compliance would be forthcoming. This was not enough to satisfy the Commission, which noted that four years after the original case, compliance measures were still at a preliminary stage. The Commission concluded that Kouroupitos waste site remained a danger to public health and the environment (*Europe Environment*, October 5, 1999).

The next step in the legal process was the issuance of a reasoned opinion, which was then offered by the Commission on August 6, 1996, where it argued that Greece had failed to fulfil its treaty obligations. Greece was given an additional two months to comply, and that it also faced fines should it fail to do so, as allowed by Article 171(2). Greece replied, tardily, on November 11, 1996, that it did have a national plan, which required both regional and local action. Furthermore, the national plan did meet the requirements of the two directives in question. Specifically referring to the Kouroupitos waste site, the Greek authorities argued that they had intervened directly with local officials in order to resolve the problem, and that they were drawing up separate management program for that site. The authorities noted that steps had been taken to construct a mechanical recycling plant and a landfill site, which together would resolve the of waste management problems in the area. In late August of 1997, about nine months later, Greece sent yet another letter asserting that preliminary approval had been granted for the location of the landfill site and that the study relating to the environmental impact of the mechanical recycling plant had been completed. These dilatory efforts on the part of Greece were not enough to convince the Commission of the seriousness of the plans, and on November 17, 1997, the Commission decided to initiate further proceedings against Greece, specifically requesting that a fine of

€24,600 per day be assessed for failing to respect the earlier ruling (*ECJ*, C-387/97).

In a preliminary hearing of the case, the ECJ's Advocate-General Damaso Ruiz-Jarabo Colomer argued, after examining the nature of the infringements, that the fine should be reduced to €15,375 a day. The Advocate-General noted that the ECJ's duty was to consider the facts and legal definitions as well as to assess the suitable and in proportion to aim being sought. Any review must be restricted to verifying the facts, determining whether an error of assessment was made, and calculating whether the principles of proportionality and equal treatment were observed, as far as the penalties proposed by the Commission were concerned. His charge is to outline the limits of the discretion of the Court of Justice keeping in sight the reason for the proceeding itself, which is not to punish, but to encourage the reluctant Member State to apply the judgement handed down. The amount should be in proportion to the scale of the offense and enough to act as a deterrent to future non-compliance (*European Report*. October 6, 1999 *European Report*, June 10, 2000).

In its landmark ruling of 4 July 2000, the ECJ rendered its judgement on three particular points. First, as of late 1998 waste was still being dumped in an uncontrolled manner. Second, given the fact that little information was forthcoming from either the Commission or Greece, the ECJ noted that it could not be proven that the latter hadn't failed fully to comply with the directives on hazardous waste. Thirdly, Greece's track record in this case did not suggest an organized and coordinated system for controlling waste, but rather its *ad hoc* interventions led the court to conclude that Greece had failed to implement the necessary measures to comply with either of the two directives at hand. The ECJ noted that the duration of the infringement was "considerable" (C-387/97). The ECJ's ruling split the difference between the Commission's figures and the Advocate General's imposing a daily fine of  €20,000 on Greece for non-compliance with the previous judgement (C-45/91). It was the first time that the Court had used the power under Article 228 of the EC Treaty to fine a member state.

From July 4, 2000 to July 31, 2001, when the Commission decided to close its long-running pursuit of Greece concerning the Kouroupitos waste dump, Greece had paid out €3,600,000. It paid the remainder of the total fine of €5,400,000 in January and February in April and May of 2002. Environment Commissioner Margot Wallström, commenting on the Commission's decision to close its investigations, noted that Greece had built a temporary waste storage area in Messomouri and preparations for a permanent waste management scheme were underway, with construction of a composting plant and a landfill site in Korakia scheduled to begin in late summer of 2001. These claims were verified by the Commission, which had sent two independent experts to the area. After inspecting the site area at the end of June, 2001, they reported in early July 2001. She said she was "satisfied that the illegal dumping has been stopped by the Greek authorities, but there is still a big clean-up job to be done. I will be contacting the Greek authorities shortly to hear what their plans are for remedial work on this site" (*CEC Press Release*, IP:01/1150, July 30, 2001).

The Commission handled the case in a very careful way, necessitated by the fact that this was the first time it had sought out financial penalties for non-compliance, even though it had the power to do so through treaty mandates. Commission caution was evidenced by the involvement of numerous Commission officials as well as the length of time required to bring closure to the case. Over the course of the case, EP parliamentarians continually posed written and oral questions to the Environment Commissioner, pointedly asking about progress in the case and the EP was particularly interested in financial penalties. Immediately after the case closed, the President of the EP Environmental Committee, Caroline Jackson (EPP-EE, United Kingdom), noted that "We [the EP] are disappointed that it has taken so long for this issue to be resolved. And we thought that the Commission was ultimately reluctant to pursue the financial penalty option. We feel that sanctions should be applied more often and in a more active way" (DG-Environment, Environment for Europeans, October 2001: 4). However, having once exercised the option, and also having discovered that member states will pay fines, the Commission will likely be less hesitant to pursue this option in the future. As noted in the *Official Journal*, the Kouroupitos case created not only a strong precedent for further efforts in Greece, where many problems raised by uncontrolled landfill sites exist, but also for other member states "where problems of similar nature occur" (*OJ* C 134 E/99, June 6, 2002). At the end of 2002, there were 1,330 cases concerning the uncontrolled disposal of waste that were being followed by the Commission. A new directive on the landfill of waste (1999/31/EC) made the Commission charge easier, as it specified the minimum requirements for design, operation, closure and after-care of landfills.[9]

## NAFTA – Backgrounder

As noted above NAFTA has three routes for supranational monitoring and enforcement of environmental policies or policies that have environmental implications: processes begun at the member country level, the citizen submission process, and processes taken through Chapter 11. The first involves a member country filing complaints about another country's persistent failure in enforcing their environmental laws. To date this route has not been pursued, and is unlikely to be used to its full extent in the future, due to the long and convoluted process necessary for fines to be imposed. As far as the citizen submission route is concerned, the CEC has issued few "factual reports." Over twenty-five complaints have been filed, mostly against Mexico or Canada, with only a few being filed against the US. These "factual records" are one of the few mechanisms that the CEC has to protect the environment, and member countries try very hard not to suffer the embarrassment that comes with their publication. Recently, it has been more aggressive in its role about warning member countries of the consequences of not taking action to protect the environment. The CEC has been at pains not to focus solely on Mexican complaints, but as Mexico has had traditionally weaker enforcement mechanisms, it has been forced to operate more openly on environmental issues.[10] Until 2000, however, only two factual records had been developed, one dealing with a cruise ship terminal in Cozumel, Mexico and the other dealing with the impact of a hydroelectric dam construction on fish habitat in British Columbia, Canada.

As for the cases which have been brought to arbitration under Chapter 11, several have been environmental in nature, and they have created a large amount of controversy. The first case concerned the US corporation Ethyl, the manufacturer of the fuel additive MMT, which Ethyl claims boosts fuel efficiency in automobiles. Ethyl took the Canadian government to an arbitral panel over a change in Canadian law which outlawed the manganese-based gasoline additive. Ethyl claimed that the Canadian ban effectively expropriated the investments that Ethyl had made to supply the Canadian market, as the additive was mixed with gasoline only in Canada. It had already been banned from use in US fuel products. While the Canadian federal government's motivation was public health concerns over possible health hazards of MMT, it did not ban MMT on the basis of health concerns as Canada's Environmental Act did not cover this type of additive. Instead, the government did it via trade laws, as the MMT was imported from the US. Alberta also challenged the federal government's removal of MMT from the market by using the Canadian Agreement on Internal Trade. An internal Canadian panel ruled in Alberta's favor, making the federal government's ban illegal before the NAFTA panel reached its conclusion. The Canadian government settled with Ethyl for a reported US$13 million and removed the ban, as well as publicly declaring that there was no scientific basis for prohibiting MMT.

A more recent case concerns health hazards relating to another gasoline additive called MTBE. Methanex, a Canadian company, manufactures methanol, which is used in MTBE. Ex-California Governor Gray Davis ordered a phase out of MTBE by December 31, 2002 in the state. This action prompted Methanex to file for arbitration against the US, claiming about US$1 billion in potential losses, a figure based on the drop in the company's stock value following the California announcement and lost potential profits. The case has not yet been resolved, and the central question in the case concerns whether the removal of MTBE would actually improve public health in California. Under the NAFTA Chapter 11 rules, if a product is shown to have public health hazards, then "expropriating" this market should not result in compensation as the expropriating measure does not constitute a trade measure.

*NAFTA Hazardous Waste Case Study*

The Metalclad case is the most widely reported case concerning environmental policy in NAFTA and has numerous parallels with the EU's Kouroupitos waste case. A Mexican company, COTERIN, had obtained authorization from the

Mexican federal government to develop a hazardous waste landfill in Guadalcazar, San Luis Potosi (SLP) in Mexico. COTERIN had already been operating a hazardous waste transfer facility there and had been given assurances from the SLP government that the facility development would not be blocked. Subsequent to the authorization, COTERIN was bought by Metalclad, a waste-management operating out of Newport Beach, California. Metalclad proceeded with construction, based on extensions of the federal governments permits. After being audited by the federal government in 1995, Metalclad was given permission to proceed so long as it took remedial actions to clean up waste from the site's earlier use, and create an environmental buffer zone around the facility. However, the municipality of Guadalcazar denied Metalclad's application for a local construction permit and an injunction judicial was issued to halt operations. As a result of local action, Metalclad filed for arbitration in January 1997. An arbitral panel met in May 1997 and found that Mexico was in violation of Chapter 11. It ruled that Guadalcazar had no right to withhold the construction permit, given that permission had already been granted for COTERIN. The panel also objected to the manner in which the decision was made, as the municipality had not allowed Metalclad to make its case. The arbitral panel essentially said that if Guadalcazar had followed the accepted procedure in Mexico for denying construction permits, then Metalclad would not have had a case.   In the Metalclad case there was a clear expectation that the important permits to have in hand were the federal permits, and given these permits, the company had every expectation that the project would go ahead. The arbitral panel did add that federal governments were obligated to remove all doubt and uncertainty about all relevant legal requirements applicable to NAFTA investors. The estimate of the direct investment in the facility, US$16.7 million was awarded to Metalclad. The Mexican government immediately made clear its intention to challenge the panel's decision. In a further effort to halt Metalclad's activities, in September of 1997, the Governor of SLP issued an Ecological Decree (September 1997) declaring a 600,000 protected zone on the grounds that the site contained a rare type of cactus.

The impact of the case was felt beyond the borders of San Luis Potosi, as local governments in all NAFTA member countries worried about their ability to question the environmental impact of direct foreign investment. Indeed, some have interpreted the arbitral panel's findings as totally undermining the ability of local government to make policy concerning local issues related to the environment. The case clearly points to procedural issues, however, as the reason for "expropriation" of investments, as here Chapter 11 provisions relating to the "fair and equitable treatment" of foreign investors apply. The Mexican government appealed the case. Because of the arbitral process chosen, the appeal took place in another country, and was finally heard by the Supreme Court in British Columbia, Canada. The appeal findings were released in May 2001, where the court ruled that there was no evidence of violation of NAFTA rules concerning either the environment or direct foreign investment prior to the

Ecological Decree, but that after this time it was patently clear that Mexico had expropriated Metalclad's investment. The BC Supreme Court did state in its decision that the right of a local government to regulate on environmental and public health grounds was not in question in this case, leaving open future challenges to NAFTA on environmental grounds.

## Comparative Analysis and Theoretical Considerations

*Analysis*

In both case studies non-governmental, sub-national, national and supranational actors were involved. In both cases the ultimate solution was found at the supranational level, but the process of arriving at a solution was radically different. However, what is distinctly different about the EU case is the fact that there were several well-developed supranational environmental directives in effect that bound all member states into a regulatory regime. In the NAFTA case, national environmental laws were irrelevant. More importantly, supranational trade laws were the ultimate grounds upon which the arbitral decision was made.

Table 6.2 shows the main features of these policy regimes, from the viewpoint of conflict resolution and enforcement. It is clear that the characterization of environmental policy in the EU is as an integral component of supranational policy competencies, where as in NAFTA, environmental policy is clearly a member country issue, unless it impinges on trade or FDI issues.

One issue that does arise relates to why the NAAEC lacks member country to member country complaint procedures, given the institution's enforcement ability through arbitration. One reason is found in the nature of environmental regulation in the US and Canada. Both member countries have relatively high environmental standards, resulting in little legal friction between these two nations. Another reason may be political. There is a great deal of reticence on the part of both the US and Canada to pursue Mexico for non-compliance with its own laws, given that Mexico has undertaken to improve its own environmental compliance, and has taken steps to upgrade its environmental programs to be more in line with the rest of NAFTA.[11]

## Table 6.2 Supranational Process, Enforcement, Compensation and Arbitration

| Item | EU | NAFTA |
|---|---|---|
| **Process** | Directives: supranational to member state | NAAEC: intergovernmental Chapter 11: investor to member country |
| **Scope** | Throughout the EU | Only in relation to trade or FDI issues |
| **Ability to arbitrate** | Informal arbitration between Commission's Legal Division and member state on behalf of investor /corporation | Arbitration through NAAEC between member states Arbitration through Chapter 11 provisions between investors and member states |
| **Ability to enforce** | Commission has the power to enforce legislation and suggest fines based upon its internal analysis | CEC has no ability to enforce or fine – only "factual record" |
| **Ability to compensate/fine** | Commission has ability to take repeat violators to the ECJ. | NAAEC arbitral panels can fine up to 0.0007 percent of trade |
| | The ECJ imposes all fines | Chapter 11 arbitral panels can compensate (usually up to FDI amount) |

*Theoretical Reflections and the Future*

Two competing approaches are available to assess the institutional development of the EU and NAFTA with respect to the environment, that of intergovernmentalism and historical institutionalism. Intergovernmentalism suggests that nations do not give up sovereignty, per se, but rather pool it, to work together more efficiently. Inside the "normal" operations of the organization, voting rules are usually established that allow for member states to maintain strong veto powers when national interests are threatened (Moravcsik, 1998). In the case of NAFTA, the provisions limiting the ability of the CEC to act as anything more than as an advocate for the environment illustrates the importance of intergovernmentalist arguments. The CEC cannot propose legislation, nor effectively enforce it. When deciding whether to investigate claims against either private actors or national members, the CEC's voting rules requiring two of the three states agreeing to move forward is a significant hurdle. The limited number of investigations and cases, to date, suggests the importance of these decision-making rules in working against supranational activity. It also suggests that the political will and desire to integrate through the pooling of sovereignty is seriously lacking in NAFTA. Intergovernmentalism also suggests that the more powerful nations will seek to use these same rules to achieve their interests, either by creating policies that benefit them disproportionately or preventing the loss of sovereignty.

Historical institutionalism stresses that the relationship between institutions and individual behavior needs to be seen in broad terms. Policy outcomes are not totally dependent on the power relations between actors, instead institutions structure collective behavior, which in turn generates distinct outcomes that are distinct from the interests of the most powerful actors. Most importantly, over time institutions lose their reference to their past, and as a consequence may only be loosely linked to their original intentions. At the same time, these institutions are capable of shaping a new future, which may guide policy away from the preferences of the creators (Hall, 1986; Immergut 1998). Pierson (1996) accepts the explanatory value of intergovernmentalism in looking at the EU, but notes that gaps in the ability of the member states to effectively control, reign in, or otherwise order the supranational organizations emerge because of four factors: the autonomous decisions of European supranational actors, restricted time horizons, the large potential for unanticipated consequences, and the likelihood of changes in the preferences of member state governments (Jordan, 1999; Bulmer, 1998; Marks, Hooghe, and Blank, 1996; Pierson, 1996; Pollack, 1997).

The implications for NAFTA in each of these areas is more difficult to ascertain, but are nevertheless important. The supranational organizations in NAFTA remain largely undeveloped, but bureaucracies can expand over time, accumulating political powers. In the case of the CEC, it may be expected to play a larger role in resolving disputes as transboundry pollution problems between the US and Canada, such as acid rain and acidification, become more important. When comparing the EU and NAFTA, there is the potential of parallel institutional development. The mandate of the EU and its relationship to the environment was minimal, at best, during its early years and little was present institutionally that would have suggested, or supported, action in the field of the environment. Over the course of the years, as the environment ascended in importance at the member state level, the environment has achieved an enhanced status in the treaties that govern the EU. The growing need to move environmental legislation forward was recently recognized in the Amsterdam Treaty, where co-decision was extended to the environment. Indeed, the possibility of expanding enhanced cooperation, also introduced in the Amsterdam Treaty, has lately been proposed by both the Commission and the EP as a way to further advance issues relating to the environment.

Restricted time horizons are also important in historical institutionalism. When decisions need to need to be made quickly, member states or countries will often agree to compromises that achieve a short-term solution, but leave long term possibilities to the supranational institutions. This has often been the case with the

EU, and may also turn out to play an important role in the development of NAFTA. Over the years both the Commission and the ECJ were institutions interested in developing supranational integration in general, and environmental provisions in particular. As a result of the cooperation of the two organizations, legislation led to the development of the supranational laws that would come to govern this policy area. The ECJ has rendered decisions that supported the policy preferences of the Commission, most specifically the *Commission v. Denmark* (more commonly known as the *Danish Beer Bottles* case) and the above-mentioned *Walloon Waste* case, both decisions that have prioritized environmental issues over trade.

While the institutions of NAFTA are clearly not as developed nor powerful vis-à-vis the member countries, other opportunities exist in NAFTA that did not exist in the EU. In the EU, non-governmental organizations can only petition the Commission and the member states to bring suits before the ECJ, as non-governmental organizations do not have the power to bring suits before the ECJ on their own. In the case of *Greenpeace International and others v. European Commission* (1998), the ECJ ruled that these groups do not have the standing to sue, effectively limiting the power of these groups to directly challenge the Commission on environmental matters. In NAFTA, however, companies and concerned actors do have this power. As part of the sidebar negotiations over the treaty, environmental groups were given standing to sue, which may give NAFTA the potential to develop an environmental mandate quicker than was in the case of the EU. Indeed, the member states' willingness to accept the legitimacy of the ECJ's rulings was vital to the development of the EU. Integration through legal rulings remains a strong likelihood for NAFTA, especially given the fact that few decisions rendered to date have been accepted by both state and non-state actors.

The potential for unanticipated consequences, and the likelihood of changes in the preferences of member state governments are also important provisions for historical institutionalism, but much harder to predict. The importance of environmental accidents (such as Chernobyl) played a role in creating an environmental consciousness in Europe which cannot be overlooked. For years environmental groups and governmental entities have been calling attention to the environmental degradation along the Mexico-US border, citing statistics on hazardous waste emissions and the concomitant impact on public health. Changing governmental preferences can also play an important role in NAFTA, especially if Mexico, and to a certain extent the US, are able to pay more attention to the environment. In the former case, national efforts over the past decade have moved the environment onto the political agenda, whether it be issues of deforestation in the south of the nation or poor air, or water and sanitation standards in the major cities. The need to protect its rich natural environment, and the need to maintain biodiversity has also been raised by environmental groups in Mexico, which has been heeded by a more receptive Mexican government. As for the EU's expansion into the central and eastern Europe, there may be future parallels between the NAFTA's experience and the EU, as lower standard nations must the expectations of the *acquis*. This has already proven to be difficult for many nations, which are also dealing with the after effects of the communist period, generally not noted for high environmental consciousness.


## Conclusions

Environmental policy is the one policy area where supranational institutions maintain some interests and competencies in both the EU and NAFTA. It is therefore useful to compare the development, monitoring, and enforcement of policy between the two regional blocs of countries.

Our findings were that in neither of the regional trading blocs was environmental policy wholly elevated to the supranational level, although in the EU the Commission does establish minimum standards along the lines of the *acquis*. In terms of construction of policy, the Commission does have powers as a supranational bureaucracy, powers that are not present in its NAFTA equivalent, the CEC. Both bureaucracies monitor the environment by collecting and compiling data. The Commission is able to gather tremendous amounts of data from the member states, as most directives have timetables that require reporting of data. Member states are often late in reporting, but the Commission does have the power to induce reporting through the initiation of legal proceedings. It is usually the case, as it is with the CEC, that too much data is available. Both institutions are chronically understaffed and under resourced, making information management a challenging exercise. The CEC, while an institutionally weak body, is able to gather a great deal of environmental data directly from governmental sources. In terms of enforcement of policy, the Commission has greater powers again, and can take member states to the ECJ. The CEC has no power of enforcement, but it does have an intergovernmental arbitral role in establishing tribunals whenever there is a dispute between NAFTA member countries about persistent failure to implement domestic environmental law. NAFTA does possess a feature that is lacking in the EU, however, that of an investor – governmental arbitration route under Chapter 11. Although this does not speak directly to the environment, it has been closely linked with environmental matters in several instances, and does not automatically undermine the ability for NAFTA member countries to develop and enforce environmental laws.

In terms of the development of policy in both trading blocs, an attempt was made to characterize both the EU and NAFTA as a blend of intergovernmentalism and historical institutionalism, with more emphasis in NAFTA on intergovernmentalism. As for the development of the NAFTA institution, it would appear that there is considerable opportunity for the institution to enhance its role in environmental policymaking and enforcement. If through time it begins to take on a more supranational identity and international environment problems become more salient to the general public and governments, the CEC is likely to play a more important role in settling disputes.

## Notes

1  The preamble states that the NAFTA member countries will "undertake [trade liberalization] in a manner consistent with environmental protection; promote sustainable development; [and] strengthen the development and enforcement of environmental laws and regulations".

2  The EEA is not directly involved in the policymaking process, but the Commission does have liaison personnel that ensure the two entities work in a cooperative manner. The chief role for the EEA is as the "environmental" conscience of the Union. Since its rather awkward inception in the late 1980s, it has spent considerable amount of time urging the EU to move more quickly on raising environmental standards.

3  It originally had its offices in Dallas, Texas, USA.

4  This provision only applies to the US and Mexico, as Canada agreed that fines assessed against it would be assessed through the courts.

5  As Gaines (2000) notes, all these conditions need to be satisfied.

6  The three used in NAFTA are a) the International Center for the Settlement of Investment Disputes (ICSID) Convention (World Bank sponsored rules) b) the additional facility rules of the ICSID, if one of the party is not a party to the ICSID Convention; or c) the UNCITRAL Arbitration rules (UN sponsored rules).

7  This is a point made quite forcibly in the CEC's own working paper (CEC, 1998) which discusses the institutional interactions between the NAFTA supranational bodies.

8  EC Treaty Article 171 (Maastricht) to Article 228 of the European Commission Treaty (Amsterdam).

9  It should be noticed that two cases concerning the application of a directive were before the ECJ in 2002 under the Article 228 procedure, the application of Directive 76/160/EEC in the United Kingdom (C-85/2001) and in Spain (C-278/2001).

10 For example, one complaint maintained that the Mexican government authorized operation of a hazardous waste landfill less than 4 miles from the city of Hermosillo, Sonora, when according to regulations it should have been at least 25 miles away. The Mexican government responded that the submitter did not exhaust all available domestic remedies, and in any case, the landfill was authorized before the regulation in question existed.

11 For example, in May, 2001, Mexico undertook to sign the Stockholm Convention on Persistent Organic Pollutants (POPS) to phase out 12 persistent organic pollutants that threaten human health and the environment.

## References

Alesina, Alberto, Angeloni, Ignazio and Ludger Schuknecht (2001), "What does the European Union Do?", Unpublished manuscript, Harvard University, October.

Börzel, Tanja. 2001. Non-Compliance in the European Union: Pathology or Statistical Artefact?" *Journal of European Public Policy*, 8: 803-24.

Bulmer, Simon. 1998. "New Institutionalism and the Governance of the Single European Market." *Journal of European Public Policy*, 5: 365-86

Clarkson, Stephen. 2000. "Apples and Oranges: Prospects for the Comparative Analysis of the EU and NAFTA as Continental Systems", *EUI Working Paper RSC* 2000/23. Florence, Italy: EUI.

*Commission of the European Communities v. Greece.* 2000. Case C-387/97. ECR I-5047.

Commission of the European Communities. 2001. Environment for Europeans. DG-Environment. Luxembourg: Office for the Publications for the European Community.

Commission of the European Communities. 2002. "Written response to EP Question concerning Greece Waste", *OJ* C 134 E/99, June 6.

Crowley, Patrick. 2002. "European Integration after EMU: What Next?", in Crowley, P., *Before and Beyond EMU*, London: Routledge, pp.157-180.

Earnshaw, David and David Judge. 1996. "Early Days: The European Parliament, Co-decision and the European Union legislative Process Post-Maastricht", *Journal of European Public Policy*, 2: 624-649.

*European Report*. 1999. October 6. Lexis: European Information Service.

*European Report*. 2000. June 10. Lexis: European Information Service.

Gaines, Stanley. 2000. "NAFTA Chapter 11 as a challenge to Environmental Law Making – One view from the United States", paper presented at EnviReform conference "Civil Society Participation in NAFTA", November 2000, University of Toronto.

Garman, Julie and Louise Hilditch. 1998. "Behind the Scenes: An Examination of the Importance of the Informal Processes at Work in Conciliation", *Journal of European Public Policy*, 5: 271-284.

*Greenpeace International and others v. European Commission*. 1998. Case C-321/95. ECR I-1651.

Hall, Peter. 1986. *Governing the Economy*, Cambridge: Polity Press.

Hayes-Renshaw, Fiona and Helen Wallace. 1997. *The Council of Ministers*, New York: St. Martin's Press.

Hogenboom, Barbara. 1998. *Mexico and the NAFTA Environmental Debate*, Utrecht, Netherlands: International Books.

Immergut, Ellen. 1998. "The Theoretical Core of the New Institutionalism", *Politics & Society*, 26:5-34.

Jans, Jan. 1996. "The Development of EC Environmental Law", in Gerd Winter (ed). *European Environmental Law*, Aldershot: Dartmouth.

Jordan, Andrew. 1999. "Lock in or Watered Down?"

Judge, David. 1993. "'Predestined to Save the Earth': The Environment Committee of the European Parliament", in David Judge (ed). *Green Dimension for the European Community: Political Issues and Processes*, London: Frank Cass.

Judge, David (ed). 1993. *Green Dimension for the European Community: Political Issues and Processes*, London: Frank Cass.

Judge, David, David Earnshaw and Ngaire Cowan. 1994. "Ripples of Waves: The European Parliament in the European Community Policy Process." *Journal of European Public Policy*, 1: 27-51.

Marks, Gary, Liesbet Hooghe and Kermit Blank. 1996. "European Integration from the 1980s: State-Centric *v.* Multi-level Governance", *Journal of Common Market Studies*. 34: 341-378.

McCormick, John. 2001. *Environmental Policy in the European Union. New Environmental Policy in the European Union*, New York: Palgrave.

McKinney, Joseph. 2000. *Created from NAFTA: The Structure, Function and Significance of the Treaty's Related Institutions*, Armonk, NY: M.E. Sharpe.

Moravcsik, Andrew. 1998. *The Choice for Europe: Social Purpose and State Power from Messina to Maastricht*, Ithaca: Cornell University Press.

Nugent, Neill. 1995. "The Leadership Capacity of the European Commission", *Journal of European Public Policy*, 2: 603-623.

Nugent, Neill. (ed). 1997. *At the Heart of the Union*, London: Macmillan Press.

Peters, B. Guy. 1994. "Agenda-setting in the European Community", *Journal of European Public Policy*, 1: 9-26.

Peterson, John. 1995. "Decision-making in the European Union: Towards a Framework for Analysis", *Journal of European Public Policy*, 2: 69-93.

Pierson, Paul. 1996. "The Path to European Integration: A Historical Institutionalist Analysis", *Comparative Political Studies*, 29: 123-163.

Pollack, Mark. 1997. "Delegation, Agency, and Agenda Setting in the European Union", *International Organization*, 51: 99-134.

Stevis, Dimitris and Stephen Mumme. 2000. "Rules and Politics in International Integration: Environmental Regulation in NAFTA and the EU", *Environmental Politics*, 9: 20-42.

Wallace, Helen and William Wallace (eds.) 2000. *Policy-Making in the European Union*, Oxford: Oxford UP.

Zito, Anthony. 2000. *Creating Environmental Policy in the European Union*, London: Macmillan Press.

Chapter 7

# The Uses and Abuses of the Euro in the Canadian Currency Debate

Paul Bowles, Osvaldo Croci and Brian K. MacLean

## Introduction

In the late 1990s, some prominent Canadian economists – notably Thomas Courchene, Herbert Grubel, Richard Harris, and Robert Mundell – began arguing that a North American common currency would solve the problems underlying the growing gap between U.S. and Canadian real GDP per capita.[1] They succeeded in provoking a lively economic policy debate that occurred in parallel with the launch of the euro. The purpose of this chapter is to examine the parallels with the European case made by both sides in the economic policy debate that peaked in the 1999-2002 period.

The body of the paper begins by providing an understanding of the European case. Then the second section outlines our interpretation of the major developments in the birth of the euro. The third section, the core of the chapter, examines in detail the use of European parallels in the Canadian currency debate. We start by providing a brief overview of the protagonists in the debate. We then continue by arguing that the euro provided a "temporal spur" for the Canadian discussion but that it was only one among several important factors. We argue further that the proponents of a North American common currency relied very little on the European experience to support their case for the need for a common currency. Where they did use the European experience, however, was in their analysis of the institutional form that a common currency in North America might take. We argue that the opponents of a North American common currency were correct in viewing this as an inappropriate usage of the European parallel. In the concluding fourth section, we summarize our findings and argue that the most important parallel between the European and North American forces for a common currency is that both were driven primarily by politics.

## The Road to European Monetary Union[2]

In Europe – or, more precisely, in twelve out of the fifteen countries forming the European Community (EC) – a common currency, the euro, replaced national currencies on January 1, 2002. The process leading to the adoption of a common currency was long and complex. This section retraces its three most salient phases, each characterized by a distinct objective, and analyses the reasons and driving forces behind each of these objectives.

The EC did not devote much attention to monetary issues in its early years because the common market operated with practically fixed exchange rates, by virtue of its member states belonging to the Bretton Woods exchange rate system. When this system began to unravel in the late 1960s, it became evident that exchange rate fluctuations could pose a problem for the proper functioning of the common market, and would be particularly disruptive for the administration of the Common Agricultural Policy (McNamara 1998: 98-104). To remedy the problem, as well as to facilitate trade and promote further economic and political integration, in 1971 the EC adopted an ambitious plan (the Werner Report) for economic and monetary union to be achieved in stages by 1980. The first stage, a modest scheme known as the "snake" limited the range of exchange rate fluctuations of the participating currencies, was launched in April 1972. As for the objective of trying to establish a regional zone of stability in the midst of global monetary turbulence, member states added their pursuit of conflicting macroeconomic policy goals during an unprecedented period of stagflation. While Germany, for instance, pursued a restrictive monetary policy to control inflation, other member states implemented expansionary policies to try to encourage growth and employment. The result was that the "snake" ran immediately into trouble. A wave of currency speculation pushed half of the participating currencies outside the established exchange rate margins and by 1974, the "snake" was reduced to a limited Deutschmark zone. Consequently, the goal of achieving monetary union was abandoned, although not for long.

In April 1978, German Social-Democratic Chancellor Helmut Schmidt and French President Valéry Giscard D'Estaing resurrected the idea because both thought that adoption of a quasi-fixed European exchange rate system would help them attain preferred domestic economic policy objectives. Schmidt wished to adopt an expansionary policy with a view to the 1980 elections but had to overcome the doubts of some members of his coalition government and the Bundesbank's traditional commitment to price stability. As he saw it, German participation in a managed exchange rate system would slow the appreciation of the mark (and thus help German industry retain competitiveness) and act as a constraint on the Bundesbank, pushing it towards the adoption of a less restrictive monetary policy. For Giscard D'Estaing committing the franc to a managed exchange rate system was a way to enlist French industrialists in the struggle against inflation by convincing them that they could no longer hope to maintain international competitiveness by means of periodic devaluations and, hence, encourage them to resist any wage increases not reflecting improvements in productivity (Oatley 1997: 48-56). The outcome of this Franco-German initiative was the European Monetary System (EMS) that began to operate in March 1979. Its central component was the Exchange Rate Mechanism (ERM), limiting the exchange rate fluctuations of most member currencies to plus or minus 2.25 per cent of predetermined parities. The EMS proved more successful than the 'snake', although some currencies were repeatedly obliged to leave it, and then devalue before rejoining.[3]

In 1987, EC member governments ratified the so-called Single European Act (SEA) that aimed at "completing" the common market by removing all remaining non-tariff barriers to the free movement of goods, people, services, and capital by the end of 1992. The success of this initiative gave new impetus to the integration process and enabled the European Commission to put again on the EC agenda the project of economic and monetary union (EMU) to be achieved in three stages. The official justification for the project was that monetary union was a natural and logical complement of a single European market. Once a single market was in place, EC member states would have to confront the dilemma of what Cohen (1993) called the "unholy trinity", i.e. the inability of governments to simultaneously achieve the objectives of capital mobility, exchange-rate stability, and monetary policy autonomy. After 1992, in fact, the EC would be an area characterized by complete freedom of capital movements and a system of quasi-fixed exchange rates (the EMS), deemed necessary to facilitate intra-Community trade and thereby promote greater economic efficiency. Hence, it was illusory for member states to believe that they could retain the ability to conduct autonomous national monetary policies. The inconsistency of these three elements had already manifested itself during the 1980s, when some member states had either opted for flexible exchange rates and withdrawn from the EMS (e.g. the U.K.) or had been occasionally obliged to resort to capital controls (e.g. France and Italy). After 1992, however, the instrument of capital controls would no longer be available. Hence, if governments wished to retain their ability to make autonomous national monetary policy, they had to return to flexible exchange rates. If, on the contrary, they were willing to relinquish whatever national autonomy they retained in monetary policy, then they might as well move from the EMS to full currency union.

Though a case could be made for returning to flexible exchange rates on the grounds that Europe did not appear to be an 'optimum currency area' (Eichengreen 1997), a number of factors combined to provide favourable conditions for the re-launch of the currency union project.[4] First, and perhaps most importantly, currency union was the solution favoured by EC officials, especially within the Commission (Verdun 1999), as well as by those political leaders who perceived the *telos* of the process of European integration to be the formation of a European federation. Officially, EMU was justified on the arguments that the single currency would lead to greater efficiency for the single market, eliminate transactions costs, and provide a stimulus to growth and employment (Padoa-Schioppa 1987; Cecchini 1988; Commission of the European Communities 1992;

Emerson 1992; Temperton 1998). The contention was also advanced that monetary union would solve the "unholy trinity" dilemma by transforming an already weak national monetary sovereignty into "enhanced joint monetary sovereignty" (Commission of the European Communities 1996: 12-15). There is no doubt, however, that the view that the adoption of a common currency would promote a European identity, and thus contribute to the consolidation of the EC as a political union,[5] was paramount in the minds of the promoters of the project (Shore 2000: 87-122). It was this realization, coupled with a divided public opinion, which led British and Danish politicians to opt out of EMU.[6]

A second and important factor was that throughout the 1980s European political elites, including social-democratic ones, had moved away from traditional Keynesian policies and converged towards neo-liberal ones. Their penchant for "minimum government" made agreement on an SEA built around deregulation and liberalization easier, while their preference for low inflation facilitated agreement on the structure of EMU, particularly on the choice of the status (independence) and main objective (price stability) of the European Central Bank. Even trade unions supported currency union, limiting themselves to argue that as a counterweight to the perceived deflationary bias of EMU, the EC should make an explicit commitment to promote employment. A specific title to this effect was introduced in the 1997 Treaty of Amsterdam.

A number of more circumstantial variables also played a significant role in the choice of currency union.[7] For example, the fall of the Berlin wall, and the consequent prospect of German reunification, led some member states to regard reinforcement of EC institutions as the best way to avoid an institutionally weak EC being dominated by a bigger Germany. The solution of a currency union was particularly appealing since Germany (or, more precisely, the Bundesbank) was already perceived as playing a hegemonic role in the EMS (Giavazzi and Giovannini 1989). Germany, for its part, traded its initial reluctance to adhere to EMU, and thus relinquish the mark, in exchange for unqualified support of reunification on the part of its EC partners. The adoption of a single currency was also regarded as necessary if the EC wished to be able to compete with the United States (U.S.) as an equal on the world stage. It was, after all, the perception that Europe was increasingly lagging behind the U.S. in economic growth that had led to the adoption of the SEA. Finally, and perhaps most importantly, domestic political and economic considerations also played a significant role. In Italy, for instance, EMU, and particularly the need to meet the criteria for admission to its third stage, was regarded as an 'external constraint' that would help Italy bring its public finances under control by supplying clear objectives for fiscal policy and a supranational surveillance upon progress to attain them (Croci and Picci, 2002).

To conclude, EMU was officially justified as a logical next step after the completion of the common market, a step that would reduce transaction costs and thus increase trade, and stimulate economic growth. These arguments, however, would have been not as successful – after all, good economic counter-arguments also existed, most importantly that EMU would deprive national governments of their ability to use interest and exchange rates as instruments of economic policy – had it not been for the fact that EMU was also, and primarily, a *politically* driven process. First, there was the desire on the part of EC officials to make another significant step forward in the process of integration, a step that arguably had the potential to increase Europe's role and visibility on the world stage as well as contribute to the formation of a European-wide 'imagined community'. Second, and most important, national leaders that could have blocked the project did not because they saw EMU as an external factor that would help them attain domestic objectives (e.g. fiscal restraint in Italy, political reunification in Germany).

## The Canadian Currency Debate and the Euro

### The Protagonists

Before analysing the details of the Canadian currency debate, it is useful to provide some brief background information on the "players" in the debate. The euro was, as indicated above, a central political issue in Europe in the 1990s. The debate over the euro was informed by "expert opinion" – typically economists – but involved also political parties, pressure groups, and even the public at large since, at least in some cases, its adoption was the subject of popular referenda. The scope and intensity of the debate in Canada instead has been of a much lower order. In Canada, the debate has mainly been between a relatively small group of economists either working in academia or for major financial institutions. The currency debate has not been high on the Canadian political agenda although it has made sporadic appearances, largely at the behest of the Parti Québécois and the Canadian Alliance, and has reached the public mainly because of press coverage, especially by the two national newspapers, the *National Post* and the *Globe and Mail*.

As noted in the introduction, the leading proponents of a common currency have been Thomas Courchene, David Laidler, Herbert Grubel, Richard Harris, and Robert Mundell, all prominent academic economists. The proposals for a common currency were made by Courchene and Harris (1999) in a jointly authored work produced for the C.D. Howe Institute and Grubel's proposal (1999) was published by the Fraser Institute, both leading right-wing "think tanks". The leading proponents are associated with the conservative end of Canada's public policy spectrum. This is especially true of Grubel, a former Reform M.P., and Mundell, a long-time supply-side economist who publicly endorsed the economic program of the conservative Canadian Alliance in the 2000 federal election.[8] They have been joined in their support for a common currency with the U.S. by some private sector economists, most notably, Sherry Cooper, a strongly pro-U.S., pro-business economist at BMO Nesbitt Burns and a regular commentator in the financial press.

The leading opponents of a common currency have been economists with Canada's banks, most notably John McCallum when he was chief economist with the Royal Bank,[9] and economists with the (central) Bank of Canada, such as John Murray and Lawrence Schembri, all with strong academic credentials.[10] Successive Governors at the Bank of Canada, Gordon Theissen and David Dodge have also periodically entered the debate by affirming their belief that Canada's flexible exchange rate system has served the country well. Other opponents can be found on different ends of the policy spectrum. Among them one should mention Mario Seccareccia, an economist at the University of Ottawa, whose work was published by the left-leaning think tank, the Canadian Centre for Policy Alternatives, and David Laidler, an internationally-known monetary economist with the University of Western Ontario, and a Canadian Bankers Association Scholar and Fellow-in-Residence with the C.D. Howe Institute. The range of political opinion found among the opponents should not be surprising because, although Courchene, Grubel, Harris and Mundell are prominent academic economists, their proposals are not particularly in keeping with mainstream academic opinion, which leans strongly towards flexible exchange rates for all but the smallest of the high-income countries.[11]

## The Context

The Canadian currency debate of the late 1990s owed a good deal to the impending birth of the euro. The EU's decision to proceed with the launch of the euro focussed attention in many parts of the world on exchange rate and currency arrangements. Canada was no exception. The euro project has had a profound influence on the credibility of common currency arrangements and has acted as a catalyst for, and has provided credence to, proponents of common currency arrangements for North America. The advent of the euro led many to speculate that the world is inevitably moving towards the use of fewer currencies.[12] Even opponents of monetary integration, such as John McCallum, conceded that if the world moved towards the use of three key currencies, an independent Canadian dollar would not survive as a fourth. The EU example shaped the intellectual agenda and made common currency arrangements the intellectual fad of the late 1990s even though, as Pomfret (2002: 2) has pointed out, the collapse of the rouble zone meant that Europe as a whole "had more independent currencies in 2002 than it had in 1991." This, plus the Canadian origins of Nobel Laureate Robert Mundell, widely described as the intellectual father of the euro and regularly featured in the news because of his Nobel Prize award, served to raise the issue of monetary integration to a higher level of public debate than might otherwise have been expected. The "temporal spur" given by the euro to the Canadian debate was explicitly recognised by many of the participants in the debate. For example, Courchene (2001: 1) notes that "it was the advent of the Euro in January 1999 that unleashed a veritable flood of interest, papers and conferences on the evolution of Canada-US and North American currency arrangements." The birth of the euro was therefore important in focussing attention on monetary unions and provided a trigger for the Canadian currency debate but it was not the only factor. At least four other factors played a role in placing currency arrangements on the public agenda.

The first of these was that the debate took place in a political environment where the Canada-U.S. exchange rate had fallen sharply since 1991, which was often portrayed as being just before the Liberals took power at the federal level in 1993. Pro-business think tanks and political forces in Canada, including numerous business columnists, moreover, had repeatedly used depreciations in the Canadian dollar as an opportunity to criticize the status quo and argue for more business-friendly policies.[13] Before Finance Minister Paul Martin's February 1995 federal budget, the depreciation in the Canadian dollar was met with calls for social program spending cuts to eliminate the federal deficit, bring down federal government debt, and prevent Canada from supposedly hitting the "debt wall" and currency collapse.[14] Later in the decade, after substantial cuts to social program spending had been achieved, the focus shifted to using the depreciation in the Canadian dollar to call attention to the desirability of corporate and personal income tax cuts to make Canada more "competitive" with the U.S.[15] In this political environment proposals for a common currency with the U.S. were naturally given a high level of news media attention because they fit in with the long-standing news media theme of treating the depreciation of the Canadian dollar as a serious Canadian public policy problem.[16] The fallout from the Asian financial crisis, which saw the Canadian dollar hit an all-time low against the U.S. dollar in 1998 (although it fell to further lows in 2001 and 2002), added more grist to the mill.[17]

A second factor behind the Canadian currency debate was the emergence of the public perception in Canada that the U.S. was once again home to a highly dynamic economy. From the mid-1990s, when the Federal Reserve Board under Alan Greenspan decided to put to the test the hypothesis that the U.S. unemployment rate could not be allowed to fall below 6 percent or so without triggering a surge in the inflation rate, and until 2000, the U.S. enjoyed exceptionally rapid growth in employment, productivity, and output (Baker 2000). The economic dynamism that the U.S. exhibited in the late 1990s, and the way that rapid U.S. economic growth translated into rapid expansion of Canada's net exports to the U.S. during the same period, added appeal to claims that Canada should strive to be "competitive" with the U.S., and that the two countries should become more highly integrated. Towards the end of the 1990s greater integration with the U.S. sounded much more attractive to the Canadian public than it did as late as 1993 when the U.S. was seen as experiencing a "jobless recovery" and declining in economic power relative to Japan. At that time, many Canadians attributed Canada's economic ills to the Canada-U.S. Free Trade Agreement (FTA), and even the federal Liberals campaigned against the proposed North American Free Trade Agreement (NAFTA).

A third factor behind the Canadian currency debate was the perception that the Canadian economy had become partially dollarized, a perception which permitted some observers to argue that Canada might as well adopt a common currency with the U.S. because powerful market forces were driving Canada towards full dollarization anyhow. The perception depended on anecdotal evidence such as news stories about certain corporate CEOs as well as players for Canadian professional sports teams being paid in U.S. dollars. In the absence of solid statistical studies, however, it was plausible for observers to assume, for example, that the strong upward trend in Canada's trade with the U.S. since the signing of the Canada-U.S. Free Trade Agreement would have prompted Canada's firms to increase their trade-related U.S. dollar holdings. [18]

A fourth factor is that the Canadian debate over a common currency with the U.S. took place during a period in which the sovereignty movement in Quebec came to see greater Canadian economic integration with the U.S. as a means of easing the transition costs of a move to a separate (or at least decidedly more sovereign) Quebec (Parizeau 1999: 8). Proposals for Quebec sovereignty have always raised difficult issues of what currency would be used post-independence and how continued use of the Canadian dollar could be negotiated with the rest of Canada. With the adoption of a common North American currency, the proponents of sovereignty believed that this source of uncertainty would be removed, facilitating the re-drawing of political boundaries within a larger economic unit. The pro-sovereignty Bloc Québécois introduced a motion in the House of Commons to study a common currency for the Americas in March 1999, a motion which was defeated by 175 votes to 67 but, much to the chagrin of the Liberal government, the Banking Committee of the Senate did discuss the issue one week later.

The birth of the euro, therefore, although instrumental in promoting the Canadian currency debate was only one among many, perhaps equally important, factors. We now turn to the use of the euro in the substance of the debate.

*The Economic Arguments*

Despite the relatively small number of participants in the currency debate, as indicated in section III.i, summarising the debate is no easy task because of the range of arguments that have been used, especially by the proponents of a common currency who have on occasion adopted an "everything but the kitchen sink" approach. Here, we focus on what we take to be the substantive parts of the debate.

The economic arguments of the proponents of monetary union are largely the same as those that would be advanced in favour of a fixed exchange rate, a currency board, or dollarisation (i.e. the unilateral adoption of the US dollar by Canada). The proponents recognise this but argue that of these four options, the monetary union option is the most attractive. It is preferred economically to a fixed exchange rate since the increase in capital mobility over the past decade has made fixed exchange rate regimes more difficult to sustain, an argument which can also be extended to the case of currency boards, and only a monetary union or dollarisation offer economically sustainable hard currency fix. A monetary union is politically preferred to dollarisation because it offers the possibility of Canada retaining some voice in continental monetary policy making, an argument to which we return in section III.iv below.

There are four central economic arguments made by the proponents of monetary union.[19] The first is that the volatility of Canada-U.S. exchange rates has inhibited cross border investment and trade, and therefore reduced economic growth. Faced with exchange rate uncertainty, firms plan conservatively and therefore investment is lower than it would be in an environment of greater certainty. Thus, the argument runs that further integration requires a more stable currency regime (Courchene and Harris 1999).

The second main argument used by proponents of a common currency relates to the effects of the secular decline of the Canadian dollar against the U.S. dollar over the past 25 years or so.[20] Specifically, the argument is that the flexible exchange rate regime has served Canada badly, allowing its staple producers and manufacturers to seek solace in a depreciating exchange rate rather than in making the productivity-improving investments that Canada is deemed to need.[21] That is, a depreciating exchange rate is argued to have insulated Canada's manufacturing and resource sectors from competitive pressures enabling them to minimise productivity-enhancing investments and slowing down the structural transformation of the Canadian economy. In short, a depreciating dollar had cushioned "lazy manufacturers" in Canada.[22] This argument has some parallels – although Canadian proponents did not draw on them – to the reasons that led Giscard D'Estaing to launch the EMS proposal in 1978. Then it was argued that a fixed exchange rate system would force French industrialists to pay more attention to the curtailment of wage inflation. For Courchene and Harris, a fixed exchange rate system would force Canadian industrialists to pay more attention to productivity-enhancing investment.

The third argument was a more general version of the productivity argument and was based on the view that monetary union would not only change the investment behaviour of Canadian industry but would also have wider impacts on Canada's institutional structure making it more 'flexible' and 'efficient'. A common conservative critique of the Canadian institutional framework has been that, in comparison to the U.S., Canada is less flexible, less dynamic and relies more on a welfare state (both from a firm and worker perspective). Implicitly, the argument is that Canadian economic institutions and policy had 'failed' with the result that Canada had a persistently higher level of unemployment, and a lower productivity growth rate than the U.S. It is this more generalized failure that the proponents of a common currency have sought to address. If adjustments to differential economic performance by the U.S. and Canada could no longer be channelled through the exchange rate, then they would have to be addressed by greater flexibility in other markets such as the labour market. Tying in with the U.S. monetary order would therefore force Canadian institutions to adapt and to become more like those in the U.S.: labour markets would need to become more flexible (for some this implies a reduction in trade union power), firms would need to be more innovative, structural change would have to occur more quickly, and government would be generally less interventionist. It is for these reasons that the currency debate found a wider resonance in the conservative media, especially the *National Post*, which has been at the forefront of the arguments for pro-business policies over the past decade such as lower government spending and lower taxes.

The fourth economic argument was that patterns of resource endowment and industrial activities had already resulted in the emergence of significant cross-border regional economies. Thus, Courchene and Harris (1999: 16), for example, argued that the similarities of regional economies across the Canadian-U.S. border, rather than East-West economic similarities, indicated that Canadian regions had at least as much interest in a stable exchange rate with neighbouring U.S. regions as with other Canadian provinces.

The economic arguments presented by the proponents of monetary union therefore did not appeal to European experience, even where parallels were available. The focus was very much on a common currency as a way of addressing the perceived dynamism and superior performance of the U.S. economy relative to the Canadian economy; it was the Canada-U.S. comparison rather than any analysis of the European case, which drove the argument.

The opponents of monetary union were similarly focussed although they did make marginally more use of the European example in their arguments. Firstly, to counter the view that a flexible exchange rate had inhibited Canada-U.S. trade, opponents pointed out that there had in fact been a substantial increase in trade between Canada and the U.S. during the 1990s. In 1989, when the NAFTA was signed, Canadian exports to the U.S. totalled US$108 billion and accounted for 73.5 per cent of Canada's total exports. By 2000, however, exports to the U.S. had risen to $359 billion and accounted for 85 per cent of Canada's exports.[23] The fact that exports to the U.S. had surged under a flexible exchange rate regime was used by opponents to argue that common currencies were *not* required to spur trade integration.[24] That is, it was argued that the European model of monetary integration was not necessary to reap the benefits of increased trade and investment integration.

As for the "lazy manufacturers" hypothesis, this was rejected at both the theoretical and empirical levels. At the theoretical level, the hypothesis implied that Canadian firms were not profit maximisers, and therefore the hypothesis was inconsistent with one of the basic tenets of neoclassical economics. Empirically, it was argued that Canada's inferior productivity performance was due to performance in just two sectors of the economy and could not, therefore, be generalised to an argument about Canadian industry as a whole (McCallum, 2000: 7).[25] The argument of a wider institutional failure in Canada was countered by the argument that, whatever institutional failings there might be, they were not to be found in the monetary sphere. Canada had, as Laidler (1999) pointed out, a stable "monetary order" and had lower inflation rates than the U.S. for much of the past decade.[26] The monetary regime should therefore be left well alone.

The most prominent argument used by the opponents, however, was that it was Canada's position as a staple producer that justified the continued use of a national currency and a flexible exchange rate. It was argued that it is precisely because Canada relied relatively more heavily on commodity exports than most other industrialized countries that its currency depreciated in times of global economic slowdowns, as commodity prices weakened. The Bank of Canada, in its analysis, pointed out that it is this feature of the Canadian economy that distinguishes it from the U.S. economy and why a flexible exchange rate serves as a useful adjustment mechanism in the face of external shocks. (See Murray, Schembri and St.-Amant 2002). Furthermore, adopting a common currency would not remove the need for adjustments to be made; it would merely move them to areas other than the exchange rate, such as nominal wage flexibility or labour mobility, where there are likely to be, at least in the short run until labour is sufficiently weakened, more protracted struggles and higher output costs. The fact that the U.S. and Canada did not meet some of the central criteria for an optimal currency area added weight to the argument that independent national currencies and a flexible exchange rate were more appropriate.[27] These arguments concerning the asymmetries of external shocks, the asyncrhonicity of business cycles, and the degree to which labour markets adjust to shocks, can of course be found in the European debate on the effects of a common currency. This, however, represents the application of common methodologies and theories by economists on both sides of the Atlantic rather than any particular borrowing from, or influence of, the EMU common currency debate.

This review of the economic arguments has illustrated the limited role that the European experience has played in debating the need for a common currency in North America. The arguments of the proponents were not based on superior performance in Europe, a performance that might be partially attributable to its exchange rate regime. Rather, the argument in Canada was that Canada had performed poorly relative to the U.S.; it is here that the comparisons were made. The U.S. was seen as having a more dynamic economy, out-performing Canada in terms of job creation, productivity growth, and economic growth. However, while the economic case for the *need* to change the exchange rate regime was based on comparisons with U.S. economic performance rather than with Europe, the form that it should take, and its political governance structure, drew heavily on the European experience.

*The Governance Structure*

In advancing their arguments for a common currency, Courchene and Harris (1999) proposed a new common currency, the North American Monetary Unit (NAMU), while Grubel (1999) suggested the 'Amero'. In arguing for such a currency, they were clearly suggesting that Canada might be able to enter into a new currency regime with the U.S. on the basis of some presumed national equality and shared sovereignty. Courchene and Harris (1999: 22) drew explicit parallels with the European model and argued that "the easiest way to broach the notion of a NAMU is to view it as the North American equivalent of the European Monetary Union and, by extension, the euro. This would mean a supranational central bank with a board of directors drawn in part from the central banks of the participating nations." Grubel (1999: 5), in discussing the governance structure for the Amero, proposed that the three NAFTA signatories adopt a common currency with each member country appointing members to a North American central bank "governed by a constitution like that of the European Central Bank."

In making these proposals, the attempt was made to sell North America as if it was comparable to Europe and to suggest that joint sovereignty over monetary policy was possible in the same way that it was exercised through the European Central Bank. To suggest that the regional political superstructures for European monetary governance were capable of being applied to the North American case was, however, an inappropriate usage of the euro example, as opponents were quick to point out. For example, McCallum (2000: 2) argued that "the European Union model, in which independent states share decision-making and sovereignty, is alien to American thinking and American history" and he described the U.S. as being "light years" away from allowing any other country a formal role in formulating U.S. monetary policy.[28] The absence of any discussion in the U.S. about sharing a new common currency with Canada (or anyone else) is also telling.

**Conclusion**

The argument of this chapter has been that the euro was important in acting as a temporal spur for the Canadian debate on currency regimes. However, the European experience of exchange rate management under the ERM and the economic performance under fixed exchange rates played very little part in explaining why proponents of North American currency union viewed this is a desirable policy option. Rather it was the comparison of Canada with the U.S. which played the central role in the debate. If anything, it was opponents which used the European experience in a negative way by illustrating that the trade growth between Canada and the U.S. in the 1990s did not require a European style fixed exchange rate regime. Where the euro did play a prominent role in the Canadian debate was as a model for North America, although we have argued that this was an inappropriate usage of the euro example given the vastly different capacities and desires to construct regional political institutions in Europe and North America.

Our discussion has also highlighted the way in which the temporal spur given by the euro was important in the period 1999-2002. However, other important factors were also identified to explain the reasons for the timing of the debate. Two of these factors were the superior growth record of the U.S. economy during much of the 1990s and the depreciating Canadian dollar. The end of the 1990s boom in the U.S. and the rapid appreciation of the Canadian dollar in 2003 has led to a considerable dampening of the public debate in Canada over North American currency arrangements.

This should not, however, be interpreted to mean that the issue of North American currency union will remain off the table for an indefinite period. In the European case, we argued that the issue continued to resurface despite numerous interludes and setbacks caused by economic events. It kept resurfacing because it was driven essentially by political motives. For the same reason, the issue of a common currency in North America is quite capable of resurfacing at future points since it too is tied to a political agenda of achieving a more integrated continental economy and of promoting a convergence of Canadian economic institutions to those found in the U.S.

## Notes

1 Courchene and Harris are Past Presidents of the Canadian Economics Association. Mundell, the recipient of the Nobel Prize in Economics in 1999, resides in the United States but grew up in, and maintains ties with, Canada.
2 This section is an expanded revision of a section in Bowles, Croci, and MacLean (2003).
3 On these first two attempts at monetary integration in Europe, see Tsoukalis (1977), Kruse (1980), and Ludlow (1982).
4 Dyson and Featherstone (1999) provide the most thorough analysis of the origins and developments of EMU.
5 Although this contention is difficult to evaluate at this early stage, it is unlikely that the Euro will make a great contribution to the formation of a European-wide national identity. At best, having replaced national currencies, it will contribute marginally to the erosion of national identities. On the role of currencies in the promotion of national identities, see Helleiner (2001).
6 In Sweden EMU was rejected by Parliament, while Greece did not meet the convergence criteria for entry into the third stage.
7 The role of serendipity, as it were, is recognized by one of the participants in the process: "Even those of us who laboured to complement the single market with a monetary union and to embody such a transformation into a treaty held only that such a transformation was desirable and feasible, not that it was probable, or much less, inevitable. Thus we might speak of a benevolent historical conspiracy, but certainly not of inevitability" (Padoa-Schioppa 1994: 9).
8 Even Harris, the least conservative of the four, is sufficiently conservative to serve on the *Financial Post* board of economists.
9 John McCallum was a distinguished academic economist at McGill University before joining the Royal Bank, which he subsequently left to become a Liberal Cabinet Minister.
10 John Murray has held academic appointments at the University of British Columbia and Princeton University, while Lawrence Schembri was economics professor at Carleton University before being hired away by the Bank of Canada, and he maintains a connection with Carleton as an adjunct research professor.
11 See, for example, Frank, Bernanke, Osberg, Cross, and MacLean (2002: 494-495).
12 See Bowles, Croci and MacLean (2003) for more details and a critique of this hypothesis.

13 On an annual basis, the Canadian dollar fell from U.S.$0.87 in 1991 to U.S.$0.65 in 2001. The Canadian dollar was at a peak in 1991 associated with the unusually high interest rates the Bank of Canada had implemented to achieve its low inflation target, and 1991 therefore makes for a misleading starting date for calculations of the trends in Canada-U.S. dollar exchange rate (though not as misleading as using the highest daily rate from 1991). Over the period 1984-1987, for example, the Canadian dollar averaged about $U.S.0.74, which is not much different from the average value of the Canadian dollar ($U.S.0.73) over the 1994-1997 period.

14 For a critical analysis of the tactics employed in the campaign for social program cuts, see McQuaig (1995).

15 See MacLean (2000). The explanation for the decline in the Canadian dollar relative to the U.S. dollar since during the 1997-2002 period seems quite simple: the U.S. dollar had become overvalued relative to most other currencies, a fact that is widely recognized outside of Canada. For example, the 2002 edition of the "Big Mac Index" published by *The Economist* (27 April 2002), had the subtitle: "In the history of the Big Mac index, the [U.S.] dollar has never been more overvalued." To illustrate with a couple of specific examples, from January 1997 to April 2002 the Canadian dollar depreciated against the U.S. dollar by less than 14 percent, which is not much different from the 12 percent depreciation of the British pound over the same period, and is far less than the 31 percent depreciation of the Australian dollar. As 2002 unfolded, the U.S. dollar began to slide against a number of currencies, most notably the euro.

16 Both the tax cuts theme and common currency arguments received special prominence in the pages of the *National Post,* established in 1998 by newspaper baron Conrad Black.

17 For many Canadians, each new low for the Canadian dollar invited envious comparison with the strength of the U.S. dollar. They sensed that the depreciation of the Canadian dollar meant that their relative standard of living was in decline, and that it would be restored if Canadian dollar were to trade at par with the U.S. dollar.

18 More careful empirical analysis has since put a damper on this line of argument. In particular, Murray and Powell (2002: 1), in a paper which constitutes a major advance in the measurement of "dollarization" in Canada, argue that "existing data suggest that informal dollarization is proceeding at a very slow (to non-existent) pace. Indeed, by many measures, Canada is less dollarized now than it was twenty years ago, and bears little resemblance to those economies that are typically regarded as truly dollarized." See also Seccareccia (2002).

19 In our summary of the arguments for monetary union we rely mainly on the analyses presented in Courchene and Harris (1999) and Grubel (1999).

20 In recent academic analyses, it has been usual to take 1977 or so as the starting point for analysing the secular decline of the Canadian dollar on the grounds that during the six-year period of 1971-1976 the Canadian dollar had traded roughly at part with the U.S. dollar. This is certainly more sensible than taking the early 1990s as the starting point for analysis, as many media pundits have done. Canada had pegged to the U.S. dollar at U.S.$0.925 in the spring of 1962, however, and maintained the peg until mid-1970, when the Canadian dollar was allowed to appreciate. In looking at long-run trends in the Canada-U.S. dollar exchange rate, then, while a starting point of 1977 or so is customary, it is also inherently arbitrary. It establishes a period of unusually high commodity prices and hence a strong Canadian dollar as the norm against which subsequent exchange rate performance is judged.

21 See Harris (2001) for more details of this argument.

22  The argument is suspect from a standard, pro-market neoclassical perspective because by the same logic manufacturers should be spurred to increased productivity if unions impose strong wage increases upon them.
23  See Statistics Canada, "Imports and exports of goods on a balance-of-payments basis," <http://www.statcan.ca/english/Pgdb/gblec02a.htm>.
24  As Seccareccia (2002: 9) notes "already more integrated than most of the countries of the EMU, with almost 90 per cent of our trade being with the U.S., it would be difficult to envisage still further growth in what is a share that have practically reached its upper limit!".
25  The two sectors were "industrial machinery and equipment" and "electronic and other electronic equipment".
26  The issue of the performance of the Bank of Canada relative to the US Federal Reserve was debated, however, by Mundell and Friedman (2001) with the former particularly critical of the Bank's record particularly under the disastrous "zero inflation" policy implemented under former Governor John Crow.
27  See Murray, Schembri and St.-Amant (2002) for tests of the asymmetric responses by Canada, the US and Mexico to exogenous shocks. See also Crowley (2001) and Carr and Floyd (2001).
28  On the question of institutional structure, see also Buiter (1999) as well as Crowley and Rowley (2002).

## References

Baker, Dean (2000), "NAIRU: Dangerous Dogma at the Fed," *Financial Markets and Society*, Financial Markets Center (December): 1-16.
Bowles, Paul, Osvaldo Croci and Brian MacLean (2003), "Globalization and currency convergence: what do the regions tell us?" in James Busumtwi-Sam and Laurent Dobuzinskis (eds), *Turbulence and new directions in global political economy*, New York: Palgrave, pp. 169-185.
Buiter, Willem H. (1999) "The EMU and the NAMU: What is the Case for North American Monetary Union?" *Canadian Public Policy / Analyse de Politiques*, 25, 3 (September): 285-305.
Carr, Jack, and Floyd, John, (2001), "Real and Monetary Shocks to the Canadian Dollar: Do Canada and the U.S. Form an Optimal Currency Area?", Department of Economics, University of Toronto, Working Paper, UT-ECIPA-Floyd-01-02 at: <http://www.chass.utoronto.ca/ecipa/author-index.html#Carr_Jack_L_>.
Cecchini, Paolo (1988), *The European Challenge 1992: The Benefits of a Single Market*, Aldershot: Wildwood House.
Cohen, Benjamin (1993), "The Triad and the Unholy Trinity: Problems of International Monetary Cooperation", in R. Higgott, R. Leaver, J. Ravenhill (eds), *Pacific Economic Relations in the 1990s: Cooperation or Conflict?* London: Allen & Unwin, pp. 133-158.
Commission of the European Communities (1996), *First Report on the Consideration of Cultural Aspects in European Community Action*, Brussels: European Commission.
Commission of the European Communities (1992), *From the Single Market to European Union*, Luxembourg: Office for Official Publications of the European Communities
Courchene, Thomas, (2001), "A Canadian Perspective on North American Monetary Union", paper presented to NAEFA/ASSA session on "Currency Consolidation in the Western Hemisphere", New Orleans, January 5, 2001.

Courchene, Thomas, and Richard Harris (1999), "From Fixing to Monetary Union: Options for North American Currency Integration", *C.D. Howe Institute Commentary*, No. 127, Toronto, June.

Croci, Osvaldo and Lucio. Picci (2002), "European Monetary Integration and Integration Theory: Insights from the Italian Case", in A. Verdun (ed.), *The Euro: European Integration Theory and Economic and Monetary Union*, Lanham, MD: Rowman & Littlefield, pp. 215-240.

Crowley, Patrick M. (2001), "Is NAFTA an OCA?", Paper presented at the Western Economics Association meetings, Vancouver, British Columbia, Canada, July.

Crowley, Patrick M. and J. C. Robin Rowley (2002) "Exchange-rate arrangements for NAFTA: Should We Mimic the EU?" *The International Trade Journal* 16, 4 (November): 413-451.

Dyson, Kenneth and Kevin Featherstone (1999), *The Road to Maastricht: Negotiating Economic and Monetary Union in Europe*, Oxford: Oxford University Press.

Eichengreen, Barry (1997), *European Monetary Unification: Theory, Practice, and Analysis*, Cambridge, Mass.: The MIT Press.

Emerson Michael (1992), *One Market, One Money: an evaluation of the potential benefits and costs of forming an economic and monetary union*, Oxford: Oxford University Press.

Frank, Robert, Ben Bernanke, Lars Osberg, Melvin Cross, and Brian MacLean (2002), *Principles of Macroeconomics*, 1st Canadian edition, Toronto: McGraw-Hill Ryerson.

Giavazzi, Francesco and Alberto Giovannini (1989), *Limiting Exchange Rate Flexibility: The European Monetary System*, Cambridge, Mass.: MIT Press.

Grubel, Herbert (1999), "The Case for the Amero: The Economics and Politics of a North American Monetary Union," *Critical Issues Bulletin*, Vancouver: The Fraser Institute, September.

Harris, Richard (2001), "Is There a Case for Exchange-Rate-Induced Productivity Changes?" in *Revisiting the Case for Flexible Exchange Rates*, proceedings of a conference held at the Bank of Canada, November 2000, pp. 277-309.

Helleiner, Eric (2001), "One Money, One People? Political Identity and the Euro", TIPEC Working Paper 01/6, http://www.trentu.ca/tipec/helleiner6.pdf

Kruse, D. C. (1980), *Monetary Integration in Western Europe: EMU, EMS and Beyond*, London: Butterworth.

Laidler, David (1999), "What Do the Fixers Want to Fix? The Debate About Canada's Exchange Rate Regime", *C.D. Howe Institute Commentary*, 131 (December).

Ludlow, Peter (1982), *The Making of the European Monetary System: A Case Study of the Politics of the European Community*, London: Butterworth.

MacLean, Brian (2000), "A Sherry Cooper Budget," *Policy Options/Options Politiques*, (April): 21-24.

McCallum, John (2000), "Engaging the Debate: Costs and Benefits of a North American Common Currency", *Current Analysis*, Royal Bank of Canada (April).

McNamara, Kathleen (1998), *The Currency of Ideas: Monetary Politics in the European Union*, Ithaca: Cornell University Press.

McQuaig, Linda (1995), *Shooting the Hippo: Death by Deficit and Other Canadian Myths*, Toronto: Penguin.

Mundell, Robert, and Milton Friedman (2001), "One World, One Money? Symposium", *Policy Options/Options Politiques* (May): 10-30.

Murray, John, Larry Schembri and Pierre St-Amant, (2002), "Revisiting the Case for Flexible Exchange Rates in North America", paper presented at conference on Exchange Rates, Economic Integration and the International Economy, Ryerson University, Toronto, May 17-19.

Murray, John and James Powell (2002), "Dollarization in Canada (The Buck Stops There)," paper presented at conference on Exchange Rates, Economic Integration and the International Economy, Ryerson University, Toronto, May 17-19.

Oatley, Thomas H. (1997), *Monetary Politics: Exchange Rate Cooperation in the European Union*, Ann Arbor: University of Michigan Press.

Padoa-Schioppa, Tommaso (1994), *The Road to Monetary Union in Europe: The Emperor, the Kings, and the Genies*, Oxford: Clarendon Press.

Padoa-Schioppa, Tommaso, ed. (1987), *Efficiency, Stability, and Equity: A Strategy for the Evolution of the Economic System of the EC*, Oxford: Oxford University Press.

Parizeau, Jacques (1999), "Globalization and National Interests: The Adventure of Liberalization", in Brian MacLean (ed.), *Out of Control: Canada in an Unstable Financial World*, Toronto: James Lorimer and CCPA, pp. 3-15.

Pomfret, Richard (2002), "Monetary Integration in East Asia: Lessons from Europe", paper presented at the 8th Convention of the East Asian Economic association, Kuala Lumpur, 4-5 November, 2002.

Seccareccia, Mario (2002), "North American Monetary Integration: Should Canada Join the Dollarization Bandwagon?" University of Ottawa (February).

Shore, Chris (2000), *Building Europe: The Cultural Politics of European Integration*, London: Routledge.

Temperton, Paul, ed. (1998), *The Euro*, Chichester: J. Wiley.

Tsoukalis, Loukas (1977), *The Politics and Economics of European Monetary Integration*, London: George Allen and Unwin.

Verdun, Amy (1999), "The role of the Delors Committee in the creation of EMU: an epistemic community?" *Journal of European Public Policy*, 6, 2: 308-328.

Chapter 8

# Possible Arrangements for Exchange Rates in a Modified, Extended or Replaced NAFTA

Patrick M. Crowley and J. C. Robin Rowley

## Introduction

The acceptance of a single currency for many European countries is a momentous development. The slow process from which this single currency emerged had extended over a considerable period of time and it was often characterized by forceful political infighting, a pronounced degree of external derision, and the adversarial strains imposed by extended negotiations before awkward compromises made agreement over relevant commitments possible. The effort was often challenged by hostile attempts to derail the ongoing process by opponents active within and outside the currency bloc. In the present European environment, the issues as to whether and where further momentum for a continuation of the integration process might occur seem to have been clearly resolved – an earlier comment on those particular issues is provided by Crowley (2001). Now in a wider context, the experience of the European Monetary Union (EMU) has begun to stimulate interest in the feasibility of extending prospects for economic and political integration in North America and elsewhere, and also in the principal considerations – economic, political, legal and administrative – that might significantly affect the character of any process of integration over the other geographical locations.

In North America, some influential observers have indicated that the North American Free Trade Agreement (NAFTA) substantially increased trade among the three signature parties. Helliwell *et al.* (1999), for example, offer a positive assessment of subsequent growth in this cross-border trade. NAFTA arrangements seem also to have given strong encouragement over the last decade to additional labour mobility (usually movement to the US from its two partners, especially with professionals shifting from Canada and unskilled labour migration leaving Mexico), to foreign direct investment (FDI), and to other capital flows. The initial agreement between Canada and the US in 1989 was facilitated by the shared experiences under the Canada-US auto pact of 1967. After the later extension to

Mexico (and perhaps further encouraged by the changes in presidential politics in the US, at least for some period before the re-emergence of stronger protectionist elements during the most recent Bush era), the magnitudes of trade flows into the US from both of its partners have been compatible with earlier anticipations of growth at rapid rates – though such rates of growth were obviously driven too by other visible developments, while the adverse responses for some particular industries, occupations and geographical regions demonstrate those severe transitional difficulties and perceived inequities that can foster political interventions and frustrating obstacles to harmonious international relations.

Past theoretical discussion has identified a 'classic' sequence for structural adjustments here. This sequence has often been attributed to historical processes for international agreements on integration. It involves a simple 'domino' imperative, whereby the initial agreements to integrate trade are presumed to gradually give way with the emergence of large 'common markets' and then perhaps subsequently to a more comprehensive economic union and to common currencies for the constituent countries. There is no inevitability that this sequence be followed. Indeed the provisional focus of recent US administrations appears to be a tentative search for a substantial 'broadening' of national participation through another agreement with other American countries. This broadening could take the form of a so-called 'Free Trade Agreement of the Americas' (FTAA).

The early years of the Bush administration in the US have offered mixed signals so it is difficult to be confident in predicting the directions that might be taken to install future institutional arrangements. Initially, however, it seemed that the new, somewhat modest, search for some broader bases of national participation ('very' modest after the 'war on terrorism' was declared) was granted precedence over an alternative desire for a 'deepening' of the existing NAFTA arrangements. Irrespective of this choice of focus, it could be inevitable – if only because of geographical proximity – that both broadening and deepening of the existing regional agreement on integrated trade will occur in the foreseeable future. Present attention might therefore be fruitfully directed towards a consideration of how, and in what particular circumstances, an enlargement or enhancement of past arrangements can occur.

As illustrated throughout the process of integration in Europe, major political elements play a crucial role in determining the pace, sequencing and specific outcomes of this development – a role that many economists, because of the way in which the abstractions of their discipline have evolved in the last few decades, find difficult to reconcile with the conventional features in their theoretical analyses of the future development of NAFTA. The relative primacies of alternative political elements markedly differ over time and across geographic boundaries, and they are generally affected by dynamic path-dependence and simple inertial influences driven by the idiosyncratic political environments faced by participants. Initially, the US administration appeared to have an ambiguous (but highly visible) pursuit of *ad hoc* measures to 'normalize' the presence of illegal Mexican workers in the US, at least to some degree, instead of pressing on with any firmer attempts to establish a clear programme for further integration. Substantial doubts in regard to the seriousness of the administration's interest in trade negotiations have been encouraged by careless presidential comments such as his assertion that "border relations between Canada and Mexico have never been better" (Joint Press Conference with Canadian Prime Minister, September 2001) and by his dismissive reluctance to visit Canada, the largest trading partner of the US.

On the other hand, the interested parties in Canada have promoted a vigorous debate (still largely ignored in the US) concerning the feasibility and desirability of a 'North American Monetary Union' (NAMU) being pursued with greater enthusiasm. The Canadian debate has been energized by three events: (a) the inception of the euro and its immediate consequences, (b) an unprecedented, unsustainable decline in the relative value of the Canadian dollar, which occurred despite persistence of large surpluses (somewhat energy-driven) in its trade with the US – a decline later partially reversed when very large government deficits re-emerged in the US during the war on terrorism, seemingly without any effective opposition to huge levels of supplementary spending by the federal government – and (c) the dependence associated with a further growth in the relative proportion of the US component in Canadian trade, beyond even the high historical levels.

Mexican leaders too seem intent on fundamental change, and their commitment to change has prompted suggestions for movement towards freer labour mobility and for active consideration of the creation of a NAMU. Many of the principal activists in Canada and Mexico are much more interested in deepening the NAFTA agreement than their counterparts in the US but, given the obvious imbalance of power involved here, the pace and direction of any further efforts toward a greater degree of integration must inevitably be dominated by the ambiguous agenda now found within the US Congress and the Bush administration in Washington and in those geographical areas (such as the 'rush belt') perceived by their political representatives to have been adversely affected by the earlier efforts at integration. Clearly too, in any direct comparison with historical experiences of the EU, the weak institutions and modest power structures of bureaucracies established for the NAFTA markedly reduce the potential for generating an 'internal dynamic' for change similar to that which had fostered integration during the Delors presidency of the European Commission in the 1980s.

The European template for integration involves a variation on the potential stages of integration identified by Balassa (1961). After introducing the Single Market Act in 1986 (with its provisions mostly acted on six years later), the EU used the existing exchange-rate mechanism (ERM) of the European Monetary System (EMS) as a basic part of the Maastricht Treaty to stimulate the new path toward more economic convergence. An extensive justification for a single currency was documented in association with the slogan of 'one market, one money' by the European Commission. Thus the primary basis for supporting monetary integration was contained in a series of forceful claims that such integration would permit a fuller realization of the benefits of a single market. Once a widespread commitment to economic convergence was viewed as largely achieved (the end of the 1980s), the time for entrenchment with some appropriate measures in the Maastricht Treaty had come. These special measures legally clarified major features of the transitional process and set definite conditions for the EMU. In this treaty, the ERM of the EMS was explicitly identified as one of five economic criteria that might lead national members of the EU towards an effective single currency. The ERM remains a criterion for membership of EMU, and the official spokesmen for several member states (notably the Netherlands, Belgium and Austria) maintained that membership of the ERM fostered the convergence of their economies with that of Germany, and it had led them to a much easier transition to the EMU than was experienced by other member states such as Italy and France. A second mechanism (centred around the *euro* rather than the *ecu*) is already available as a contingent device for potential use in determining possible convergence by new candidates among Eastern European countries.

In terms of further integration within NAFTA, the Canada-US relationship is more likely to be an initial point of departure rather than the relationship between Mexico and the US because of the relative longevity of existing agreements, the closer match for states of economic development, and the inevitable severity of concerns over structural adjustment and political stability in Mexico (Clarkson, 2000). This situation may justify our preference for first dealing with the Canada-US relationship before seeking an extended perspective. The following discussion re-addresses the feasible options for new exchange-rate arrangements within NAFTA. As far as we can determine from existing literature – apart from a few observations by Courchene and Harris (1999) and Grubel (1999), which are rare exceptions – these feasible arrangements have not received much attention from economists in frameworks that acknowledge the need for a comprehensive political-economy screen.

The discussion also deals with the possible dynamic for integration processes that follows from the adoption of special exchange-rate arrangements. Three distinct sections follow below. As charted and assessed by Little (2000), Frankel (1999) and Fischer (2001), there is considerable scope for different choices in regard to rival exchange-rate schemes, irrespective of whether they occur as part of a regional trading bloc or not. In one section, some arguments for moving away from the current status quo in the narrow Canada-US context are reviewed. Then, in the next section, the possible choices among rival configurations for a future exchange-rate regime linking the two countries are considered, and also some of their obvious implications from a simple political-economy perspective are incorporated. The subsequent section extends the comments beyond those arrangements limited to Canada and the US to include Mexico and the rest of the Americas.

*Do Particular Arrangements for Exchange Rates Really Matter?*

The conventional bipolar debate over the relative advantages and disadvantages of any fixed or flexible exchange rates is well established and its use continues unabated in much theoretical debate – although it can now be sensibly expanded to include a host of so-called 'intermediate' choices. The principal findings of the extensive research during the last half century or so are three-fold: (a) the choice of an exchange-rate regime does matter, (b) there is no 'right' or optimal choice when considering the two poles of fixed or flexible exchange rates, (c) the 'better' choices can depend on idiosyncratic economic circumstances, the historical conditioning of inherent relationships, and institutional credibility as well as other factors that are far from consistent across national situations and perhaps not invariant over time. Frankel (1999) inferred from an analysis of 'recent' trends in exchange-rate regimes that there appears (at least to him) to be a partial movement towards the 'periphery' – that is, both fully fixed and fully flexible exchange-rate regimes have been gaining in popularity during recent decades, while the intermediate regimes with some degree of both fixity and flexibility have become less popular than they were in the past.

Although fixed exchange rates find little support among many North American economists and political representatives, such rates with limited variability (or 'credibly fixed' rates) continue to find ample support among their counterparts in both developing countries and European circles. If there were a compelling case for either polar view of fixed or free exchange rates – a sensitive case that recognizes the real complexities for discretionary governance of monetary policies, and that also acknowledges the various forms of structural interdependencies across boundaries, radical new concerns about the current significance, magnitude and fluidity of international capital flows, and other related matters from an adequate political-economy perspective – surely a consensus would have emerged during the interval that has elapsed since the Bretton-Woods system was introduced immediately after World War II. However, achievement of some consensus here is severely handicapped by the deep fractures generated by partisan advocacy and perhaps too by an undue reliance on excessively restrained trade models, which omit too many of the features that are significant to political interests.

**Benefits and Costs of Fixing the Exchange Rate**

Several important economic consequences of credibly fixed exchange rates have been clearly identified. The apparent benefits to individuals from adopting fixed exchange rates include (a) a potential reduction of foreign-exchange risk on temporal contracts, with lower uncertainty and a reduced need for exchange-rate hedges, (b) increased trade, which Rose (1999) found to be quite significant, and (c) facilitation of foreign direct investment. In addition, but with a somewhat lower degree of confidence, we can suggest that (d) Canadian capital markets might further benefit from a fixed exchange rate when more 'certainty' is perhaps assured for asset values, and (e) the relative attractiveness of Canadian equities in the US may be enhanced, as also might the attractiveness of domestic Canadian assets to those Canadians who have (collectively) been acquiring US assets in order to resist profit depredations associated with a persistent depreciation of the Canadian dollar over some recent years.

Macroeconomic benefits, due to the elimination of exchange-rate shocks, can be substantial when earlier volatility of rates has been high. These shocks can induce corresponding shocks to both productive activity and employment, and thereby can inhibit economic growth, create adverse business conditions, and foster a climate of political discontent or *ennui*. Many of the perceived macroeconomic costs of exchange-rate fixity are attached to strong concerns that stress an expected loss of monetary sovereignty that is usually attributed to a potential emergence of concomitant obstacles to weaken monetary policy – obstacles which are presumed to curtail the effectiveness and responsiveness of the banking authorities to deal with financial dislocations, to make credit shortages more likely to occur, and to strengthen other adversities covered by the primary mandates of many central banks. If 'asymmetric' shocks afflict a country, changes in an exchange rate might conceivably provide a resistant 'buffer' to those shocks so that some timely changes in the exchange rate could potentially reduce the economic impacts of adverse developments.

From a domestic perspective, when fixed exchange rates are maintained and options for monetary policy are narrowly defined, it is often accepted as an article of faith that monetary policy is directly tied through the exchange rate, as represented in the theoretical perspective of Giavazzi and Pagano (1988). Further consideration suggests that the occurrence (and severity) of good or bad effects depends on a host of determinate factors: (a) the incidence and magnitude of asymmetric shocks, (b) general synchronicity of cyclical fluctuations across major trading partners, c) perceived credibility of all monetary authorities in question, (d) the range of alternative measures that are readily available to these banking authorities, (e) the interaction or relative independence of trade and capital flows, and (f) many other relevant elements that impinge on economic performance – such as product diversion due to trade activity, including the spatial relocation of economic activities and corresponding modifications to previous supply chains, as well as that diversion reflected in the quantities of different outputs – and on institutional effectiveness.

## Benefits and Costs of Adopting a Single Currency

Accepting an explicit and firm commitment to a persistent system of 'irrevocably-fixed' exchange rates (that is, a commitment to reliance on a single currency) leads to a different group of benefits and costs for countries that are involved. Among major considerations here are (a) the elimination of some foreign-exchange costs, (b) the associated costs in real resources of converting currencies, (c) the one-time expenses of switching to the new currency, (d) those administrative costs produced by the need to convert provisions in previous contracts that were denominated in old currencies, and (e) some miscellaneous costs linked to 'vending' operations.

The elimination of foreign-exchange costs could, at least in theory, be easily estimated by the bid-ask spreads in the foreign-exchange market – this spread is often held to represent competitive 'rentals' of the physical and human resources now employed in the exchange of those currencies which will become redundant once a monetary union is fully implemented. But since the character of any existing foreign-exchange market is very difficult to reconcile with the idealized form of a perfectly competitive market, actual spreads may inadequately represent the social opportunity costs of exchanging currencies. There may indeed be some 'excess profits' (relative to the competitive image) made by participants in foreign-exchange markets. Of course, most companies tie up human and physical resources in the exchange of currencies so associated costs in real resources of converting currencies incurred by those companies that trade might exceed a contemporary bid-ask spread in a foreign-exchange market. Authors of a document prepared at the European Commission (1990) sought to estimate such costs in real resources within the EU context, but there is little doubt their numerical estimates were probably inadequate.

Immediate costs from the adoption of a single currency are reviewed by Dowd and Greenaway (1993). Their constituent elements include (a) in-house costs of creating parallel accounting systems for dealing with the new international currency, (b) the 'menu costs' of converting current price lists into the new currency, (c) the legal costs of converting provisions of existing contracts into that currency, (d) the 'learning costs' (as expressed in the time spent in assimilation, training and administration) introduced when dealing with a new currency, and (e) miscellaneous costs associated with the one-time conversion, apparently mundane costs that fall outside convenient categories, such as practical costs of adjustments to vending machines. Benefits expected to occur in capital markets are probably similar to those cited above for fixed exchange rates.

Once a common currency has been firmly chosen by a bloc of countries, there are further costs – those associated with revisions to fiscal arrangements and employment provisions, and revenues from *seigniorage*, for example – that might be incurred by business corporations and governments at various levels. One cost stems from the reconciliation of variations in different regimes for sales taxes. Canadian and US taxes are collected within different frameworks, with the former relying on a value-added tax system and the latter using a simple sales-tax format. These systems also exhibit markedly different bases for coverage between the countries and they reflect pronounced internal disparities across provinces and states, the normal collection agencies. There may have been trade 'distortions' between the two countries since the costs of paying extra taxes were offset by a 'weak' exchange rate between them. In the context of NAFTA, the presence of higher levels of indirect taxes in Canada (which seem likely to persist in the absence of some major transformations of federal-provincial fiscal relations and provincial priorities and even constitutional revision) might encourage the 'creative' shipment of goods to the US as a potential means of avoiding due tax payments when the costs associated with currency exchange are eliminated.

Another potential cost arise from the need to re-deploy those human resources that were formerly involved in the foreign-exchange market, both in terms of redundancy claims from former employees to the affected companies and in terms of greater levels of unemployment benefits and retraining costs for government departments as well as in skill losses and other wastage of human capital. For governments themselves, *siegniorage* revenues are likely to be foregone. If the single currency to be adopted were the US dollar, which seems inevitable, there is scope for a modest variety of sharing arrangements for the revenue from *seigniorage* with eventual choice among them essentially determined by political pressures rather than economic ones. Many researchers assume that similar agreements to those already reached by American authorities with Argentina and Ecuador could be replicated in the Canadian context.

If a single North American central bank were established (with many of the remaining functions of the Bank of Canada and the Canadian financial regulators somehow absorbed within an enlarged Federal Reserve System, a hypothetical development that is seriously bedevilled by complex obstacles), it is possible that *seigniorage* revenue might be divided on a similar basis to that adopted for participating countries in the EMU. However it is impossible to justify any firm impressions of what could emerge from a real political settlement that might be reached among the federal governments, their lower-level counterparts, their primary institutions and other interested parties. Economists have little to contribute here. They have been markedly weak in dealing with the evolution and structural design of institutions, with the emergent properties of interactive processes in general, and with the profound impact of social and political factors in particular. Their conventional 'black box' models lack relevant features, as already noted, and the narrow definition of 'rational conduct' found in most of these models seemingly dismisses as irrational many of the concerns that will ultimately be reflected in the details of any political settlement. Perhaps, before offering their myopic advice on potential impact of structural transformations, economists should be required to read the account by Macmillan (2001) of political deliberations prior to (and following) the Versailles Treaty or the recent commentaries of their experiences in international organizations by some prominent US economists. Strong parochial interests in the US Congress and the disturbing influence of pressure groups under US trade law have already affected, perhaps weakened, the functioning of both the NAFTA and the WTO. Recent comments in Congress and elsewhere indicate no apparent willingness to share *seigniorage* revenue with Canada (or any other country) were the process of further integration to advance.

In terms of evident benefits, there are clear advantages relating to a lower level of exchange-rate volatility between the Canadian and US currencies. Reduction of uncertainty and lower costs in purchase of exchange-rate hedges for trading currencies must be recognized – although the costs of most forward contract costs are small, usually amounting to a few basis points. On a national level, proponents of more integration suggest a number of microeconomic benefits are likely to occur. These benefits seemingly stem from what is perceived to be the inevitable encouragement of a more stable monetary environment for business planning purposes, as pursued too by advocates of inflation targets to guide the priorities of banking authorities. These benefits are believed to find expression in easier union-employer negotiations, formulation of pricing policies, and other areas of economic interaction. There is an obvious danger in focusing attention solely on the transitional period for monetary integration. The overall net welfare effects of adopting a single currency must depend not only on the immediate non-repetitive costs of change but also on the net gains or losses that will arise from operating with a single currency over the indefinite future. In the European context, the Commission has claimed that these net welfare effects will be positive, but this claim could reflect mere wishful thinking since there is little *a priori* evidence to validate the claim or provide a quantitative framework for its appraisal (Buiter, 1995).

## NAFTA and the EU Context

In reviewing possibilities that the Canadian exchange rate can be fixed or a single currency adopted for Canada and the US (essentially 'dollarization'), significant differences between the EU context and that faced by NAFTA should be noted:

- While all member states of the EU have intense trade connections with each other, Canada and the US have a more asymmetric relationship — Canada has a high dependence on the US as an external market (and the US depends on considerable energy imports from Canada) but the US exports to Canada are far less important. A similar disparity applies to their capital markets.
- Europe adopted a *new* single currency whereas North American integration would probably require adoption of an existing one. In Europe, it might have been advantageous to adopt that currency (the German mark) with the highest usage but this choice was unacceptable on political grounds to most member states. For an extended NAFTA, the retention of the US dollar would reflect the facts that Canada can only offer a weak counterbalance to the political and economic power of the US, the unique international hegemon, and that the US populace would not accept a replacement for its currency. The US authorities will only consider

arrangements by which other countries subordinate any contrary domestic preferences in order to adopt the US dollar.

- In considering precedents, it is difficult to imagine Canadian negotiating authorities could obtain a 'significantly better' deal than their predecessors.

- Cultural and linguistic diversity in the EU moderates the role of labour mobility as a 'valve' for offsetting the impacts of asymmetric shocks or asynchronous business cycles. However, apart from broad controversies affecting Hispanics in the US, the principal cultural disparity between Canada and US is the maintenance of the French language use in the labour market (supported by federal politicians, and even more forcefully by the Quebec provincial government), a visible barrier to labour mobility but a relatively small barrier overall.

*Alternative Arrangements*

Despite the substantial reservations expressed above, it seems worthwhile to speculate on the possible options for exchange rate arrangements in the NAFTA bloc, however remote they are from current implementation. Three broad strategies can be separated: a deliberate commitment in the form of dollarization with a new currency introduced or with exchange-rate fixity; use of deliberate constraints involving the explicit establishment of exchange-rate rules, and perhaps the creation of an autonomous institution with sufficient power and independence to oversee the implementation of such constraints; and a reliance on flexible exchange-rate options that are bound up with implicit (unannounced) 'shadow' target zones. Each of these strategic options is considered in turn.

*Deliberate Commitment*

Under this strategic category, several alternative configurations in the North American context can be clearly identified:

- Dollarization of the Canadian economy, a *de facto* recognition that the US dollar is to the sole active currency for NAFTA.
- Negotiated adoption of a new NAFTA currency, say the *amero*.
- Symmetric binding of the partners to an agreed fixed exchange rate between them, perhaps with a distinct institution to oversee intervention, devaluation/revaluation, and other matters.
- Asymmetric binding to a chosen fixed exchange rate − for example, the Bank of Canada is required to consistently choose the relative level for the Canadian dollar and to defend that value for the currency whenever necessary. Alternatively, a currency board can be established.

All of these configurations need to be evaluated, their difficulties should be identified, and significant concerns arising from their implementation duly recognized.

As noted by Courchene and Harris (1999), *de facto* dollarization is already expanding within the Canadian economy as many firms adopt US dollar accounts to conduct business when the bulk of their dealings are with their US counterparts. A more stringent *de jure* form requires granting the status of legal tender to the US dollar in Canada. Achievement of this form would be difficult even after lengthy negotiations of Canadian authorities with their opposite numbers in the US government and the Board of Governors of the Federal Reserve. Although the jurisdictional situation within Canada remains unclear, it is certain that the federal authorities would be compelled to seek explicit, transparent, comprehensive and unprecedented provincial support from other levels of government before entering any substantive negotiations – much more support than was thought necessary when the earlier trade agreement was announced, and affected by concomitant searches for compromises in regard to other contentious issues that presently endanger many contacts among the central government and the provincial governments.

At the international level, a series of agreements or a treaty would require: (a) an adequate expansion in the supply of the US currency so that the existing Canadian dollars can be retired from circulation, (b) agreement on an Canadian entitlement to a share of *seigniorage* revenue, (c) a transparent agenda and explicit timetable for reconciling current differences in the regulatory functions, activities and mandates of the two central banks, (d) some clarification of how payments due on federal and provincial government bonds would be denominated and how confidence in such bonds would be secured, and (e) an explicit programme that indicates how Canadian interests will be safeguarded, perhaps by the creation of another Federal Reserve Bank based in a Canadian city, by some other explicit representation within the governance of the Federal Reserve itself, or a formal consultation process. The agreements would have to be accompanied by a multitude of documents indicating relevant changes in other operational practices, the *minutiae* of central banking. Although current agreements with South American countries have not granted special status to foreign supplicants, it seems non-viable for any Canadian government to yield on the major issue of obtaining a significant 'voice' in the ultimate banking authority that may emerge after integration. Undoubtedly any profound change in the status of the Bank of Canada would attract acrimonious and persistent political debate, some nationalistic in tone and some opportunistic.   The general impression is that this particular configuration is unlikely to occur, given the strong perception evident within the Canadian populace that its sovereignty is already much challenged in many areas of economic, social and political endeavour and given the reluctance to simply become yet another small voice in an American empire.

The second configuration, championed by Grubel (1999), seeks the adoption of a new North American currency and perhaps the establishment of a new central bank. If the authorities in Canada and the US want to adopt of a new common currency, a series of formal agreements or a treaty would again be necessary. This option is influenced by both the structure of the EMU and the drastic revisions in banking governance that followed the establishment of the ECB, including the reassessment of roles to be set for individual national central banks. The new North American counterpart of the ECB, it has been suggested, would have control of monetary policy and exchange-rate policy. Some claim that it would require designated independence in significant respects from intervention by the Canadian Department of Finance and the US Treasury Department. The Federal Reserve Board of Governors and senior officials from the Bank of Canada would have due representation on the board of the new bank according to some pre-determined (negotiated) formula or agreement. Presumably too, given historical practices in Canada and the US, some lines of formal and informal communication with political authorities would have to be established – perhaps including testimony before Congressional committees, *ex officio* representation for fiscal officials, and other indirect means of reconciliation with the responsibilities of other players.

Although quite attractive to a few Canadian observers, there are substantial problems with this strategic option within the NAFTA context:

- NAFTA has no culture or historical experience of institutional construction, and the sovereignty of the national state is one of the tenets held dear by the US populace and authorities, at least in regard to US sovereignty. No equivalents exist in North America for the European Council, ECOFIN, European Commission, or European Parliament to fulfill their roles in determination and implementation of fiscal policy, coordination, or democratic oversight and accountability within an expanded NAFTA context, as noted by Buiter (1999).
- The US dollar remains the predominant or hegemonic currency. Many US citizens seemingly associate the 'strength' of the US dollar with sovereignty and national identity, and they are essentially inward looking so they tend to primarily stress the significance of their internal or partisan issues. It is therefore unlikely that they would give up a familiar national symbol, the dollar, for something less identifiable with US hegemonic leadership and national myths.
- The EMU took a long time to acquire its present shape. The ERM and the single market were important stepping-stones that underpinned the dynamic process that produced the current EMU. The NAFTA, although largely an area of freer trading, still has tariff schedules for various goods and services, and many industries have been protected from competition by perceived pressures of national interests (banking and defence industries, for example). Clearly NAFTA remains far from being a single market in practice.

The functioning of the ERM induced European governments to develop a sustainable culture of dialogue and compromise – an interactive environment of cooperative endeavours – on many important operational issues. Both the single market and the ERM prompted a greater degree of economic, political and monetary convergence, and they strengthened the resolve of the EU governments to establish some practical mechanisms with which to coordinate activities, to permit cooperation, and to provide effective communication for the day-to-day performance of the single market and the ERM. These governments also sponsored facilities by which unanticipated events could effectively be dealt with. Apart from conventional consultations among diplomats, the trilateral NAFTA dispute-settlement panels, and basic contacts among some modest environmental or technically-focused agencies (for example, between the two national statistical agencies), no extensive record of cooperation and coordination on the European scale is identifiable for North American governments and bureaucracies despite the history of lesser forms of cooperation in many forums set up for bi-national dialogue and complaint resolution.

Symmetric binding to an agreed fixed value for the exchange rate (our third configuration) would require a written agreement with the US in which various contingencies are clearly specified, penalties for persistent non-compliance are determined, and the scope for short-term mismatching severely curtailed. Within Canada, the interested parties for the agreement would clearly be the Bank of Canada, the Department of Finance, and representatives from other departments with direct responsibilities over international trade and financial flows – all mediating the wishes of the federal Cabinet. The situation must be somewhat more complicated for the US, where the main interested parties would include the Federal Reserve and the Department of the Treasury but where any proceedings might also be subject to influential congressional oversight and committee hearings. Complications abound in the hostile climate that supported withdrawal of 'fast track' commitments and the imposition of supplemental obligations on the trade commissioner and other official agencies. The agreement would not need to take that form of a formal treaty. Its contingencies would have to specify fundamental detail – those governing operational mechanisms for changing the bilateral peg, the level of commitment that would be required for defence of a chosen peg, and any subordinate mechanisms for borrowing funds that would be available to provide support for such defence, for example. Clearly whenever the US authority acknowledges that it has a strong interest in maintaining a particular peg, then a joint intervention would have a greater chance of success in maintenance than if any monetary authority acts in isolation.

Political awareness has, not surprisingly, encouraged the belief among some Canadian observers that no US agency would declare an interest in tying US hands with a commitment to intervene merely in order to defend the value of the currency of another currency. This belief undeniably carries a lot of weight although it is not difficult to find illustrations of US interest groups achieving the fulfilment of remarkable goals through such means as implicit logrolling. It is therefore not inconceivable (though perhaps unlikely) that, given the large volume of exports to Canada, a group representing an export lobby could manage to affect the crafting of an agreement and, hence or otherwise, affect the passage of some enabling legislation through the Congress. Even when a symmetric agreement has emerged, there is of course no guarantee of permanence or of adequate resilience in face of a sustained pattern of adverse economic developments.

The fourth configuration for deliberate commitment is an asymmetric binding of the exchange rate. Canadian authorities must commit themselves, to the extent they are able, to a policy of persistent defence for the value of the Canadian dollar against the US dollar at a pre-announced level, without any concomitant requirement for the US authorities to directly support their efforts. The implementation of this strategic option may only require a joint announcement by the Bank of Canada and the Department of Finance (similar to the publicity of that launched the radical shift to an inflation target process a decade ago). One perceived advantage for some Canadian producers here is that Canadian authorities might be persuaded to choose an undervalued exchange rate that could allow the exporters to retain a competitive advantage, at the cost of inflating the prices of imported goods. Two major disadvantages arise from the potential drain of reserves that may occur during any stubborn defence of a given exchange rate – the possibility of a drain that could exhaust (perhaps even exceed) the exchange resources that any central bank is prepared to muster (or capable of mustering with temporary assistance for third-party central banks, for example) – and from the stimulus given to substantial speculative activity when support for a given peg loses its credibility and the corresponding opportunities are searched for speculative gains.

*Deliberate Constraint*

Under this option, two possibilities are worth considering, each reflecting the European template for exchange-rate management:

- A bilateral NAERM, a negotiated North American mechanism for exchange rates.
- A unilateral ERM.

In the case of a bilateral negotiated NAERM, where the arrangement is modelled on the ERM, the items to be negotiated by the two partners would include: (a) the central parity to be used, (b) the margins of fluctuation around this central parity that are allowed, (c) the level of divergence from parity after which intervention becomes obligatory, (d) the onus for intervention, (e) the process for seeking a change in the central parity, and (f) the institutional arrangements and general means for producing sufficient amounts of dedicated borrowing in order to support intervention. The central parity to be used would obviously be jointly determined and the relevant considerations already cited would again come to bear. Margins of allowable fluctuation are very important in determining the degree of latitude and autonomy for monetary policy that is permitted under the arrangement, as indicated by Svensson (1994).

Historically, the EU has set four different margins of fluctuations in the ERM; namely, +/- 1% (for the Dutch guilder), +/- 2.25% (the norm used during the period 1979-1993), +/- 6% (the margin assigned to the Italian lira and Spanish peseta), and +/- 15% (the range used for all participants after 1993 to 1999, and the current margin for use in the ERM2). The very narrow band of +/- 1% would probably be excessively tight for a NAERM, and that of the +/- 15% band too loose, so perhaps an intermediate range would be considered more appropriate for the North American economies. The permissible level of any divergence, beyond which active intervention was deemed necessary in the European context, was initially established by a specific indicator, but this technical device was soon judged to be technically flawed. Subsequently an intervention in the EU was stimulated when an exchange rate approached the edge of its margin for fluctuation. Perhaps in the less complex environment of a bilateral NAERM, the divergence indicator could be set quantitatively, at +/- 9% say. The onus for intervention would then fall on both of the administrative agencies, the Bank of Canada and the Federal Reserve, to act – while the determination of any appropriate responses (including the size of any intervention and attendant market strategies) would be primarily left to officials of these two agencies, possibly but not certainly without much in the way of explicit oversight by either national government.

The process for seeking a change in the referential central parity is also important in establishing and maintaining an adequate degree of confidence in the arrangement with foreign-exchange markets. Sufficient speed of response is of the essence in most adverse circumstances, and many realignments in Europe appear to have been managed without adding further turbulence to foreign-exchange markets. The EU member states normally had their finance ministers and central bankers meet (either directly in person or indirectly through teleconference calls over a weekend) to determine any realignments of the system. Partisan bargaining was sometimes intense with the German representatives usually insisting that any realignment affecting the Deutschmark should not fully compensate for the accumulated inflation differential. Implementation of the realignments, however, was usually successful – apart perhaps from particular instances occurring either in the early years of the ERM or around the time of the crisis in 1992/1993. Presumably a similar interactive arrangement could be readily adopted in a NAERM without much practical difficulty. The new innovation would, in essence, be a modest extension of the current consultative process that links the deliberations and major actions of the two central banks.

In terms of borrowing facilities, the EU had short-term financing available to it – financing that would permit the 'affected' countries to intervene (when deemed necessary) in support of their own and other currencies. If a similar system were to be adopted in a NAERM, management would presumably occur on a bilateral basis. Implementation of a new agreement for management of exchange rates would not necessitate the creation of new oversight institutions. However, if the arrangement were subsequently expanded to include more countries, the need to create a 'North American Monetary Institute' might arise with its mandate focused on the management of borrowing and surveillance procedures of NAFTA/FTAA economies. The European Commission fulfilled this type of bureaucratic task in Europe during the 1980s and 1990s, after which the European Monetary Institute (EMI) operated its own surveillance procedures during the 1994-99 period. In terms of the immediate political considerations, an establishment of the NAERM might appear to raise markedly different ones than those expected from the alternative option of a symmetric deliberate commitment. In terms of a unilateral ERM, similar considerations would apply – although credibility for any arrangements would be reduced.

There are other wider issues of concomitant activities, asymmetric responsibilities, targeting effectiveness, and announcement or honeymoon effects that need to be addressed here:

- At the inception of the ERM in 1979, the member states of the EU imposed and enforced capital controls, which seems to have enhanced credibility. Such controls were phased out from 1983 onwards, in association with the development of a 'new' ERM. If capital controls are to be implemented in the context of a NAERM – whether they are negotiated at the national level in a bilateral forum, or else declared unilaterally by a partner – a wider constituency may be involved during an establishment process. Interactive consultations are necessary in order to provide a broad consensual agreement among many 'interested parties', including provincial governments in Canada, who have substantial financial autonomy relative to their federal counterpart. Any persistent reliance on capital controls would require implementation of a complicated deposit scheme that can be promptly enforced and legally validated if challenged. Political environments in the two countries and the firm commitments by their national governments to maintenance of relatively mobile capital make easy implementation of this deposit scheme seems unlikely.

- Consider the use of particular interest rates to defend exchange-rate parities, a strategy often employed in the ERM. The Federal Reserve is not likely to target US interest rates in order to deal with adverse situations affecting the Canadian dollar exchange rate – onus for remedial action would presumably fall only on the Bank of Canada. In recent years, that central bank has sought to encourage (confidence-building) changes in interest rates as a means of reducing a long decline in the value of the Canadian currency, but there was no expectation this activity could, would or should be pursued to the extent that occurred in Europe in the early years of the ERM.

- Severe uncertainties surround the influence that any potential changes in the Bank of Canada's targeted instruments affecting (short-term) interest rates can have on subsequent developments in the foreign-exchange markets. Most evidence suggests that this particular influence is attenuated by other developments, plagued by imprecise time horizons, and possibly weak.
- Transitory 'announcement effects' are associated in theoretical models with 'honeymoon effects' for policy measures – illustrated by Krugman (1991) in a treatment of 'target-zone' mechanisms and connected with the credibility of monetary authorities. A honeymoon effect could allow exchange rates to behave a little differently than they might under a fully flexible regime. The reputations of authorities encouraged by sensible implementation of monetary and exchange-rate policies may induce reluctance among market participants to test the authorities' voracity. Thus a less challenging environment might prevail. Again evidence on this matter is either sparse or mixed in its implications, though Pansard (1999) cites possibly insubstantial effects for small realignments. With the NAERM, the possibility of beneficial honeymoon effects remains unclear.

Although the ERM was originally conceived as an arrangement for exchange rates, the Treaty of Maastricht of 1991 transformed the arrangement into a potential temporary arrangement that would serve as a criterion for entry into EMU. This secondary role induced political pressures that sought to avoid realignment of currencies – the Treaty stipulated that currencies should not realign for two years before entry to the EMU, a condition which ultimately led to crises for exchange rates of 1992 and 1993. Within NAFTA, the NAERM could be conceived either as a means to an end (a criterion for adopting the US dollar) or as an end in itself. Obviously questions arise here. If the ERM had not been incorporated as a criteria for EMU, would the historical crises been averted? These crises were considered an indictment of adjustable peg arrangements. Could the actual arrangement not be flawed, but rather the operation of the arrangement at fault? Given this latter possibility, if a NAERM were to be established as a pre-requisite for adopting a common currency, then margins for fluctuation should be set at a wider range than would be appropriate if the NAERM were to be an end in itself.

*Flexible Exchange-Rate Options*

There are four configurations to evaluate in conjunction with strategic options for flexible exchange rates:

- A 'shadow' or implicit target zone.
- Some modest degree of intervention stimulated by either the size of the change in exchange rate, or by movements relative to a shadow target.

- The *status quo* in which no prescribed target zone exists for either the level of exchange rates of for changes in them.
- Complete neglect.

Use of a shadow target zone would be a practical means of implementing one of the configurations assessed in subsection (2) above, with the zone of acceptable experience being unannounced. There are two clear precedents for this type of policy – a secret agreement among the G7 countries that was made within the Plaza Accord of 1985, and the implicit targeting of narrower bands that took place following the collapse in 1992/1993, which ultimately led to the adoption of a wide band of +/- 15% for the ERM. In the first of these situations, the policy met with little success since contemporary exchange rates were very volatile. Also although the policy was not openly announced, the agreement on target zones was leaked to the press so participants in foreign-exchange markets soon identified where trigger-points for intervention were located. In the second situation, the policy was successful for most ERM currencies. Even when currencies broke through the implicit bands, few significant consequences seem to have afflicted monetary policies.

A potential advantage of adopting this strategic option is that the defence of bands may not be seen as crucial to the credibility among market participants of an exchange-rate policy. Over time it might become apparent that a shadow target zone exists but provided actions associated with revaluation or devaluation seem to be timely and sensibly managed, then the policy's existence and its trigger points for intervention might be obscure for the markets. Obviously if the general reputation of the monetary institution is not much affected by the credibility of its exchange- rate policy, there can be no honeymoon effect here. The disadvantage of this option occurs when participants in the foreign-exchange markets detect a trigger point for intervention, and infer the policy in effect. Then the 'game is up' and some other device is required. In political terms, a covert arrangement between the US and Canada authorities would be difficult to hide, not least because other institutions and agents must be involved, and contrary to past attempts to demonstrate transparency. Given the considerable hazards of a leak, a credible policy might have to be unilaterally based, but even then sufficient secrecy would perhaps be impossible to sustain.

The second configuration is basically a 'dirty' float. It can arise as a secret 'internal' policy or in the form of explicit announcements to the effect that remedial actions of monetary authorities are to be determined by an undesired range of values for the exchange rate or by excessive destabilizing volatility. Advantages come from a greater stability that might be encouraged by the strategy (although evidence on potential success is mixed), while the disadvantages stem from market challenges to the credibility of the policy-makers and their particular actions as reflected, for example, in insufficient or adverse responses to major announcements.

The *status quo* configuration continues present policy with few significant adjustments to past behaviour – a lengthy justification is offered by Murray (1999), and support indicated by Crow (1999) and Laidler (1999). Their main premise is that the Canadian dollar is highly dependent on the levels of commodity prices. To the extent that such prices are volatile, the Canadian dollar will continue to attract adjustments relative to its US counterpart. The final configuration requiring complete neglect would make the Bank of Canada, after due consultation with the Federal Department of Finance, abstain from any further intervention in order to affect exchange rates. The decision would be made known by an initial declaration of its intent and by the confirmation of subsequent practice.

## Beyond Canada-US Agreements

Consider now the extension of deliberate configurations to include Mexico, and also some implications of the replacement of the NAFTA by a FTAA. The extension of a deliberate commitment to involve Canada and Mexico would only be sensible if the US was forcefully involved in establishing a NAFTA-wide policy for exchange rates. There are several reasons underlying this assertion:

- Credibility of the Banco de Mexico in the financial markets does not match that routinely attributed to the Federal Reserve or the Bank of Canada despite sustained efforts over the last decade by the Banco to restore confidence (since the Peso crisis of 1994), nor is this disparity likely to end within the foreseeable future.
- Mexico is a relatively new partner in the formal integration process, without a positive historical record on which to draw. The country is ill-placed in terms of its present reconciliation with the provisions of NAFTA, so it would be premature to move beyond that adjustment process towards the pursuit of a single market or an exchange-rate agreement with Canada and the US.
- Merchandise trade between Mexico and the US is of significant magnitude but much is restricted to sourcing from the *maquilladora* plants in northern Mexican states. Actual degrees of economic and financial integration are substantially lower than exists between Canadian and the US entities. The rationale for an expansionary policy is therefore not compelling. Inappropriate timing is evident for an ERM-type arrangement since the Mexican currency has been far more volatile against the US dollar than has its Canadian counterpart. Inclusion of the Mexican peso in a formal arrangement could be destructive. The subsequent frequency of effective devaluations must reduce the essential credibility needed for that arrangement, unless Mexican authorities choose to dollarize or a single currency is proposed for North America – chances of the latter seemingly remote.

There are few guidelines as to whether a particular country is suited to the adoption of a monetary policy of another country. One framework is associated with the 'optimal currency-area paradigm' introduced by Mundell (1961) and refined by MacKinnon (1969).

In considering the current Mexican situation and its feasibility of joining a US currency bloc, an exploration by Bayoumi and Eichengreen (1994) indicates Mexico and the US do not share symmetric economic shocks. Recent research by Crowley (2001a) too suggests Mexican business cycles have very different characteristics to those experienced elsewhere in North America. Such empirical findings mean that the transition to a new economic arrangement would be difficult. Mexico has no pressing reasons to abandon its own currency – in contrast to Ecuador say – so there is presumably little justification for that country to unilaterally adopt the US dollar in place of the domestic alternative. With regard to political dimensions however, if the US government recommended a US dollar bloc for an expanded NAFTA and then offered to provide offsetting concessions – a partial voice in the determination of monetary policy and compensatory payments for seigniorage losses of adequate magnitude and duration, for example – then the apparent costs of lost monetary sovereignty might be diminished, while the perceived economic benefits of faster integration with more credibility, and the other benefits cited earlier, could enhance the acceptability of stronger deliberate ties.

The expansion of the NAFTA to a FTAA is complex option and it remains unclear whether an eventual FTAA must inevitably subsume the NAFTA. Would differential conditions be set for the constituent members of a FTAA? Would the new agreement require a 'level playing field' among members, or would the initial signatories of a comprehensive pact (Canada and Mexico) be given tariff concessions that are not made available to subsequent FTAA countries? Equal treatment reflects a broadening aspect of integration rather than a deepening one. This choice would reduce chances of introducing additional joint initiatives in the arena of exchange-rate coordination, whereas differential treatment implies the two basic agreements are separate legal entities and a further deepening of the NAFTA arrangement remains feasible. Costa and De Grauwe (1999) offer an instructive analysis and useful analogies to illuminate aspects of further integration beyond the EMU format.

A final consideration, often ignored in appraising the NAFTA context, is the role of economic agreements in promoting a political dynamic that can spill over into other areas of political endeavour and policy interest, as identified by Wessels (1997). The fact that potential responses to wider concerns raised by the illegal immigration of Mexican labour to the South West US and Texas are now being considered (sometimes tentatively and in a somewhat haphazard fashion, and occasionally in bold presidential announcements that challenge existing immigration procedures) by the US administration and Congress might lead, for example, to closer and more effective attention being given to other significant matters that are raised by their Mexican counterparts and domestic American groups, and thus serve to stimulate the pace and incidence of a progressive dynamic for further integration throughout North America.

## Concluding Remarks

Our discussion is summarized in the accompanying table. Significant differences of structure, historical experience and political pressures or priorities separate the European Union and the NAFTA composite. Some economic observers, particularly a few that reside in Canada, have initiated debate on the relative merits of adopting a NAFTA-wide policy for governing exchange rates. Current configurations of the NAFTA remain far from those normally associated with an idealized vision of a free trade area because of substantial barriers to trade that exist both between the NAFTA countries and within them. Verifiability of many arguments being offered remains indeterminate. A huge deficiency is the apparent weakness associated with a myopic focus on abstract economic theory rather than a sensitive reliance on a wider multidisciplinary perspective that deals with some aspects of interaction of political, social, spatial, legal and demographic dimensions with economic ones – multiple dimensions that must surely be influential in framing any possible choices among strategic options for integration policies. Introduction of a new exchange-rate regime may assist the growth of contiguous cross-border trade for NAFTA countries, but we must not presume that this initiative provides strong encouragement for any dynamic processes of integration in the absence of a better economic intelligence for an adaptive international environment.

## Note

This chapter was based on an earlier article that was published as "Exchange Rate Arrangements for NAFTA: Should we mimic the EU?" in the *International Trade Journal* in 2002 (Crowley and Rowley, 2002)

## References

Balassa, R. (1961), *The Theory of Economic Integration* (Homewood, IL: Irwin).
Bayoumi, T. and Eichengreen, B. (1994), "Monetary and Exchange Rate Arrangements for NAFTA", *Journal of Development Economics*, 43: 125-65.
Buiter, W. (1995), "Macroeconomic Policy during a Transition to Monetary Union", *CEPR Discussion Paper 1222*.
Buiter, W. (1999), "The EMU and the NAMU: What is the Case for North American Monetary Union?" *Canadian Public Policy*, 25(3): 285-305.
Clarkson, S. (2000), "'Apples and Oranges'. Prospects for the Comparative Analysis of the EU and NAFTA as Continental Systems", *EUI Working Paper RSC 2000/23*.

Courchene, T. and Harris, R. (1999), "From Fixing to Monetary Union: Options for North American Currency Integration", *C.D. Howe Commentary*, June.

Crow, J. (1999), "Canadian Exchange Rate Policy", *Canadian Public Policy*, 25(3): 315-19.

Crowley, P. (2001), "Beyond EMU: Is there a logical integration sequence?" Paper presented at the ECSA-US meetings, Madison, WI, May.

Crowley, P. (2001a), "Should NAFTA adopt NAMU", Paper presented at the Western Economics Association meetings, San Francisco, CA, July.

Crowley, P. and Rowley, R. (2002), "Exchange Rate Arrangements for NAFTA: Should we mimic the EU?", International Trade Journal, 16, 4: 413-451.

Costa, C. and De Grauwe, P. (1999), "EMU and the Need for Further Economic Integration", in (ed) W. Meeusen, *Economic Policy in the European Union* (Cheltenham: Edward Elgar).

Commission of the European Communities (1996), *Reinforced Convergence Procedures and a New Exchange Rate Mechanism in Stage Three of EMU*, Communication from the Commission to the Council, COM(96) 498 final, Brussels.

Dowd, K. and Greenaway, D. (1993), "Currency Competition, Network Externalities and Switching Costs: Towards an Alternative View of Optimum Currency Areas", *Economic Journal*, 102: 180-9.

European Commission (1990), *Economic and Monetary Union: The Economic Rationale and Design of the System*, Working Document of the Commission, Presented to Finance Ministers, March, Brussels.

Fischer, S. (2001), "Exchange Rate Regimes: Is the Bipolar View Correct?" *Finance and Development* (Washington, DC: International Monetary Fund) 39(2): 18-21.

Frankel, J. (1999), "No Single Currency Regime is Right for All Countries or at All Times," *Essays in International Finance No. 215* (Princeton NJ: Princeton University Press).

Giavazzi, F. and Pagano, M. (1988), "The Advantage of Tying One's Hands", *European Economic Review*, 32: 1055-82.

Grubel, H. (1999), "The Case for the Amero: The Economics and Politics of a North American Monetary Union", *Critical Issues Bulletin* (Vancouver: Fraser Institute).

Helliwell, J., Lee, F. and Messinger, H. (1999), "Effects of the Canada-U.S. FTA on Interprovincial Trade", Unpublished paper, Industry Canada.

Krugman, P. (1991), "Target Zones and Exchange Rate Dynamics", *Quarterly Journal of Economics*, 56(3): 669-682.

Laidler, D. (1999), "Canada's Exchange Rate Options", *Canadian Public Policy*, 25(3): 324-32.

Little, J.S. (2000), "Mapping the Economy: A World of Difficult Currency Choices", *Regional Review* (Federal Reserve Bank of Boston), 10(1): 6-8.

Macmillan, M. (2001), *Paris 1919* (New York; Random House).

McKinnon, R. (1969), "Optimum Currency Areas", *American Economic Review*, 53: 717-55.

Mundell, R. (1961), "A Theory of Optimum Currency Areas", *American Economic Review*, 51: 657-75.

Murray, J. (1999), "Why Canada Needs a Flexible Exchange Rate", *Bank of Canada Working Paper 99-12*.

Pansard, F. (1999), "Target Zones and Small Realignments", *Economic Letters*, 64(3): 625-7.

Rose, A. (1999), "One Money, One Market: Estimating the Effect of Common Currencies on Trade", Unpublished manuscript, University of California, Berkeley, USA.

Svensson, L. (1994), "Why Exchange Rate Bands: Monetary Independence In Spite of Fixed Exchange Rates", *NBER Working Paper W4207*.

Wessels W. (1997), "An Ever Closer Union? A Dynamic Macro-Political View on Integration Processes", *Journal of Common Market Studies*, 35(2): 267-99.

**Regimes and Their Implications**

| Level of Commitment | Regime | Treaty/ Agreement? | Institution Building? | Monetary Policy Independence? | Credibility? | Political Acceptability? | Increased Trade/Foreign Direct Investment? |
|---|---|---|---|---|---|---|---|
| Deliberate Commitment | Dollarization | Y | (Y) | None | Y | ✘ – Canada Y – USA | Y |
| | New currency | Y | Y | Shared | Y | (Y) – Canada ✘ - USA | Y |
| | Symmetric binding | Y | ? | Some with realignments | (Y) | (Y) | Y |
| | Asymmetric binding | Internal | ✘ | Yes with realignments | ? | (Y) | Y |
| Deliberate Constraint | Bilateral NAERM | Y | (Y) | Some | (Y) | (Y) | Y |
| | Unilateral NAERM | Internal | ✘ | (Yes) | ? Depends on realignments | ((Y)) – Canada | (Y) |
| Flexible Exchange Rate Options | "Shadow" target zone | (Y) | ✘ | (Yes) | ? Depends on leaks | (Y) | ((Y)) |
| | Triggered intervention | Internal | ✘ | Yes | ? – depends on frequency | (Y) | (((Y))) |
| | Status quo | NA | ✘ | Yes | (Y) | Y | NA |
| | Complete neglect | NA | ✘ | Yes | ✘ | ✘ | ✘ |

# PART IV

# POLICIES FOR
# NATION-BUILDING

Chapter 9

# National Identity: European Union and Canadian Policies in Comparative Perspective[1]

Edelgard Mahant

## Introduction

Does the state have a place in the culture of the nation? Is a common culture a necessary, or at least a useful component of the nation-state? Does the survival of the European Union, as a political system, depend on the existence or creation of a common European culture? These are the questions that will be discussed in this chapter.

Before turning to these questions, though, I pose another one. Is the European Union, as led by the Commission, Councils and Parliament, seeking to become a European super-state? Such a "eurosceptic" question may sound outdated in 2004. The concept of the United States of Europe faded from Europe's political agenda over a quarter of a century ago. Since the publication of Ernest Haas's *The Uniting of Europe* (Stanford University Press, 1958), the idea that the European Union is *sui generis*, a supranational community which is neither state, nor nation, nor international organization has become a truism. It is, therefore, surprising that the EU has, until recently, been analysed primarily in terms of international relations theory, neglecting comparative politics and the literature on nationalism (Cram 2001, p.235; Hix, 1999, pp.1-5). This chapter argues that although the Union is not a state, much less a nation-state in spite of repeated denials to the contrary, many European political leaders continue to act as if they want the Union to be or become a nation-state. Besides the push for common policies in almost every field of governmental activity, from monetary to foreign and cultural policy and the attempt to draft a European constitution, "political actors in the Union have adopted traditional nation-building strategies by fashioning emblems such as the European flag, passport, driving licence, the European anthem and European sporting occasions" (Laffan 1996a, p.97).

But what is culture? It is a term that cannot be satisfactorily defined because it has different meanings. In a sociological context, culture has at least two different but related sets of meanings. In its wider sense, culture "is a set of values that guide [*sic*] the actions of individuals and the interaction of people within a society" (Harrison 1997, p.31). The term "political culture" falls within this definition, as does Karl Deutsch's (1980, pp.11-14) definition of nationalism as "a community of shared meanings". Tom Henighan adds three further definitions of culture: the anthropological concept of a cultural community, culture as art, and culture as learned tradition. These three approaches to a definition of culture are related. The anthropological cultural community survives because it passes its culture on to the young and to new members. Art (including literature) is one aspect of this tradition. Yet the appreciation of art is not limited to any one cultural community. Shakespeare's plays, classical Indian dancing and the music of the Beatles, to mention only three examples, have been appreciated by many different people of a great variety of cultural traditions. The last example introduces yet another distinction, that between mass and elite cultures, which Henighan (1996, p.2) calls entertainment and aesthetic cultures, a categorization which leaves out yet a third category, that of traditional folk cultures. It would seem, though the matter remains to be demonstrated, that governmental cultural policies have tended to favour culture of the aesthetic and folk varieties, leaving entertainment culture to support itself ( – although there are notable exceptions).

A nation-state, by definition, includes a national culture, and that culture is in turn assumed to be one of the means by which the sense of national identity which helps to keep the nation-state functioning as a legitimate political institution is created. In an article comparing national and European sources of identity, Anthony Smith (1992, p.60) defines a nation as a:

> human population sharing a historical territory, common memories and myths of origin, a mass, standardized public culture, a common economy and territorial mobility, and common legal rights and duties for all members of the collectivity.

Later he adds a common language or related languages and a common religious tradition as sources of national identity (Smith 1992, p.68-70). Kevin Dowler (1997, p.330) goes several steps further than Smith when he argues that a culture and the resulting sense of identity are a matter of national security to states such as Canada which have neither defined frontiers nor an autonomous national economy:

> From the perspective of security, identity is simply one of the desired outcomes of state security aims. The governmental administration of culture should be seen as a set of 'tactics' to enhance security and ensure the continual reproduction of the Canadian state. Beyond the question of brute space and issues of sovereignty ... appears the question of managing the population .... Culture is, from this perspective, a regime ... that functions as a form of security.

Tom Henighan (1996, p.91), like Dowler a professor at Canada's Carleton University, agrees.

Culture is the most inspiring, the most provocative and creative form of national defence, that one can imagine. Canada should support arts and culture because our nation cannot survive as an integral and independent entity without them.

In other words, culture is needed for a government to maintain the loyalty of and to control its people. These are not merely the ravings of ivory-tower academics. In 1961, a Canadian Royal Commission on Publications wrote that "the communications of a nation are as vital to its life as its defences, and should receive at least as great a measure of national protection" (Schwanen 1997, p.10). Think what the artistic community could do with the national defence budget!

The modern nation-state system is thus based on the assumption that each sovereign nation-state enjoys a predominant national culture. This culture, in ways which have not been fully explored or analysed, is in turn both the source and the consequence of a national value system in a reciprocal process whereby the evolution of the culture leads to the evolution of the values, which in turn feeds back into the development of the culture. A common value system not only creates the sense of legitimacy which allows the government of the state to function without the frequent use of repressive measures, it also helps a government to set priorities in, for example, the making of social policy (Closa 1995, p.489; Sørensen 1996, pp.3, 15, 53).

In many cases the identification of citizen and government extends further than a common value system would require. Nationalists and governing elites have demanded that citizens find their *primary* identity in the state. If nationality is a person's primary source of identity, it follows that most people would – or perhaps should – have one and only one nationality. Furthermore, since a sense of identity is a characteristic many persons strive to obtain and retain, they will go to some lengths to maintain that identity. People have on occasion been asked to die for their family or their religion, their community or ideology. Millions have died for their "nation"-state and have, in many cases willingly, made that sacrifice (Habermas 1992, p.5; Closa 1995, p.491; Sørenson 1996, p.53).

How can such a powerful sense of identity be created and maintained? Most governing elites believe that a common culture is one of the primary factors which leads to the creation of a common identity. They have accordingly attempted to create or foster a national culture where they found that one did not yet exist to the requisite degree. This is a good example of how the human mind so often makes that apparently small yet sometimes dangerous leap from the empirical to the normative, from the "is" to the "ought."[2] The nineteenth century assumption that a common culture *was* a characteristic of aspiring nations (Italy, Germany) became the twentieth century value judgement that a nation-state *ought* and needs to have a common culture.

Nineteenth century nationalists, such as Mazzini and Herder, argued that the existence of a common culture is a pre-existing fact which calls for the establishment of a nation-state. Today, Habermas (1992, p.3) distinguishes between such "prepolitical communities" and the "republican *praxis*" of learned citizenship. However, the nineteenth and especially the twentieth century have seen the creation of states which did not have a pre-existing common culture (Canada, the Sudan, Nigeria, South Africa) or which share a culture with one or more neighbouring states (most of the Latin American republics [Harrison 1997, p.26]). In many such states, governments have attempted to create, foster and/or preserve national cultures, presumably to create a sense of legitimacy and identity. The process by which governments create or foster a nationalism which may not have preceded the state, or does not exist to the degree the elites consider necessary for the successful governing of the state, has become known as *nation-building* (Deutsch 1963, pp.1-16). This paper examines the examples of three states, Luxembourg, Ireland and Canada, whose governments have perceived the need to protect or foster a national culture. The three states were chosen as examples because each shares a language with one or more larger neighbouring states, a factor which may cause governmental elites to perceive a need to foster a national culture.

After examining the measures which each of the governments has used to support a national culture, the paper turns to the European Union and its cultural policies. The main question to be examined is the extent to which the cultural policies of the European Union are or are not equivalent to the nation-building policies of states. That is, is the Union involved in a process of nation-building with a view to the creation of a European nation-state, or is the Union's cultural policy designed to contribute to the creation and/or maintenance of a European identity which will be inclusive and multi-layered. A concluding section then evaluates (a) the extent to which such European efforts may or may not contribute to the creation of a European identity; and (b) the relationship between the concept of a European identity and the goals of the European Union.

An important aspect of the study of cultural policy concerns the degree to which cultural policy is meant to influence culture according to its various definitions. When governments make cultural policy, they usually mean policies affecting the fine arts, such as literature, painting, film and music. But even that pragmatic definition has its complications. There is also the problem of the development of media which convey culture (from print to film to radio, television and the internet), which has also caused an overlap between cultural policy and media and telecommunications policy.

Governments that enact and implement cultural policies, as well as the proponents of such policies, often make the assumption that a national culture constitutes a necessary component for the continued existence of the state. Henighan (1996, p.4) writes that the Canadian national vision, made manifest, articulated and shaped by its culture, is in danger, and that the danger is coming from the "universal entertainment culture" that is largely a product of the American media and entertainment industry. He continues by stating that "art and culture [are] morally central to common social life, as the carriers of values and visions that could serve the whole society." In a similar vein, Rick Salutin (1988, p.209),writing about the 1988 Canadian-American Free Trade Agreement, asks:

what are we supposed to write our books about ... when there is no distinctive Canadian society left; when our country has been absorbed into the glittering American market place .... Culture is not about culture or literature, or art; it is about the way a people lives in social and national groupings. What is the point of being a writer or artist in Canada when Canada is no longer distinctive and in control of its own destiny? The fight was never to save Canadian culture; it could only be to save Canada.

## Canada[3]

Apart from Quebec, north of the Rio Grande, the English language is the principal means of communication across all parts of North America. Canadians never felt tempted to abandon English, no matter what they thought about the United States, though Canadians do also rely on policies of bilingualism and multiculturalism to help distinguish themselves from Americans. The discussion which follows deals exclusively with federal government policies and is largely limited to English-language Canadian culture, since it is English-Canadian culture which, like that of Ireland and Luxembourg, appears threatened by the culture of a larger neighbouring state of the same language.

After the War of 1812 there were efforts to use fewer textbooks of American origin in Upper Canadian schools, and some Protestant churches severed their administrative ties with parent bodies across the border. During the 1920s, legislation limited the importation of American magazines, and during World War II, the Canadian government, to save foreign exchange, banned the importation of all American comic books. The 1936 creation of the Canadian Broadcasting Corporation was also meant to promote Canadian culture.

Since World War II, support for Canadian culture has ebbed and flowed. The Canada Council, created in 1951, continued the task of subsidizing Canadian culture that had begun with the creation of the CBC and the National Film Board. In 1976, legislation meant to protect Canadian magazines put the Canadian edition of *Time* magazine temporarily out of business. Since the 1950s, various broadcasting acts have limited the amount of foreign content on Canadian radio and television and have favoured Canadian over American advertisers. The 1988 Free Trade Agreement "grandfathered" most (not all) of Canada's cultural protection measures, and the 1993 NAFTA continued this exemption. The main difference between the NAFTA and the FTA with respect to culture is that the FTA allowed a government that felt its trade had been injured by a cultural exemption to impose restrictions of "equivalent commercial effect" whereas the NAFTA allows retaliation by similar "discriminatory rules or procedures". This will limit Canadian (and Mexican) access to the American market, but will also allow Canada some leeway in protecting its cultural industries (Gestrin & Rugman 1993, p.8; Tawfik 1994, pp.15-16, 24, 41).

In 1991 the Canadian government adopted a new Broadcasting Act which was meant, among other factors, to reflect the reality of North American free trade.

The Act defines the mandate of both the CRTC, which regulates broadcasting, and of the CBC, the publicly-owned broadcaster. The CRTC is to "safeguard, enrich and strengthen the cultural, political, social and economic fabric of Canada" and to "encourage the development of Canadian expression". It is instructed to ensure that "each broadcasting undertaking shall make maximum use, and in no case less than predominant use, of Canadian creative and other resources" (though some exceptions are permitted). The CBC is instructed to provide programming which is both "predominantly and distinctively Canadian" and to "contribute to shared national consciousness and identity" (Canadian Radio and Telecommunications Commission 1991, pp.50-52). In 2000, in response to budget cuts as well as the rapid influx of specialty channels and the internet, the CBC outlined a three-pronged mandate: to provide distinctive, high-quality Canadian programming; to leverage all available assets to re-invest in and support Canadian programming; and to maximize the use of partnerships and strategic alliances in support of CBC programming goals and initiatives (Standing Committee on Canadian Heritage 2003, pp.184-5).

Most Canadians agree that the protection of Canadian culture is both a necessary and a worthwhile purpose of government policy. Current government policies in aid of Canadian culture can be classified into five major categories. First there are the regulatory measures, such as the "Cancon" (Canadian content regulations), which have existed since the 1930s in various forms. Private TV broadcasters, for example, are required to show at least 60% of Canadian programming, more during the evening, but during "prime time" most of them show considerably less Canadian programs than these figures would suggest. A recent variation of *Cancon* has allowed some broadcasters to substitute additional Canadian content on some channels or stations for more, Canadian content on others. Another regulation orders Canadian cable companies to substitute Canadian commercials when the same program is shown in Canada and the US at the same time (*Globe and Mail* 11 Oct. 1996; Schwanen 1997, p.16). In yet another controversial measure, the Canadian government has encouraged broadcasters to sensitize their programs to a so-called "V-chip" which would allow families to block out violent or sexually explicit programs (*Globe and Mail* 18, 19, 20 Jan. 1996, 29 Feb. 1996; Austen 1996, p.16; Lorimer 1992, pp.73-79). In 1999 the CRTC changed the rules defining *Cancon* to reflect hours of programming only, excluding production values by cost. This led to a severe decrease not in quantity but in the quality of Canadian programming (*The Hill Times* 1 Dec. 2003).

A second set of measures consists of trade protection. The 80% tax the Canadian government imposed on the proposed split-run edition of *Sports Illustrated* in 1995, as well as a similar measure directed against *Time* in 1976, fall into this category as does the provision that does not allow Canadian advertisers to deduct as a business expense advertising aimed at Canadian but placed in American-owned magazines or on American radio or television stations (*Globe and Mail* 16 Sept. 1996).

A third set of measures relates to investment, since, according to a 1987 Canadian government statement, there is a "demonstrable link between ownership and cultural performance in Canada" (Audley 1994, p.12). The liberalization of investment in Canada provided by the Free Trade Agreement and NAFTA does not apply to cultural industries. Investment policies have allowed the Canadian government to prevent the expansion of an American bookstore chain, (ironically) named *Borders* into Canada (*Globe and Mail* 9, 10 Feb. 1996). During the negotiations on the stillborn Multilateral Agreement on Investment (MAI), the governments of Canada (and of France) insisted on an exemption for cultural industries (*Globe and Mail* 8 Dec. 1997). In 2003 the Standing Committee on Canadian Heritage recommended that current foreign ownership rules, which allow for up to 47.6% foreign ownership in the case of a holding company which owns broadcasting or telecom operations, be maintained (Standing Committee on Canadian Heritage 2003, p.420).

A fourth way of promoting culture consists of direct subsidies. The Canada Council systematically awards these subsidies, supposedly according to merit, but such subsidies have been sharply reduced as a result of recent efforts (federal, provincial and municipal) to contain government spending (*Globe and Mail* 1 Mar. 1995; *Macleans* 30 Sept. 1996). Nevertheless, film, television, literature and publishing as well as the fine arts generally still enjoy a measure of government subsidy throughout Canada, both directly in the form of grants and indirectly through such measures as investment tax credits or the former postal subsidies granted to Canadian magazines (Lorimer 1992, pp.73-79; Audley 1994, pp.14-18; Schwanen 1997, pp.29, 31). The Canadian Film or Video Production Tax Credit (CPTC), for example, designed to "encourage Canadian programming and to develop an active domestic production sector," is a fully refundable credit for up to 12% of the total cost of an eligible production (Standing Committee on Canadian Heritage 2003, p.146).

Fifth, because of the perceived need to limit government spending, the Canadian government has in recent years turned to a number of mixed and *ad-hoc* measures to protect Canadian culture. The dispute with the United States over Country Music Television (CMT) was resolved by allowing the ousted American producer to buy a part ownership in the Canadian broadcaster of country music (*Winnipeg Free Press* 9 March 1995; *Globe and Mail* 9 March 1995, 24 Jan., 7 Feb., 7 March 1996, 9 Aug. 1996; Acheson & Maule 2001, pp.206-19; *About Telesat* 2003). Other measures tax blank tapes and order Canadian radio and television stations to pay royalties to Canadian performers whose works they broadcast (*Globe and Mail* 27 April 1996).

Since the NAFTA came into effect, on January 1, 1994, the number of Canadian-American disputes about cultural industries seems to have increased. There have been disputes about the refusal of the Canadian government to allow an American bookstore chain to expand into Canada, the CMT dispute, both mentioned above, and continuing problems about content regulations for cable television. In retaliation, the American government refused permission for Telesat

Canada to beam programs rebroadcast from its satellite into American homes, even though American firms, who cannot find space on American owned satellites, were eager to find space on the Canadian one. These restrictions were not lifted until December 1999, when in an agreement with the World Trade Organization (WTO), the US Federal Communication Commission allowed US broadcasters to rent space on Telesat's satellites (*Globe and Mail* 30 Jan., 4 July, 12 Sept. 1996; *About Telesat*, 2003). In January 1996, the American movie industry launched a court challenge against a Canadian government regulation that limits the number of foreign films that can be shown on direct-to-home satellite services (*Globe and Mail* 30 Jan. 1996; *Montreal Gazette* 8 July 1995). In an unusual move between two countries which tend to settle their disputes bilaterally, the American government asked a WTO panel to find the Canadian tax on split-run editions of magazines illegal. In July 1997, the panel decided in favour of the American government, and in 1999 Bill C-55 struck a compromise limiting the amount of Canadian ad space a split-run could have (*Globe and Mail* 26, 27 May 1999).

## Ireland

With few exceptions, people in both parts of the Anglo-Irish dyad speak English. They share a common literature and history and an open border. Residents of the United Kingdom are as indifferent to Radio Television Eire (RTE) as Americans are to the CBC or CTV, but residents of the Irish Republic, if anything, are more devoted to the BBC than Canadians are to NBC or CNN. As RTE has some programs in the Irish language (principally newscasts), and as most viewers have a minimal knowledge of the Irish language, the temptation to watch British channels becomes particularly strong.

There is an analogy between the Irish Republic's situation and that of Luxembourg. Both, in a sense, are part of a triangle. Belgium is not the world's largest French-speaking country, and there is considerable French as well as Belgian influence in Luxembourg. The United Kingdom is not the world's largest English-speaking country, and there is considerable American, as well as British, influence in Ireland. Residents of Dublin ride on double-decker buses and watch the BBC and other British channels, but they also watch *Dallas* and *Happy Days* on RTE and *Little House on the Prairie* was a favourite during the Reagan years. Network 2 has carried *Raggedy Ann and Andy*, *Ghostbusters*, and *Lassie*. Nor is Irish television limited to programs from the United States, the United Kingdom, and Ireland. The Australian program *Home and Away* was another favourite on Network 2. RTE radio, faced with new competition from commercial stations, differentiated itself from its competition by playing country-and-western songs from Texas.

British television is directly accessible in Dublin, along the east coast, and in areas close to Northern Ireland, but Irish authorities wanted Irish people to identify with Irish heroes and Irish interests. So steps have been taken to maintain a distinct Irish culture: subsidies are made to Irish publishers and artists through the government financed Arts Council, there are a few Irish language television programs, the bilingual signs, and Irish language instruction in schools. In the early years of the Republic, the government followed strict policies of censorship (inspired largely by the Catholic Church) and "cultural protectionism." In 1960, the Irish government created Telefis Eireann (Irish Television), a further development of the state radio corporation which had existed since 1926. RTE's original mandate included "restoring of the Irish language and preserving and developing the national culture." The amended 1976 version is less emphatic – it requires RTE to "reflect the varied elements which make up the culture of the people of the whole island," to show "special regard for the elements which distinguish that culture and in particular the Irish language," and, in an interesting addition, to "have regard... and understanding of the values and tradition of" other countries, "including in particular ... members of the European Economic Community." The 1988 legislation allowing for the establishment of commercial radio and television stations similarly requires commitments to "promote Irish 'culture' and to respect 'good taste', and 'decency'." Taoiseach Sean Lemass, leader of the Fianna Fail party – the more nationalistic of Ireland's two dominant parties – explained "that television was an instrument of public policy." Cabinet ministers could have access on demand, said Lemass, and the Dublin government could censor "subversive and illegal organizations" (Murphy 1988, p.149; Barbrook 1992, pp.203-208, 214; Chubb 1982, p.71).

Financing comes from license fees and advertising revenues. This last may have strengthened British influence in Ireland. According to cultural historian Terence Brown (1987, p.261):

> The advertisements are sometimes British-made on behalf of British products, sometimes Irish-made on behalf of British products, while Irish-made advertisements on behalf of Irish goods and services, where a company can afford it, are created for an audience accustomed to British advertising techniques. One effect therefore of extended viewing of the national television channels (a second channel began broadcasting in 1978) is a sense of Ireland firmly within the British commercial sphere of influence.

In 1980, RTE was showing more imported programs than any other EU television network. Since 1980 there has been a reversal, as RTE has learned that Irish viewers prefer some home-made programs (Gibbons 1988, pp.221-234). By the 1990s, half of its programming was made in Ireland. At the same time, commercial operators, finding it hard to survive RTE competition, are calling for a levelling of the playing field (that is, help for them as well as RTE) – again, of course, in the name of Irish culture (Barbrook 1992, pp.208-211, 219-221).

Although a few Irish nationalists prefer the Irish language to English as a matter of principle, Ireland's language laws are tepid as compared with, for example, Quebec's Bill 101. Though the constitution declares Irish to be the national language, for the most part Ireland is an English-speaking country, the exception being the Gaeltacht in Ireland's far west and distant north (county Donegal). In the 1920s many considered it logical that a revival in the Irish language would be a by-product of the newly created Irish Free State, that Ireland without the Irish language was not really Ireland. And as of April 1922, it was decided that Irish was to be the only language for the first two grades of government-financed schools. Teachers in such schools were to allow singing only in Irish, and to use Irish as the only language of instruction for history and geography. In addition, students were to spend one hour per day studying grammar and vocabulary. Because the Irish lessons left no time for science and other subjects, these efforts rapidly failed and English continued to expand at the expense of Irish. As recently as 1961, a Fianna Fail politician described the idea that school children would not have to pass Irish to obtain credit for other subjects as "national treachery" (Brown, 1987, pp.43-78). Yet by 1973 the government abolished the requirement that all university entrants had to successfully complete Irish courses, though they still have to study the subject. That was the year when Ireland was joined the European Community, where French or German would be more useful than Irish.. Nevertheless, passing an examination in Irish remains a condition for certain professional and civil service positions.

The Irish historian John Murphy suggests a certain tension between those of his compatriots who write in English and those who write in Irish. Those who write in English, he suggests, tend to find traditional Irish life somewhat myopic (1988, p.153). The works of William Butler Yeats, nevertheless, demonstrate that one could write in English, be an ardent Irish nationalist and become well known and appreciated outside Ireland. Some Irish nationalists believe that their culture is so distinct that it does not need to express itself in a separate language; others say that Catholicism helps to distinguish them from the British. It did not help the Irish language that the Church did not encourage the use of Irish, first because it believed the language to be an "uncouth" peasant language, and later because Protestant missionaries used Irish. Yet Irish remains a source of national identity since it is used on state and ceremonial occasions, as Latin was once used by the Catholic Church (Keogh 1995, pp.247-248; Easson 1990, p.71; Hutcheson 1987, p.308; Comerford 1989, pp.21-40.)

Use of the Irish language continued to diminish after World War II. Brown (1987, p.268) estimates Irish was the mother tongue for fewer than 70 000 people in 1966, perhaps 32,000 by 1975. Tourists who visited the Gaeltacht required services in English, as did multinational corporations which built factories there. Radio na Gaeltachta, established in 1972, broadcasts only twenty-five hours a week in Irish (Brown 1987, p.269). English-language programming dominates RTE as well. According to Brown, in the twelve month period from 1 October 1975 until 30 September 1976, there were only 131 hours of Irish language television (10% of all programming), 58 hours of which were newscasts. There were only three hours aimed at children. By 1975, fewer than three per cent of the students in Irish secondary schools were choosing to write their mathematics, history and geography exams in the Irish language. In 1983, Ireland's equivalent of Quebec's Régie de la Langue Française, the Bord na Gaeilge, noted: "Today, some sixty years after the foundation of the State, only 1 per cent of our population can be said to be native speakers using Irish as their normal day-to-day language in Gaeltacht areas" (Brown 1987, pp.271-2, 352). In spite of its language legislation, Ireland has become a predominantly English-speaking country.

## Luxembourg

Luxembourgers have their own language, called Letzeburgesch, a German dialect related to both Dutch and Swiss German. All three languages, Letzeburgesch, French and German, have been used in Luxembourg for as long as those languages have existed. In 1859, the poet Michel Lentz wrote a national anthem in Letzeburgesch (on the occasion of the construction of the first railway line) (Newcomer 1984, p.13). After World War I there was tremendous pride in being distinct, and the poet Lucien Koenig (1888-1961) led a school of nationalists who wrote in the language.

Like Canada and Ireland, Luxembourg has language laws. According to the constitution of 1868, "the use of the German and French languages shall be optional" and "their use cannot be limited" (Calmes 1989, p.403). The Nazis outlawed French and promoted German, which led the Luxembourg resistance to use Letzeburgesch. After the war, the government promoted the use of French, but there was no officially defined national language. From 1948 until 1984 the relevant legislation read: "The use of languages for administrative and judicial purposes shall be determined by law." In 1984, after some attempts by German neo-Fascists recalled the Nazi efforts to Germanize Luxembourg, the government passed a language law declaring French, German and Letzeburgesch to be national languages. According to Article I of the 1984 law "the national language of Luxembourg is Letzeburgesch" and Article II says that French is the language of legislation. Article III permits French, German or Letzeburgesch as languages of communication for administrative and legal purposes. Citizens can communicate with authorities in any of these languages, and "as far as possible" the authority figure is supposed to reply in the same language (Calmes 1989, pp.403-404; Bossaert 1992, pp.77-78).

The actual use of the three languages presents a fascinating mix. Most Luxembourgers are trilingual in the spoken languages, a majority can read all three languages, and have taken the use of several languages for granted since they formed part of the Austrian and Dutch empires (Bossaert 1992, pp.66, 91). Newspapers are primarily in German, though there are also French-language articles, and many of the classified ads are in Letzeburgesch. There are daily radio broadcasts in Letzeburgesch and, since 1991, the weekly noon-hour Letzeburgesch news program has been supplemented by an hour long nightly news magazine. Other than that, Luxembourgers watch French or German programs, which may or may not originate in Luxembourg. The production of radio and television programs beamed into neighbouring countries where the media tend to be treated as means of nation-building, if not political control, is one of Luxembourg's principal industries. Luxembourg has less than 400,000 in population, yet forty million Europeans regular tune in to Luxembourg-based radio or television stations (Schroen 1986, pp.67-68; Bossaert 1992, p.83; Weber 1994, pp.148-151).

French is the language of administration and, for the most part, of politics, though the trade unions tend to use German or the local language (Schroen 1986, pp.6-7). In education, all children have one year of teaching in Letzeburgesch. German is introduced in the second year, French in the third. In the academic high schools, French tends to predominate up until the time students write their final examinations, whereas German is more common in the technical schools. In 2001 Luxembourg's Minister for Higher Education announced plans for a Luxembourg university. Before that, Luxembourgers who wanted to continue their studies past the first year of university usually went to France (Bossaert 1992, pp.72-73; Clyne 1995, pp.51-55).

There is limited government subsidization of culture. From 1950 to 1977, the government aided the creation of a standard dictionary of the language; it subsidizes a local language and folklore society and one national newspaper, but gives only limited subsidies to broadcasts in the local language. The media are expected to earn money for Luxembourg! On September 26, 2002, the Minister of Education sounded almost apologetic as she asked teachers to observe the European Day of Languages (*Journée européenne des langues* 2002, author's translation):

> our children learn at least two foreign languages and only 2% of Luxembourgers speak only Letzeburgesch. Nevertheless, since learning languages is of vital importance for the youth of our country, Luxembourg's schools should celebrate the European Day of Languages in their fashion.

The Ministry of Education subsidizes the publication of books in and research into the Letzeburgesch language and is also supporting creation of a computer "spellcheck" system for that language. Since 1985, there has been a revival of publishing in Letzeburgesch, especially in children's literature. A number of translations of Dutch and French children's favourites as well as some indigenous Luxembourg books have appeared (Schroen 1986, pp.67-68; Bossaert 1992, pp.83-87; "Renaissance in Letzeburgesch" 1992, p.37).

As in all European countries, there is some subsidization of culture as such, including folk dance and theatre. In April 2002, the Minister of Communication announced increased subsidies for the film industry. While most of the money is meant to attract foreign film makers to Luxembourg, the minister expressed the hope that some of the money would be used to make a Luxembourg film to be shown at the Cannes film festival (*Lancement du site www.filmfund.lu* 2002, Film Fund Luxembourg 2002).

## The European Union

The European Union performs some of the functions formerly carried out by national governments, but does so without the benefit of national identities or national cultures. Yet many of the Union's leaders have limited their vision to the analogy of the pre-existing nation-state; that is, they have tried to build a European federal-state (*Bundesstaat*), which would cap the existing nation-state system, much as the creation of Canada united the existing British North American colonies.[4] According to Brigid Laffan (1996b, p.6), "there is a tendency among those who favour the development of a strong polity at the European level to seek to recreate familiar institutional configurations at the supranational level of government." Thus while expressing their continued support for national and sub-national cultures, European elites have also been pursuing the elusive goal of a European identity. Hedetoft (1990, p.17), a Danish academic, points to the schizophrenic attitude of European leaders on the issue of identity: they pay lip-service to the idea of European identity while rejecting it "as a form of rival emotionalism." Let us first see what European leaders have said and second what they have done in this respect.

European Union pronouncements on culture are schizophrenic. On the one hand, there are proclamations of the need to build a European cultural identity. Colette Flesch, then European Commissioner in charge of cultural issues, told a 1995 conference that Union "action taken ... demonstrates the existence of a common sense of belonging and the progress already achieved on the way to union." Doris Pack (Group of the European People's Party 1995, pp.30, 43, 44), the Coordinator of the European Parliament's Committee on Culture, told the same conference that

> It is becoming increasingly accepted that the political, economic and social unification of Europe has no long-term prospects unless Europe comes to terms with its own cultural identity. Attempts are being made to achieve via cultural policy what European economic policy has so far failed to deliver, namely a genuine feeling of identity with and citizenship of the European Union. ... European culture's most distinctive feature is its combination of unity and diversity, separateness and openness.... European culture is also characterized by the development of democracy, the rule of law, philosophy, religion and humanism.

These comments demonstrate not only the persistence of the nation-state analogy, but also the schizophrenic nature of much of the commentary on cultural policy. In 1990, the Commission, in a report on audio-visual industries, claimed that "the commitment of citizens to the European idea depends on positive measures being taken to enhance and promote European culture in its richness and diversity" (Hutchinson 1996, p.6). Only occasionally do European Union decisions allow us a glimpse behind the correct and cautious jargon of the intentions of the European policy-makers: in 1994, Article 2 of the Decision creating the now defunct Raphael program lists one of the objectives of the program, "to contribute to the affirmation of a European citizenship through greater knowledge of heritage" (Commission of the European Communities 8 July 1996, pp.1f and 9; *Annual General Report of the Activities of the European Union* 1994, par. 716).

In recent years, EU pronouncements on culture have taken on a more cautious tone. Article 151 of the consolidated Treaties of Rome and Maastricht sounds as if it comes from a traditional inter-state treaty (Treaty Establishing the European Community 1997, pp.107-108):

1.     The Community shall contribute to the flowering of the cultures of the member States, while respecting their national and regional diversity and at the same time bringing the common cultural heritage to the fore.
2.     Action by the Community shall be aimed at encouraging cooperation between Member States and, if necessary, supporting and supplementing their action in the following areas:

- improvement of the knowledge and dissemination of the culture and   history of the European peoples;
- conservation and safeguarding of cultural heritage of European significance;
- artistic and literary creation, including in the audiovisual sector.

Paragraph 5 of the article specifies that decisions with respect to cultural policy are to be adopted unanimously, and this in an institution which adopts its budget by majority vote.

A November 2001 Council resolution (*Cultural/Audiovisual Affairs* 2001) on culture takes a slightly more assertive stand with respect to culture as a means to integration:

1.     Whereas the European Community contributes to the flowering of the cultures of the Member States, while respecting their national and regional diversity and at the same time bringing the common cultural heritage to the fore, and whereas this imperative respect for the cultural diversity underpins and sustains the Europe of culture in accordance with the principal of subsidiarity;
6.     Whereas the common dimensions and mutual knowledge of cultures in Europe, in a society based on freedom, democracy, solidarity and respect for diversity, are essential components of citizens' support and participation in European Union;
7.     Whereas, with this in mind in particular, culture constitutes a very important factor in the development and consolidation of the process of integration of the European Community...

The resolution concludes with a mild call for cooperation. The joint European Parliament and Council decision creating the Culture 2000 program echoes some of the phrases included in the later Council resolution, but takes a generally stronger stand on the importance of cultural cooperation (*Établissant le programme 'Culture 2000,'* author's translation):

1.      Culture has an intrinsic values for all the peoples of Europe, is an essential element of European integration and contributes to the affirmation and vitality of the European model of society as well as to the influence of the Community on the international stage.

5.      The full adhesion and participation of citizens in European integration assumes a greater demonstration of their common values and cultural roots as a key element of their identity and belonging to a society based on freedom, democracy, tolerance and solidarity. There is need for a better balance between the economic and cultural aspects of the Community so that these two aspects may complement and reinforce one another.

The 2003 Draft Treaty Establishing a Constitution for Europe states that "The Union shall contribute to the flowering of the cultures of the Member States, while respecting their national and regional diversity and at the same time bringing the common cultural heritage to the fore" (Article III-181).

In short, Europe's leaders want it all – regional, national, European and global values and culture. The programs established to date suggest that they are also trying to do a bit of everything, though with very limited resources. In 1995, the principal of the College of Bruges estimated that only 0.014% of the EU's budget is devoted to culture (Group of the European People's Party 1995, p.39). In 2002, the EU devoted .08% of its budget to education and culture combined (*Budget by Policy Area* 2002), and with this money the EU has conducted a number of cultural programs. A few examples from the cultural field follow. (I have not included strictly educational exchanges and programs, such as the ERASMUS program and the program of endowed Jean Monnet chairs [Delegation of the European Commission 1994]).

In the regulatory field, the Union has, like Canada, Ireland, Britain and France, adopted content rules. A 1989 Decision (*Economist* 1989, p.48; Delegation of the European Commission 1992; Hutchinson 1996, pp.7-8), which came into force in 1991 and was renewed in 1995 (*Economist* 1995, pp.42-43; *Europe* 1995; *European* 1995; *Annual General Report of the Activities of the European Union 1995*, par.656 and *1996*, par.635; "L'audiovisuel européen" 1995, pp.16-17) and 1997 (though only after unsuccessful French efforts to tighten and strengthen it) orders television broadcasters to show no more than 49% non-European content, though it adds "where practicable" and "by appropriate means." The same directive set daily and hourly maximums for advertising time, ordered broadcasters to buy at least 10% of their programming from independent producers, and eliminated all barriers to the retransmission of broadcasts originating anywhere within the EU. The Commission claims that from 1992 to 1994 the number of European channels broadcasting a majority of European programming has increased from 70 to 91 ( – it does not say whether the number of channels over all has increased). The Union is also considering regulations that will equip television sets with the "V-chip" mentioned above. The 1997 revision (Directive 97/36/EC 1997; "The new 'Television without Frontiers' Directive" 1997) of the directive requires "events of major importance" (read sports events such as soccer matches) to be broadcast unencrypted, allows pharmaceutical companies to sponsor programs while withdrawing that right from tobacco firms, and insists that programs addressed to "minors" must not "contain any incitement to hatred on grounds of race, sex, religion or nationality."

In addition, the European Union is spending small amounts of money (small in relation to its total budget) on programs to encourage the development of European television and the preservation of and dissemination of the European heritage. A program entitled MEDIA promotes the production and distribution of European-made audiovisual works. MEDIA at first scattered its resources widely, supporting everything from cartoons to such commercial successes as *Cyrano de Bergerac* and *Four Weddings and a Funeral*. What appear to have been one-time only grants in December 1995 supported the development of wide-screen broadcasting in seven member states (the highest grant being ECU 940,000 to the Danish national broadcasting service). In January 2001, MEDIA (MEDIA Programme of the European Union 2003), equipped with a budget of 400 million ECU, instituted a series of support measures dealing with:

> the training of professionals, the development of production projects and companies; the distribution of cinematographic works and audiovisual programmes; the promotion of cinematographic works and audiovisual programmes; the support for cinematographic festivals.

Since then, requests for development funds have increased by 120%: 352 projects were submitted in 2001, 574 in 2002 and 778 in 2003 ("Audiovisual Policy: Mid-Term Review of MEDIA Programme Recommends Adaptations"). The European Union has also encouraged and to a limited extent supported the European Broadcasting Union's efforts to create a European news channel.

The Culture 2000 program mentioned earlier has a budget of just €167M for five years. Culture 2000 supersedes three earlier programs, Ariane, Kaleidoscope and Raphael, while attempting to continue their work. Ariane supported the translation of literary works into less widely used languages and supported some book publishing. Kaleidoscope supported cultural exchanges and artistic and cultural activities of Europe-wide significance. The Raphael program was designed "to upgrade and conserve the fixed and movable heritage," to try and devise European standards for the conservation of the European heritage, and ensure "public access" to that heritage (Hjavard 1993, pp.71-94; *Europe* Dec. 29,

1995; *Annual General Report of the Activities of the European Union* 1994, pars. 718, 719; 1996, pars. 629, 637; 1999, pars. 677, 680; Commission of the European Communities 8 July 1996, 12 July 1996 and 29-30 May 1996; Hutchinson 1996, pp.10-11).

While promoting European culture and identity, the Union has been attempting to measure the results of its efforts. Since 1982 it has been asking Europeans whether they identify themselves as European, or citizens of Europe, or nationals of both Europe and their own country. The questions vary, but the results are fairly consistent, with just over half of the citizens of member states thinking of themselves as nationals of both their country and Europe. Luxembourgers and the French are consistent: they think of themselves as Europeans and national citizens. The lowest scores are less predicable; depending on the wording of the question, the British, the Danish, the Irish and the Dutch are least likely to think of themselves as European. Both the Irish and the Dutch are surprises. In the case of the Irish, it could be the government's insistence on maintaining the concept of an all Irish citizenship (residents of Northern Ireland have the option of obtaining Irish passports) that drives out the idea of a European citizenship. Overall, the older, more affluent and more educated Europeans are likely to think of themselves as European, a cruel irony compared with the aspirations of the early leaders of European integration who had seen European unity as a cause for the young. On the other hand, the young are somewhat more likely to be proud of being European. In an interesting question in 1986, *Eurobarometre* asked Europeans what made them feel European. A common culture was a distant fourth on the list, after the sense of having overcome past rivalries, freedom to travel and even the adventure of building a united Europe (*Eurobarometre* June 1987, p.A12; *Eurobarometre* Spring 1995, p.66; "EOS Gallup Europe," July 1995; "European Opinion Research Group," 24 May 2002).

## A European Political System – With or Without a European Culture?

A national culture, including one or more national languages, has by definition been accepted as an essential characteristic of the nation-state. That same nation-state was *the* defining political institution of the modern age: it was neat, tidy and all inclusive to its citizens, exclusive to all others. All the world's inhabitants, except a few unfortunate stateless persons, were meant to enjoy the benefits of a nationality, which included the enjoyment of a national culture. There are signs that European citizenship as defined in the revised Maastricht Treaty was meant to become an exclusive citizenship of this type (Sørenson 1996, pp. 65, 119-120) – yet this is a political system of the past.

In the past, the almost total identification of the individual with her or his state was to be achieved through a powerful combination of culture, ethnic consciousness, sense of history and political pride altogether known as nationalism. This idea of a world political system in which most of the world's inhabitants identified with one nation-state or another was so simple and attractive that many commentators not only espoused it as a goal to be achieved, but also saw it as a permanent and irreversible state of affairs. Hence the stubborn insistence in many political science textbooks that nationalism is an ideology.

Nationalism is not an ideology. As Ernest Renan (cited in Hedetoft 1990, p.8) pointed out in the nineteenth century, nations and nationalism will pass, just as surely as other political systems have come and gone. The recent outburst of ethnic nationalisms in parts of eastern Europe as well as the revival of regional nationalisms in the western part of the continent is added proof of this fact. If nationalism were a primordial characteristic of humankind, then how could a British national consciousness become a Scottish one? The fact that Spaniards can become Andalusians, Italians Lombardians and Canadians Québecois only confirms the fluid nature of national identification. National identities can not only change; they could disappear from history just as they appeared two hundred or so years ago.

Although nationalism in neither permanent nor is it an ideology, it had and has potent cultural and political attraction which caused it to dominate political systems based on other sources of legitimacy (empires, feudal systems, tribes). While the nation-state system is both rationally and emotionally attractive, a powerful combination, the very fluidity of national identification and the recent trend to identification with ever smaller groups has also demonstrated the incongruous nature of national identification in a world where governing elites virtually everywhere can watch CNN and where the economic forces of the market place are operating on a world-wide basis. In such a world, the nation-state may no longer be the most attractive, much less the most effective, political system.

The excesses of fascism demonstrated the extent of immorality to which the identification of the individual with the nation-state can lead. It required another two or three decades before political thinkers began to realize that the answer to a more effective, yet democratic, political system lay in the political recognition of the fact that individuals usually enjoy several different identities. These identities can be social, economic, religious, geographical, cultural or political, and they can, of course, overlap. What is more, each of the sources of identity has sub-categories which can in turn overlap. Thus Austrians identify with Austrian culture, but also with German-language culture overall; Catalonians may identify with the political system of their city, region and nation. Once we accept that individuals may have different sources of identity, the need for a coincidence in culture and politics becomes less obvious. Individuals could identify with their political community on one level, their cultural community on another. In other words, the successful functioning of a political system does not necessarily depend on the existence of a common culture. Thus the policies which the governments of states such as Canada, Ireland and Luxembourg, have been following in an effort to promote national cultures, may be or have become unnecessary. A common culture is not a necessary component of a successful state.

Pierre Trudeau (1968, p.196) once advocated a political system based entirely on rationality, one which would function because the individual citizen *rationally* accepted the need for government(s), not because s/he emotionally identified with that system. The idea of a rationally-based political system is one that political thinkers have imagined since the time of the ancient Greeks, but it has not yet been achieved. Is it a goal that can be easily attained and maintained? In other words, is it possible for a government to govern when its citizens do not emotionally identify with the political system? That has been the case throughout much of history and may well be the case again. There will, however, be at least two major differences between a system where an emperor ruled by divine right and a post-national political system where citizens accept that governments (and similar political institutions) at various levels have the right to make decisions affecting various aspects of their lives. First, a post-national political system will be one where governing institutions fulfil many more functions than they did in prenational times. Second, citizens will expect that so-called participatory democracy will be inherent in their political systems and the making of authoritative decisions.

If territorially overlapping political systems can function without the glue of national identity, do political systems not need common or at least similar value systems? Without such sharing of values, by what standards could governments and quasi-governments decide priorities and policies? It is probably true that governance cannot succeed for any length of time without a degree of shared values within the community being governed. But these common values need not depend on culture in the sense of the arts. It may well be that the connection between culture and politically relevant values has been overstated. If we take the example of Europe, West and East, hardly anyone would dispute that a large number of cultures flower there. Yet on the political level, the Council of Europe's Court of Human Rights has quietly, and to a large extent unnoticed by academics, the media and citizens, created a common standard for the rights of the individual citizen (Merrils and Robertson, 2001). The few hundred cases dealt with by this system have led to changes in dozens of laws affecting millions of people. Yet who has seen the flag of the Council of Europe? Does the Council have an anthem? Does anyone identify with it as his or her political system? Probably not, yet the consciousness of the rights the Council has awarded may in itself become a source of identity (Closa 1995, pp. 493-494, 505). If the Council of Europe can define and continue to redefine as basic an aspect of political life as the rights of the individual and do so without the glue or identity of a common culture, perhaps the creation of a single market and a single currency do not require a common culture to sustain them.

The example of the Council of Europe and its European-wide system for the enforcement of a common standard of human rights demonstrates the importance of politically relevant values to the functioning of a system of governance. While the days of nationalism may now be waning in Europe, liberal democracy, born as nationalism's twin (1789-1848 was the period of gestation), still seems to have a long and assured future. The observance by governments of individual rights is one of the two defining characteristics of liberal democracy (majority decisions being the other one). These are the common values the Council of Europe's human rights system is enforcing, and these are the values that those who espouse liberal democracy, from Burma to China to Nigeria to Serbia are asking their governing elites to observe. This ideology and its values have become so universally accepted – even those who manifestly advocate other types of governance do so in the name of democracy – that some have absurdly claimed that liberalism is the final ideology, the political heaven from which there can be no more progress. This writer would not make such a prediction, but will predict that liberal democracy will become more widely adopted before its star begins to wane. This is the common value system and the common ideology which forms the basis of European politics.

There seems little need, therefore, for the EU to pursue the chimera of a common cultural policy. The great majority of its peoples of have the common politically-relevant value system of liberal democracy. This value system includes the value of individual human rights – that is, persons have rights *not* because they are citizens of a certain state, or are members of a nation, or of Europe, as a state writ large, but because persons affected by governmental decisions are humans whose lives and rights the governing elites ought to respect as they do their own. "People ... must be respected as people, not treated as political components" (Ward 1997, p.92; Sørenson 1996, pp.20-21). This separation of politically relevant and other values cultural values, incidentally, provides a formula whereby immigrants can maintain many elements of their culture while participating in the political life of their new country (Habermas 1992, p.17).

It is time for the European Union's leaders to act in accordance with what they probably know but do not always say – that the Union is not a political system like that of the nation-states and is not likely to become one. The nation-state system is that of an age which is coming to an end. The European Union and its leaders pride themselves on building a system for the future. A new political system will, of course, draw on the one that came before it. The core value most likely to be retained is not that of nationalism and national identity but that of democracy, political participation and human rights. Whereas nationalism may at last be approaching the absurd conclusions to which its logic leads, democratic values have not yet achieved their maximum potential.

So the leaders of the European Union would be well advised to abandon the model of the nineteenth century nation-state and the policies that twentieth century states, such as Canada, Ireland and Luxembourg, have adopted in an attempt to achieve that nineteenth century ideal. Instead, they should turn their attention to a more purely political policy puzzle: how can Europeans create a political system that combines the best of democratic control and human rights with the most efficacious of political decisions?. More specifically, how can democratic control become meaningful and effective in a world where economic decisions require ever wider geographic spheres while cultural expression often returns to regional and local levels? Much has been written about multi-layered political systems and the multiple identities of individuals; more has been said and written about Europe's democratic deficit. The European Union's complex, multi-level political system provides a good starting point for the creation of a political system through which individuals can express the "range of identities" Europeans now enjoy. According to Cram, Europe's leaders need not hunger after the "hot" nationalism of previous generations, which in any case, brought Europeans to grief. They should be content with the "banal" nationalism which combines an awareness of being European with loyalty to region and nation. Ward (1997, p.90), citing Frug, claims that only the "radical decentralization of administrative power" can empower the individual; the Union's concept of subsidiarity would appear to be a good beginning for planning such an empowerment (Meehan 1993, pp.155-159; Cram 2001, pp.237-239). Yet little practical work has been done on designing and establishing the overlapping and multi-layered political systems that can bring democratic control to various levels of governance. That could become the European Union's next cultural project.

### Notes

1   I should like to thank Glen Norton, a PhD student in political theory for lots of help with editing and updating this chapter. Glen did a great a great job and managed to become an EU specialist almost overnight.
2   Another issue, not germane to this paper, but certainly worth investigating is: Who benefits from the identification of the citizen with the state, the elites or the citizens?
3   I thank my friend and colleague Graeme Mount of Laurentian University for much of the research and some of the writing of the following two sections. E. Mahant, Are National Cultures and Identities and Optional Extra, Paper read to the Canadian Association for American Studies, Toronto, October 1996, where he spoke on the historical antecedents of the cultural policies of the three states discussed here.
4   Only recently have academics, and to a lesser extent the European political leaders themselves, imagined and tried to implement forms of governance which really do leave the nation-state model behind. The work of Liesbet Hooghe and Gary Marks (2001) on the concept of multilevel governance is particularly interesting in this respect.

### References

*About Telesat: A History of World Firsts* [online] 2003, Available:
   http://telesat.ca/eng/about_history.htm (Accessed 23 Jan. 2003).
Acheson, K. & Maule, C. 2001, *Much Ado About Culture*, University of Michigan Press, Ann Arbor.
*Annual General Report of the Activities of the European Union 1994*, July 25, 1996, untitled press release of the European Union No. 217-G.
*Annual General Report of the Activities of the European Union. 1995*, untitled press release of the European Union.
*Annual General Report of the Activities of the European Union. 1996*, untitled press release of the European Union.

Audley, P. 1994, "Cultural Industries Policy: Objectives, Formulation and Evaluation,"
     *Canadian Journal of Communication* [online] vol.19, no.3-4, Available:
     http://cjconline.ca/title.php3?page=4&journal_id=18&document=1 (Accessed 2 Feb 2003).
Austen, I. 1996, "Culture Between Commercials," *Canadian Forum* [online]
     Available:http://www.mediaawareness.ca/eng/issues/cultural/resource/austen.htm
     (Accessed 2 Feb 2003).
Barbrook, R. 1992, "Broadcasting and National Identity in Ireland," *Media Culture and
     Society*, vol. 14, no. 2, pp. 203-27.
Bossaert, D. 1992, *Das Großherzogtum Luxemburg*, Universitätsverlag Dr. N. Brockmeyer,
     Bochum.
Brown, T. 1987, *Ireland: A Social and Cultural History*, Fontana, London.
*Budget by Policy Area* [online] 2002, The European Union On-Line, Available:
     www.europa.eu.int (Accessed 23 Jan. 2003).
Calmes, C. 1989, *The Making of a Nation*, Paul, Luxembourg.
Canadian Radio and Telecommunications Commission, 1991, *Annual Report 1990/91*,
     Ottawa, Canada.
Chubb, B. 1982, *The Government and Politics of Ireland*, Stanford University Press,
     Stanford.
Closa, C. 1995, "Citizenship of the Union and Nationality of Member States," *Common
     Market Law Review*, vol. 32, pp. 487-518.
Clyne, M. 1995, *The German Language in a Changing Europe*, Cambridge University
     Press, Cambridge.
Comerford, R.V. 1989, "Nation, nationalism and the Irish Language," in *Perspectives on
     Irish Nationalism*, eds T. Hachey and L. McCaffrey, University Press of Kentucky,
     Lexington, pp.21-40.
Commission of the European Communities 29-30 May 1996, "Opinion on the Proposal for a
     Council Decision on the adoption of a multi annual programme to promote the linguistic
     diversity of the Community in the information society," Brussels.
Commission of the European Communities 8 July 1996, "Amended Proposal for A
     European Parliament and Council Decision Establishing a Community Action
     Programme in the Field of Cultural Heritage," The Raphael Programme, Brussels.
Commission of the European Communities 12 July 1996, "Communication from the
     Commission to the European Parliament on the Council common position on the
     proposal establishing a support programme in the field of books and publishing" The
     Ariane Programme, Brussels.
Cram, L. 2001, "Imagining the Union: A Case of Banal Europeanism," in *Interlocking
     Dimensions of European Integration*, ed. H. Wallace, Palgrave, Basingstoke, pp.231-
     246.
*Cultural/Audiovisual Affairs* [online] 5 Nov. 2001, European Union 2381st Council
     Meeting,Brussels,Available:http://ue.eu.int/Newsroom/LoadDoc.asp?MAX=1&BID=92
     &DID=68667 &LANG=1 (Accessed Jan.15, 2003).
Delegation of the European Commission 25 Feb. 1992, *European Community News* [press
     release] no.(92)4, Ottawa.
Delegation of the European Commission 17 March 1994, *European Community News* [press
     release] no.(94)7, Ottawa.
Deutsch, K. 1963, "Some Problems in the Study of Nation-Building," in *Nation-Building*,
     eds K. Deutsch and W. Foltz, Atherton Press, New York, pp. 1-16.
Deutsch, K. 1980, *Politics and Government: How People Decide their Fate*, Houghton
     Mifflin, Boston.
Directive 97/36/EC of the European Parliament and of the Council of 30 June 1997, *Official
     Journal of the European Commission*, No.1, 202/60.

Dowler, K. 1997, "The Cultural Industries Policy Apparatus," in *The Cultural Industries in Canada*, ed. M. Dorland, J. Lorimer & Co., Toronto, pp.328-339.

*Draft Treaty Establishing a Constitution for Europe* [online], 13 June and 10 July 2003, ArticleIII-181, Available:
http://europa.eu.int/futurum/constitution/part3/title3/chapter5/section3/ind ex_en.htm (Accessed Dec.15, 2003).

Easson, A. 1990, "The Courts of Justice of the European Communities," *Journal of European Integration*, vol.14, no.1, pp.65-76.

"EOS Gallup Europe," July 1995, Flash *Eurobarometre*, no.47, pp.21-25.

*Ètablissant le programme "Culture 2000"* 14 février 2000, Décision no. 598/2000/CE du Parlement européen et du Conseil, Journal officiel no. L603 du 10/03/2000 pp.0001-0002. (DOCI -32000D0508-bas-clx).

"European Opinion Research Group," 24 May 2002, *Eurobarometre* 2002 – Edition spèciale.

"Audiovisual Policy: Mid-Term Review of MEDIA Programme Recommends Adaptations," *European Report*, 29 Nov. 2003.

Gestrin M. and Rugman A. 1993, "The NAFTA's Impact on the North American Investment Regime," *C.D. Howe Institute Commentary*, no.42.

Gibbons, L. 1988, "From Megalith to Megastore: Broadcasting and Irish Culture," in *Irish Studies: A General Introduction*, eds T. Bartlett et al, Gill and Macmillan, Dublin, pp.221-234.

Group of the European People's Party 1995, European Parliament, Cultural Europe, Bruges Study Days, *European Digest*.

Gouvernement du Grand Duché de Luxembourg. Lancement du site www.filmfund.lu. http://www.gouvernement.lu/gouv/fr/act/0204/15biltgen.htm (Oct. 23, 2002)

Habermas, J. 1992, "Citizenship and National Identity: Some Reflections on the Future of Europe," *Praxis International*, vol. 12, no. 1, pp.1-19.

Harrison, L.E. 1997, *The Pan-American Dream*, Basic Books, New York

Hedetoft, U. 1990, "Euro-Nationalism: or How the EC Affects the Nation-State as a Repository of Identity," *European Studies* (Aalborg), no.1.

Henighan, T. 1996, *The Presumption of Culture: Structure, Strategy and Survival in the Canadian Cultural Landscape*, Raincoast Books, Vancouver.

Hix, S. (1999) *The Political System of the European Union*. St. Martin's, New York.

Hjavard, S. 1993, "Pan-European Television News: Towards a European Political Sphere?" in *National Identity in Europe*, ed. P. Drummond, British Film Institute, London, pp.71-94.

Hooghe, L. and Marks, G. 2001, *Multi-Level Governance and European Integration*, Rowman & Littlefield, Lanham.

Hutcheson, J. 1987, *The Dynamics of Cultural Nationalism: The Gaelic Revival and the Creation of the Irish Nation State*, Allen & Unwin, London.

Hutchinson, D. 1996, "The Atlantic Gulf of Comprehension: Current European Reposes to American Media Imperialism," paper read to the Annual Conference of the Canadian Association for the American Studies, Toronto.

*Journée européenne des langues* [online] 2002, Le Gouvernement du Grand-Duché-de-Luxembourg,Available:http://www.gouvernement.lu/salle_presse/communiques/2002/0 9/26langues/index.html (Accessed 23 Oct. 2002).

Keogh, D. 1995, *Twentieth-Century Ireland: Nation and State*, St. Martin's Press, New York.

"L'audiovisuel européen," 1995, *Label France*, Jan., no.18, pp.16-17.

Laffan, B. 1996a, "The Politics of Identity and Political Order in Europe," *Journal of Common Market Studies*, vol.34, no 1, pp.81-102.

Laffan, B. 1996b, The Intergovernmental Conference and the Challenge of Governance in the European Union, Paper prepared for the European Community Studies Association Conference, St. Catherine's, Canada.

*Lancement du site www.filmfund.lu et présentation du rapport annuel du Fonds national de soutien à la production audiovisuelle* [online] 2002, Le Gouvernement du Grand-Duché de Luxembourg, Available:
http://www.gouvernement.lu/salle_presse/actualite/2002/04/15biltgen/index.html (Accessed 23 Oct. 2002).

Liesbet Hooghe and Gary Marks, *Multi-level Governance and European Integration*. Lanham: Rowan & Littlefield, 2001.

Lorimer, R. 1992, "T.V., Radio and Film: Government Support for Culture," *Social Policy*, vol. 23, no. 1, pp.73-79.

MEDIA Programme of the European Union [online] 2003, Available:
http://www.europa.eu.int/comm/avpolicy/media/index_en.html (Accessed 27 Jan 2003).

Meehan, E. 1993, *Citizenship and European Community*, Sage Publications, London.

Merrills, J.G. and A.H. Robertson, 2001, *Human rights in Europe. A Study of the European Convention on Human Rights*, Juris Publishing, Manchester.

Murphy, J. A. 1988, *Ireland in the Twentieth Century*, Gill and Macmillan, Dublin.

Newcomer, J. 1984, *The Grand Duchy of Luxembourg*, University Press of America, Lanham.

O'Domhnallain, T. 1977, "Ireland: The Irish Language in Education," *Language Problems and Language Planning*, vol. I, p.84.

"Renaissance in Letzeburgesch," 1992, *Europe* (Washington), June, p.37.

Salutin, R. 1988, "Keep Canadian Culture Off the Table – Who's Kidding Who?" in ed. L. LaPierre, *If You Love This Country: Facts and Feelings on Free Trade*, McClelland and Stewart, Toronto, pp.205-211.

Schroen, M. 1986, *Das Großherzogtum Luxemburg*, Universitätsverlag Dr. N. Brockmeyer, Bochum.

Schwanen, D. 1997, "A Matter of Choice: Toward a More Creative Canadian Policy on Culture" [online] *C.D. Howe Institute*, Commentary 91, Available:
http://www.media-awareness.ca/eng/issues/cultural/resource/schwanen.htm (Accessed 2 Feb. 2003).

Smith, A. 1992, "National Identity and the Idea of European Unity," *International Affairs*, vol. 68, no.1, pp.55-76.

Sørensen, J. M. 1996, *The Exclusive European Citizenship*, Avebury, Aldershot. Standing Committee on Canadian Heritage. *Our Cultural Sovereignty: The Second Century of Canadian Broadcasting*. Clifford Lincoln, M.P., Chair. June 2003.

Tawfik, M. 1994, "The Secret of Transforming Art into Gold: Intellectual Property Issues in Canada-U.S. Relations," *Canadian-American Public Policy*, no.20.

"The New 'Television without Frontiers' Directive," 23 June 1997, DN MEMO 97/63.

Treaty Establishing the European Community, 10.11.1997, Official Journal, C340 (EUR-Lex – Treaties – consolidated).

Trudeau, P. E. 1968, *Federalism and the French Canadians*, Macmillan, Toronto.

Ward, I. 1997, "Law and the Other Europeans," *Journal of Common Market Studies*, vol. 35, no. 1, p.79-96.

Weber, N. 1994, "Sprachen und ihre Funktionen in Luxemburg," *Zeitschrift für Dialektologie und Linguistik*, vol. 61, no. 2, pp.148-151.

Chapter 10

# The Politics of Inclusion and Exclusion: Immigration and Citizenship Issues in Three Democracies

Geneviève Bouchard and William Chandler

## Introduction

Immigration and citizenship policies, by defining entry (who gets in) and membership (who belongs), set the human boundaries of any political order (Brubaker 1992, ix-xi). Both issues have become increasingly divisive within advanced democratic orders and have provided intriguing terrain for consideration of the linkage between policy and politics. This research explores the extent and nature of political and policy change in this sector by comparing developments within France, Germany and Canada.

A working framework for this investigation is presented in Figure 10.1, which schematically identifies potential linkages between migration patterns, political response and policy.

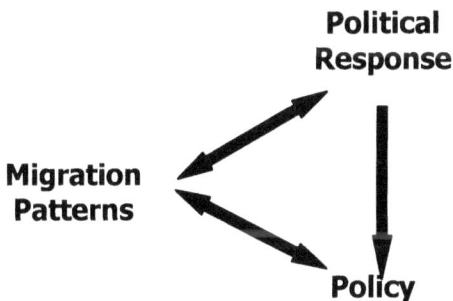

**Political Response**

**Migration Patterns**

**Policy**

**Figure 10.1   National Traditions**

Nations differ in their values and approaches to the initial entry and ultimate inclusion of foreigners.  The most basic distinction is between states of net in-migration and states of net out-migration, but within these two categories, we find mixed patterns of immigration/ emigration.  Freeman distinguishes between three national traditions: settler societies (e.g., the U.S., Canada, Australia), recent mass migration states (including France, Germany and other northern European states) and traditional sending states (e.g., Ireland, Italy, Spain, Portugal, and Greece), some of which have recently begun to experience their own immigration. He hypothesizes that settler nations will be "relatively immune to sharp swings in direction," whereas in the European nations which only in the post-war era have become lands of mass immigration, the political consequences will be "highly volatile and conflictual" (1994, 881).

Canada, as a settler nation, was created by immigrants and constitutes a classic land of immigrants in which the transition from immigrant to citizen is expected and routine. This national experience (in which all but indigenous peoples claim ancestry from immigrants) appears at first glance to contrast sharply with the traditions of both France and Germany, which historically have been largely non-receiving countries. However, a closer look shows surprising similarities between France and Canada and sharp differences between the French and German traditions. Both Canada and France are marked by high degrees of openness with respect to both immigration and citizenship, whereas Germany, with a strong heritage of emigration, has lacked an explicit immigration policy and has maintained, until recently, high barriers to obtaining citizenship.

Among European states, France exhibits a distinctive pattern of very limited emigration complemented by a relatively long tradition of immigration. From the middle of the nineteenth century, industrialization combined with a low birth rate generated a need for foreign labour. In 1850 the share of immigrants in the population was only 1 percent, but this rose to about 6.6 percent by 1931. France's legacy of empire and colonialism also shaped modern immigration and citizenship issues. In the post-war era, both the level and composition of immigrants have changed considerably. (See appendix 1: Evolution of the immigrant population in France, 1921-1999.)

The German experience has been fundamentally different. For hundreds of years, the rural and pre-industrial Germanic territories/states were sources of emigration. This began to change with late nineteenth century industrialization, which created a need for migrant workers from the east (Martin 1994, 197), but even into the twentieth century, Germany, unlike France, remained an exporter of people. However, post-1945, the Allied zones of occupation attracted millions of refugees forced from their homelands in the eastern territories taken over by Soviet forces (Frantzioch-Immenkeppel 1996, 3-4). Moreover, in direct reaction to the political persecution and genocide of the Third Reich, the 1949 Basic Law of the Federal Republic (the country's constitution, written by the Allies) established its openness to refugees. Within a few years, as economic recovery took hold, the recruitment of non-German temporary or "guest" workers and de facto immigration began to meet labour shortages.

The three countries can also be distinguished by their underlying assumptions about social integration. The French Republican universalist model proposes open citizenship rules complemented by official assimilation, a combination that presumes anyone can become French without allowing for cultural distinctiveness. Canada, by contrast, has opted for a multicultural approach to integration, while German law has officially rested on the principle that Germany is not a land of immigration.

Citizenship policy may be distinguished by degrees of inclusiveness and exclusiveness, evident in the legal requirements for naturalization. National cases can be compared in terms of three general conditions: birthright, naturalization and dual citizenship (see Table 10.1). In France, the rather open procedures for citizenship limit governmental control on expansion of the non-French population. Children born in France to non-French parents have the right to citizenship, which, under the new law, become automatic at 18 years of age. Canada, on the other hand, offers citizenship to children of non-Canadian parents without conditions.

**Table 10.1      Types of Citizenship**

|  | **France** | **Germany** | **Canada** |
|---|---|---|---|
| Basis of Birthright | Blood and soil | Blood only but reform of 2000 established both rights | Blood and soil |
| Naturalization | Low barriers (minimum 5 years) | High barriers, reduced in 2000 reforms. (8 years – previously 15 years) | Routine process (minimum 5 years) |
| Dual citizenship | Yes | Only exceptionally, until the reform of 2000 | Yes |

In both Canada and France, obtaining citizenship by naturalization is common. By contrast, the definition of who is a German traditionally has been restrictive. Neither German citizenship law nor common citizenship existed until the 1913 Reichs- und Staatsangehörigkeitsgesetz.  In the nation-building context, the original spirit of this law was fundamentally inclusive because it created a single citizenship for all German peoples from diverse cultures, regions and previously independent jurisdictions. However, it also defined citizenship by ancestry (jus sanguinis). In the modern context, the effective significance of this law became one of closure.

Constitutional provisions governing immigration, human rights and citizenship provide the formal foundations shaping issues and policy. All three nations protect basic human rights and subscribe to the principles of the Geneva Convention on asylum and refugees but have differed in operational treatment of asylum-seekers and refugees.

In the German case, inclusive humanitarianism has had two facets. The urgency of the post-war integration of expellees (Vertriebenen) and the post-Nazi moral obligation to provide refuge to those suffering from political persecution were at the base of its openness to asylum-seekers and refugees. The founders of the Federal Republic sought to offer indirect moral compensation for the violations of human rights during the Third Reich by guaranteeing the right of asylum to individuals seeking refuge from political persecution elsewhere. Article 16 of the Basic Law obliges Germany to consider claims for asylum and to permit those who satisfy the criteria to remain in Germany. This exceptionally liberal policy contributed to making Germany the most attractive and open state in Europe. From 1990 to 2000, 1,958,350 applications for asylum were initiated in Germany, with France far behind and coming fourth after the U.K. and the Netherlands with only 336,630 applications during the same period (UNHCR).

Institutional factors, especially federal arrangements, may also influence immigration politics. In the case of Canada, immigration is a joint jurisdiction (Constitution Act, 1982, section 95). However, since the beginning of the confederation, immigration has been considered primarily the responsibility of the federal government. All provinces accepted federal pre-eminence, even Quebec, until 1960. With the beginning of the "Quiet Revolution" in Quebec, the provincial government set as its two main objectives the control over the selection of immigrants and responsibility for the integration of immigrants into Quebec society. After years of intergovernmental tension, Quebec obtained the full responsibility for the selection and integration of immigrants in 1991 (Canada-Quebec accord). In German federalism, the Länder have a significant administrative role in financing and regulating foreign residents and refugees.

**Policy-Politics Linkages**

Historically, emigration and immigration were consequences of war, famine, labour needs or economic opportunity rather than intended public policy. Eighteenth and nineteenth century migrations occurred largely without governmental management or control and often prior to formal citizenship (Hollifield 1994, 145-6). The expanding capacity of modern nation-states to control borders and manage economies meant that such movements gradually became public policy concerns. Policy, either as conscious strategy or as reactive response, emerged after the immigration occurred. Until recently, immigration and citizenship have remained submerged issues, ranking low in public awareness, and therefore have been handled routinely through legal and administrative procedures.

However, as the volume and character of in-migration have shifted, mass publics in most immigrant-receiving countries have become increasingly sensitive both to the concrete implications of immigration (such as the costs of housing, education and social services) and to the more symbolic/emotive effects (especially perceived threats to national identity and the uncertain implications of a multicultural society).

In the post-war era, European policy trends have varied. Devastation in WWII briefly prompted massive population movements, but borders closed quickly, preventing east-west migrations, as the Yalta Cold War division became reality. In-migration expanded as part of the post-war economic recovery, with the early demand/pull dynamic driven by labour shortages. Workers predominantly from southern Mediterranean regions were recruited on short-term bases, often with the expectation of rotation and return. This pattern provoked neither popular reaction nor political backlash.

However, the 1973-74 OPEC oil crisis ended the "economic miracle" phase of European recovery and growth, and led to a period of stagflation marked by rising unemployment and signs of rust-belt decay in older industrial sectors. This critical turning point had direct consequences for immigration patterns as governments stopped active labour market recruitment. Although demand/pull factors ceased, many foreigners were already de facto permanent residents. Some labour recruitment did continue in seasonal sectors – agriculture and construction.

Demand-pull policies also had unanticipated consequences. Trans-national social networks helped sustain migration, notably in the form of family reunion and illegal immigration. Despite economic recessions, immigration has persisted at high levels, via refugee and asylum-seeker and illegal entrants. Governments have scrambled to redesign immigration policy. Policy shifted towards increasing priority on restricting legal immigration, combatting illegal entries including managing temporary refugee populations (Cornelius et al. 1994, 15-16). In both France and Germany, governments at first encouraged the return of foreign workers, but supply-push pressures increasingly undermined controllability. In the 1980s and 1990s, this dynamic has further intensified, accentuated by newly opened borders. The politicization of immigration and integration has correspondingly intensified (Baldwin-Edwards and Schain 1997, 8-9; Weil 1991).

## Policy Trends in Canada

The evolution of the modern Canadian immigration policy through l the end of the twentieth century comprises of four main periods. In the post Second World War era, Canada emerged as a dynamic industrial state that was principally concerned with accepting immigrants who would contribute to the growth of its population and to industrial development but who would not alter the essentially white European character of its population. The 1946-1962 period is, therefore, often portrayed as one of a discriminatory and illiberal immigration policy.

The second phase of the Canadian immigration policy, which began in the sixties, put an end to such racial discrimination and marked a turning point in the history of this country. Canada abandoned its exclusionary policy by introducing new immigration regulations in 1962 under the direction of Ellen Fairclough, the Minister of Immigration. From then on, immigration policy would be based on three major criteria: skills/contribution to the labour force, family reunion and compassionate considerations for refugees (Hawkins 1989, 641). At this time, Canada was the first of the three major receiving countries (Canada, Australia, and the U.S.) to replace its white immigration policy with a non-racist one. The adoption of the point system in 1967 also ensured that newcomers would be selected according to domestic labour-market requirements instead of discriminatory ones with respect to sex, colour, race, nationality and religion.

The third phase of immigration policy began in 1978 when the Canadian government adopted a new Immigration Act, replacing the inequities of the previous one. For the first time, this act confirmed "... the fundamental principles of Canadian immigration law: family reunion, non-discrimination, concern for refugees and the promotion of Canada's demographic, economic, social and cultural goals" (Hawkins 1989, 651). This new legislation also considerably reduced the amount of individual discretion allowed to immigration officers and attempted to institute more objective criteria for admission.

The nineties have witnessed a fundamental transformation in the direction of Canadian immigration policy. Without abandoning its fundamental principle of family reunion, immigration policy now tends to favour increasing the proportion of immigrants from the independent (economic) class. Thus, in addition to narrowing the definition of family class, the federal immigration plan of 1995-2000 focused on the financial costs of family immigration, and gave a higher priority to economic immigration. The most recent immigration statistics show that economic immigrants now constitute more than half of total in-immigration. This trend reflects the preoccupation of policy-makers to increase the percentage of economic immigration into Canada.

The Canadian immigration system has recently been under review. A first bill to attempt to reform the system (C-31) was presented to the House of Commons but died on the order paper when the 2000 federal election was called. A second bill (C-11) was accepted by the Senate, following pressure for quick approval from the then Minister of Immigration Elinor Caplan, who argued that Canada was in need of tougher regulations in the wake of the Sept. 11 terrorist attacks on the United States. Despite the fact that the new Immigration and Refugee Protection Act attempts to strike a better balance between encouraging the entry and admission of "good immigrants" and preventing "unwanted" immigration, it fully retains the fundamental intentions of the previous Immigration Act. The objectives of this new legislation include measures aimed at speeding up security screening of refugee claimants and streamlining deportation proceedings of persons designated as security risks. It also reduces the possible number of appeals and clarifies detention and deportation rules. While removing some appeal rights for non-citizens who are accused of serious crimes or are considered security risks and ordered deported, the new Immigration Act also opens a new level of appeal for refugee claimants called the Pre-Removal Risk Assessment.

Even with new legislation in place, criticisms in the country have not faded away. Some critics maintain that the new level of appeal combined with Charter rights will make it easier for people to get in and much more difficult to remove should their claim be rejected or that this new legislation will put a further strain on resources that are already insufficient. Moreover, the events of September 11 have quite significantly modified public perceptions about immigration in Canada. The linkage of border control problems to terrorism has lowered public tolerance vis-à-vis newcomers. A recent poll conducted by the Council for Canadian Unity, for example, shows that 45% of respondents feel Canada should accept fewer immigrants, up from 29% in spring of 2001. Another survey (by Léger Marketing) indicates that more than 80% of Canadians favour stricter immigration guidelines. The seriousness of the impact of the terrorist attacks on the World Trade Center and the Pentagon on public opinion toward immigration is not yet known but will certainly influence future policy decisions. In the aftermath of September 11, pressures for the greater harmonization of border controls and immigration procedures with those of the United States continue to mount as stories of border delays and reduced trade flows are publicized. There are many who argue that the current legislation does not go far enough to address security concerns and that what is needed is a North American security perimeter through which the movement of people would be regulated. The very concept of a common perimeter, however, remains only vaguely defined because it has quite different meanings among various stakeholders. While some understand it as involving complete harmonization of immigration, refugee, security and even labour mobility policies, others envisage it more narrowly, such as a sharing of security information and joint border controls. The ongoing debate on the necessity of a common security perimeter has given rise to deep differences of opinion within the political elite and the public in general and will certainly be an important issue for the next few years.

Recently, the Liberal government has taken some important steps toward harmonization. Canada and the United States have signed a Joint Statement of Cooperation and Border Security and Regional Migration Issues. This indicates that "Canada and American efforts will focus on deterrence, detection and prosecution on security threats, the disruption of illegal migration and the efficient management of legitimate travel through:

- Integrating Canadian officials on the US Foreign Terrorist Tracking Task Force;
- Visitor Visa policy review [harmonizing the list of countries which require a visa];
- Developing joint units to assess information on incoming passengers;
- Increasing the number of Immigration Control Officers overseas;
- Developing common biometric identifiers for documents;

- Developing a Safe Third Country Agreement; and
- Expanding the Integrated Border Enforcement Team (CIC)."

Following this agreement, a new bill was introduced in the Canadian Parliament in November 2002 in which Canada recognises that the United Stated is a safe third country. According to this agreement, refugee claimants who are trying to enter Canada through the United States will be sent back.

**Policy Trends in France**

After World War Two, French objectives were driven both by population goals and labour needs (Hollifield 1994, 147-8), but immigration was also shaped by decolonization and the traumatic effort to retain control over Algeria, officially an integral part of the French state. This crisis polarized France and under threat of a military takeover, and forced the French parliament to invite General de Gaulle to form an emergency government with the power to draft the constitution of the Fifth Republic. The struggle for Algerian independence culminated in the Evian accords of 1962 which resulted not only in Algerian sovereignty but in a massive repatriation of French settlers, the "pieds-noirs", with their reservoir of political resentment directed against North African migrants (many of whom had claims to citizenship) and against the Gaullist government in Paris. Coincidentally, the flow of migrants from the Maghreb and sub-Saharan Africans persisted over the next decades.

Prior to the 1970s, French immigration policy remained full of ambiguities. Policy change only began in earnest in 1974, as priorities shifted quickly to "suspend immigration and the recruitment of foreign workers, encourage as many workers as possible to return to their countries of origin, and integrate into society those foreigners and their families who had been working and living in the country for specifics periods of time" (Hollifield 1992, 74).

Efforts to curtail economic immigrants (many of whom were by this time illegal) increased in the late 1970s, although measures aimed at controlling such immigrants and tightening borders were largely ineffective. During this period, family and seasonal immigration replaced labour recruitment as the principal type of foreign migrant in Western Europe and especially in France. Moreover, because resident aliens were protected by civil and human rights, policies of zero immigration and forced return were ineffective or illegal.

In 1979 the government introduced two complementary bills to further restrict immigration. The Stoléru bill proposed discontinuing all permanent work permits. The Bonnet bill increased police powers of expulsion and detention of illegal immigrants for up to seven days. This provoked intense opposition in the National Assembly, leading to the withdrawal of the Stoléru bill (Ashford 1982, 282).

After the 1981 election, the socialist government significantly altered the policy orientation toward the treatment of foreign residents, stressing due process and seeking to expand efforts at social integration. New legislation extended the rights of foreigners and enacted a generous amnesty for illegal immigrants (resulting in 145,000 amnesty applications), reforms of residency and work permits, expansion of rights of association of foreigners and suppression of the Bonnet law on expulsion. A 1984 law on the"carte de dix ans" also regularized the status of refugees. The government further sought to establish greater control over illegal immigration. In this context, the treatment of foreigners became a higher policy priority than before and a partisan conflict over basic value issues ensued, intensifying with the involvement of civil rights groups, especially SOS-Racisme, in defence of minority/foreigner interests.

The 1986 elections brought defeat for the socialists and formation of a conservative Chirac government in the first-ever period of cohabitation. The foreigner question was now high on the policy agenda, with illegal immigration having become the most politically sensitive concern. Policy shifted sharply under interior minister, Charles Pasqua. The loi Pasqua of 1986 made entry of foreigners more difficult and their expulsion easier (Safran 1991, 235). Expulsions increased sharply by 1987. The government also introduced incentives for encourage foreigners to return to their native lands, although this turned out to be expensive and ineffective, with the notable side effect of encouraging Spaniards rather than North Africans to leave. The Socialists reclaimed the government after the 1988 elections and immediately rescinded the loi Pasqua with passage of the Rocard government's loi Joxe.

Economic recession, scandals and longevity in power had crippled the popularity of Mitterrand and his Socialist governments (under prime ministers Cresson and Bérégovoy) and led to the landslide victory for the conservative bloc (winning 484 of 577 seats) in the 1993 legislative elections. The RPR-UDF thus returned to power but again under cohabitation. The government of Edouard Balladur maintained immigration/ refugees/ illegals as high priorities, based both on public opinion and the need to block any further political advance of the anti-immigrant Front National (FN) under Jean-Marie Le Pen. Pasqua, returned as Minister of the Interior and sought to restrict further family reunification and to crack down on the problem of illegal immigrants (les clandestins). He labeled his restrictionist measures a "zero immigration policy." This involved specifically:

1. Revision of the Nationality Code to limit automatic citizenship for second generation immigrants by requiring children (between the ages of 16 and 21) of foreigners to file for naturalization and swear an oath of allegiance to the Republic. But this did not challenge the basic principle of jus soli, and its effects remained largely symbolic.
2. Reinforcement of police powers and restrictions on civil liberties of foreigners.
3. Restrictions on social benefits, including health care for illegal immigrants.
4. Increased police power to detain and deport illegals, increased powers to check the identity of "suspicious persons," and a one-year exclusion from French territory (declared unconstitutional).
5. Foreigners could no longer obtain citizenship automatically through marriage (declared unconstitutional).

6.      New restriction of family reunification (declared unconstitutional).

Warnings came from the Council of State, while the 1993 rulings of the Constitutional Council declared several provisions to be unconstitutional. All this led to a full-scale political debate over immigration and refugee policy (Hollifield 1994, 168-71). In 1995, Jacques Chirac succeeded Mitterrand as President of the Republic and appointed Alain Juppé prime minister. In the context of popular anxiety over "les clandestins," crime, and violence, the Juppé government introduced in 1997 a new exclusionary loi Debré, designed to control and expel illegal immigrants. Originally, the bill required that hosts record the departure of visa holders. This denunciation rule reminded many of Vichy collaborationist reporting of Jews and provoked protests and hot debate over a symbolically loaded change. The provision was withdrawn by the government, with most of the new law intact (certificate of entry, no automatic renewal of 10-year residency cards, police power to search workplaces for illegal employees). The law also included provisions intended to improve the troubled suburbs, and to ease rapid integration of immigrants through acceleration of naturalization, language training and job hunting

After Socialist Prime Minister Lionel Jospin took office in 1997, Patrick Weil, a specialist of migration, was asked to write a report titled "L'immigration et la nationalité." This "show(ed) openness toward the migration issue, but also confirmed some of the main tough laws of the previous government" (Ezra, 2000, 20). The Weil Report formed the basis for two new bills, one on immigration (the loi Chevènement) and one on citizenship (loi Guigou). Although those proposals were controversial and fed a bitter political debate, their adoption was facilitated by Jospin's large majority in the Assembly.

The new immigration law came into force in 1998 and aimed to control the influx of migrants more effectively while humanizing some of the French entry and residence procedures. It addressed such issues as visas, asylum, residence permits, mixed marriage, family unification and expulsion order. More specifically, this new legislation contained provisions maintaining the visa system but emphasized an obligation to justify refusal. It espoused a larger opening for certain categories of foreigners who do not represent a migration threat (e.g. people with personal or family ties in France, retirees and scientists). Furthermore, it expanded the right to asylum for freedom fighters (constitutional asylum) and for those who are threatened by civil society (territorial asylum). Inspired by the US visa provisions for highly skilled immigrants, the loi Chevènement also created a special status for scientists and scholars. Other measures aimed at easing the conditions of entry for certain highly skilled professional categories were introduced the same year.

The new French citizenship law also came into force in 1998. This allows children born in France of two foreign-born parents to apply for French citizenship at the age of 13 with parental approval if they can prove that they have resided in France for at least 5 years. Children who are between 16 and 18 years of age can apply for French citizenship without their parents' authorization. Second generation immigrants who are 18 years old will automatically become French unless they formally refuse French citizenship. Thus, the loi Guigou reinstates the right to automatic citizenship (for those of 18 of age), which was removed from the system a few years earlier with the Pasqua law.

This legislation, moreover, reduces the waiting period for non-French nationals who are married to French citizens and who want to apply for French citizenship from two to one years. The new law is also more flexible toward children born in France to parents born in Algeria before 1962, allowing them to automatically become French at birth.

In the 2002 presidential and legislative elections, popular concerns about internal security, crime and urban violence weighed heavily. The new Raffarin government's conservative majority immediately sought to take a strong hand in dealing with these fears. Minister of the Interior, Nicholas Sarkozy quickly took the leadership role. In terms of the internal problems associated with immigration, the social effects of urban poverty, including high crime and hygenic problems are most evident at the local level, where mayors are confronting everyday problems posed by growing settlements of les clandestins. They report "chauchemar" problems, with the biggest usually involving schools, which have experienced rapid increases in enrolments but without new financing. Some report enrolments of 90% foreigners (*Le Figaro* of 4-5 November 2002).

When Socialists were in government, they avoided controversy over immigration and social integration for fear of backlash. The conservatives, once again back in power as of 2002, have seen an opportunity to gain support among minority groups (and to embarrass their opposition) with Interior Minister Sarkozy having taken up some of the themes from the left. The question is is this will be short-lived symbolic politics or will it carry over into significant reforms? (Philippe Bernard, "L'immigration à front renversé", *Le Monde*, 30/10/02.)

**Policy Trends in Germany**

In Germany the official assertion that "Germany is not a country of immigration" has been contradicted by more than three decades during which the Federal Republic has taken in vast numbers of immigrants. The failure to recognize this in law has meant that there was neither a governmental strategy on entry nor a commitment to integration via citizenship. In the workplace, foreigners have enjoyed practical inclusion through the social protections of the welfare state.

Because of Germany's unique history and territorial changes, a separate body of law pertains directly to the entry, treatment and conditions of ethnic German expellees (Vertriebenen) and resettlers (Aussiedler). At war's end in 1945, some 12 to14 million were expelled from the Eastern European territories, resulting in an east-west migration of enormous proportions. Most of these forced migrants eventually settled in the British and American zones of occupation. They at first imposed a heavy burden on a devastated economy, but quickly integrated and became a vital force for economic recovery and consolidation of the Federal Republic after 1949.

The Gastarbeiter (guest worker) phase, running from 1955 to 1973, began with the recruitment of Italians to fill labour shortages in farming. As labour shortages also became evident in industry, the experiment with temporary labour importation expanded and became official policy through a series of governmental agreements between the Federal Republic and countries of origin. This recruitment presumed that such workers would be transient with rotation back to their lands of origin. As a consequence, policy was defined as a labour-market rather than an immigration matter, though in fact it led to permanent settlement. By 1964 one million guest workers had arrived (Meier-Braun 1995, 14-5; Weiner 1995, 52-5). As full employment ended with the economic stagflation of 1973-79, the government halted recruitment. This phase also marked the beginning of awareness of the need for policies of integration as family unification progressed. By the 1980s, an atmosphere of increasing tension forced a new governmental approach to laws governing foreigners. The social democratic-liberal coalition, in power until 1982, initiated a new emphasis on limitation. The new Christian democratic-liberal (CDU/CSU-FDP) majority encouraged foreign workers to return to their native lands but by and large failed to achieve the intended effect. Interior Minister Schäuble's reform of 1991 reinforced the halt on recruitment, while leaving loopholes for the filling of specific labour market shortages in selected sectors like construction. The legislation did slightly reduce the barriers to naturalization but did not deal with the question of dual citizenship.

## Asylum Policy Response

When the eastern borders of Germany opened in 1989-90, a new migration wave heightened public and governmental concerns. Existing restrictive policies on entry remained in place, while longstanding problems of the social integration of foreigners were heightened by new problems of absorbing asylum-seekers, refugees and ethnic German resettlers. Electoral advances by the extreme right, reflected preoccupation with abusers of the right to asylum (under Article 16 of the Basic Law) and generated overwhelming support for the revision of asylum policies. Because the amendment process of the Basic Law requires a two-thirds majority and because the SPD held majority control in the Bundesrat, inter-party agreement was essential. The CDU/CSU advocated significant restrictions on Article 16, as did the FDP, while also stressing the need for Europe-wide solutions. Initially, the SPD opposed this but was also anxious to avoid an unpopular stance on an emotive issue.

After long negotiations, an inter-party draft agreement was reached in December 1992. Despite strong partisan differences, a substantial policy compromise was achieved reasonably quickly. Contrary to expectations of blockage, party politics did not produce the anticipated quagmire – rather the German policy process has proved "remarkably flexible"(Henson and Malhan, 134). Under the new law, the right to asylum from political persecution remains, but with three provisions designed to curb the volume and its abuse:

1. The third state rule: The right to asylum may only be granted provided the applicant did not arrive via some "secure" third country. This proviso was the most stringent feature of the change because it allowed for sending refugees back to safe countries. Both the Bundestag and Bundesrat passed this legislation by the end of May 1993 (Martin 192-3).
2. The nation of origin rule: Citizens from nations judged to be secure can be rejected, unless they can prove persecution.
3. The airport rule: Citizens from secure nations or those with false or incomplete documents are subject to on-the-spot trial proceedings that can result in expulsion within days.

Measures also were taken to speed up the application process. The new restrictions immediately reduced the influx of asylum-seekers and by early 1994, there was a 70% decline from the same period for the previous year. The number of applicants declined further through 1995-97 to moderate levels of just over 100,000 per year and correspondingly popular concerns dissipated.

## Ethnic German Migration

From 1989-91, an inflow of almost 1 million ethnic Germans (including Volga Germans, German-origin minorities from Romania, the Baltic states and other parts of Central Europe) began to alarm Bonn and prompted initiatives to control the outflow of an anticipated 5 million ethnic Germans with claims to citizenship (under Article 116). The government's response included both new regulatory measures and treaties with several Central European and ex-Soviet republics. The new 1993 law included a quota and queue system restricting the total of ethnic Germans to 225,000 annually. It also limited development assistance, and language training for entrants (Martin 1994, 216-7). In addition, accords were negotiated with several eastern states, for example, the 1996 agreement with Kazakhstan, to encourage ethnic Germans not to migrate.

## Refugee Policy

Protection against political persecution remains a constitutional principle, but the post-unity context tested both the limits on public tolerance and the capacity of German governments to absorb large numbers of refugees. Ethnic warfare in the former Yugoslavia provoked an exceptional humanitarian crisis. In this event, Germany quickly became the primary haven for refugees. By 1994, financial strain and shortage of housing were creating pressure for returning them, but few were actually deported. However, the subsequent inflow of largely Muslim Bosnian refugees, prior to the Dayton Agreement, further strained social services and housing. Fearing eventual backlash, both federal and regional governments sought to encourage and/or oblige these refugees to leave, but with only limited success.

In 1996, the Minister of the Interior introduced a policy permitting the deportation (in stages) of many of the 320,000 Bosnian refugees, and the 16 Länder, who bore most of the costs, agreed to begin returning refugees starting in 1996. However, given the unstable situation in Bosnia, a de facto moratorium was extended until April 1997. With no place for returning Bosnians to go, this provoked appeals for delay from many leading political figures. The policy of forcible return became a public relations nightmare for the government.

## Citizenship

The traditional vision of German national identity has been that of a cultural/ethnic community in which ancestry takes precedence over birthplace. Naturalization remained uncommon, although not prohibited. Of those who initially entered as temporary workers, most eventually chose permanent residence, but very few became citizens. The closed nature of German citizenship precluded any well-defined policy objective of social integration. For historical reasons, the Basic Law (Art 116, 1) also contains special inclusive provisions that secure citizenship claims for ethnic Germans resident in former German territory as defined by the borders of 1937, and ethnic Germans and descendants (Martin 1994, 217; Weiner 1995, 53). The question of citizenship became politicized, especially after unification, by virtue of the social reality of a large foreign-born minority that remained constitutionally disenfranchised. An intense and ongoing partisan debate over citizenship opened up and is still not fully resolved. Although there were limited changes, easing obstacles to naturalization and acceptance of possible dual-citizenship status (Meier-Braun 1995, 22), the matter created an intense political stalemate that was confirmed in 1997 with Chancellor Helmut Kohl's rejection of the idea of dual citizenship.

In the 1998 federal election campaign, both the SPD and the Greens advocated a fundamental reform of citizenship law. The Red-Green 1998 governing agreement between the two parties included a commitment to a major reform of citizenship laws and was implemented without delay, once the coalition took office. The provisions in the proposed citizenship law addressed the issue of naturalization (Einbuergerung). Resident foreigners would have the right to apply for German citizenship after only 8 years' residence (far less than the previous 15). Juveniles under 18 with one parent living in Germany would be able to claim citizenship after 5 years. Children of foreigners, where one parent was born in Germany or arrived prior to age 14 will be entitled to citizenship from birth. The reforms also introduced the principle of dual nationality, under which children born of foreign parents in Germany would be able to obtain double citizenship if one parent has been born or has lived in or came to Germany prior to age 14. Although it became the primary focus of partisan controversy (leading to a Christian Democrat victory in the Land election in Hesse), the new law was adopted in the Bundestag on May 7, 1999 and was supported by both governing coalition parties and the FDP. The Bundesrat approval then followed two weeks later.

This reform fundamentally changed the restrictive 1913 citizenship law based on the descent (blood) principle, which is now complemented by the territorial (soil) principle. The settlement of the citizenship question left key aspects of immigration unresolved, though, as the debate shifted toward labour market needs. Demographic projections of a rapidly aging population foresaw a need for immigration to maintain the size of workforce. Warnings that Germany is not producing enough scientists and technical personnel from technological firms pointed to the need to attract foreign-born talent. In response to complaints that this shortfall could jeopardize Germany's economic competitiveness, Chancellor Schroeder announced a "Green Card" program intended to attract programmers and electronic engineers from outside the EU to work in Germany for up to five years. This proposal explicitly linked immigration and technological competitiveness. The political battle shifted away from whether more foreigners should be allowed to settle in Germany to how migration should be regulated. The Greens stressed that immigration policy should avoid fixed quotas and should accept immigrants on political and humanitarian grounds as well as for economic reasons.

In light of intense partisan controversy and public concerns, the government in 2000 appointed a commission to review the issue, chaired by former Bundestag president Rita Suessmuth (CDU). Both demographic and economic considerations provided the basis for the commission's report, which noted that without an increase in immigration Germany's population will likely decline from today's 82 million residents to about 60 million by 2050, and its workforce from 41 to 26 million. The shrinking and graying of the German population will have "undesirable effects" on the country's public finances, social welfare system and economy. The bipartisan commission presented its proposals in July 2001, saying that Germany needs as many as 50,000 immigrants per year. The recruitment of qualified workers should increase the labour supply, employment and thereby stabilize the financing of welfare and pensions. The commission further proposed a point system, inspired by the Canadian-Quebec selection systems, for assessing the applications of would-be immigrants. High academic or professional credentials and knowledge of German would maximize the chances of gaining permanent residency. The commission also recommended that holders of temporary work permits have the opportunity to apply for permanent residency once they have successfully established themselves in Germany. In August 2001, the Minister of the Interior, Otto Schily, introduced ground-breaking legislation that anticipated the need for more foreign workers and abandoned the tradition of preserving cultural homogeneity. However, the opposition CDU remained skeptical about the chances of reaching a consensus on how to deal with rejected asylum applicants and illegal aliens, as well as on the problem of criminality among Germany's foreign residents.

In an effort to resolve the issue prior to the 2002 elections, the Social Democrats and the Greens negotiated with the CDU/CSU to find a compromise acceptable to all parties. In anticipation of the need for CDU/CSU support in the Bundesrat, the government accepted many measures advocated by the Christian Democrats on tougher procedures for deportation, asylum, and compulsory integration courses for immigrants. On March 1, 2002, in a major step the proposal to regulate immigration to Germany, legalization was passed by a vote of 321 in favor and 225 against, with 41 members of Parliament abstaining. The law is designed to control immigration into Germany with an eye to the country's integration capacities and its economic and labour market conditions. The Bundestag vote split along clear party lines. It remained unclear whether the Bundesrat would ratify it, with the deciding vote in the hands of the SPD-CDU grand coalition in Brandenburg.

After months of wrangling, the Bundesrat culminated an intense debate by passing the country's first immigration law. However, when its president (Klaus Wowereit, the SPD mayor of Berlin) ruled that the vote from Brandenburg counted as support for the law, the CDU/CSU objected that the vote was unconstitutional because split votes are prohibited under Article 51 of the Basic Law.[1]

In preparation for the 2002 Bundestag election, the opposition CDU/CSU had the possibility of exploiting fears about unwanted immigrants, given the rancour over the new law. However, campaign organizers saw this as a risky strategy, and immigration issues were largely avoided in the campaign. By January 2003, the Constitutional Court ruled that the law was void by virtue of the irregular conditions under which the Bundesrat had approved it. The re-elected SPD-Green government faces the task of re-formulating the law. This requires a compromise with the opposition, which holds a majority in the Bundesrat.

## Politicization in Canada, France and Germany

The transformation of immigration and citizenship issues from routine administrative matters into controversial issues has intensified their partisan and electoral effects. Fears and insecurities have spread, and immigrants even if legal, are often unwanted (Cornelius et al. 1994, 5). However, political reactions and the corresponding pressure on government officials to adopt exclusionary controls have varied greatly (See Table 2). By comparison to European experience, immigration and citizenship in Canada have provoked only limited controversy, and partisan polarization has been largely absent.

The most significant exception is found in the distinctive bases of support for the Reform Party already evident in the 1993 election campaign (Nevitte et al. 1994-1995, 589). This party officially avoided explicit exploitation of anti-foreigner themes, but was widely seen as being intolerant of immigrants and minorities. The Canadian Alliance, which has grown out of the Reform Party and is now the Official Opposition of Canada, has adopted a similar policy toward immigrants and refugees. While recognizing Canada's obligation to support genuine refugees and immigration, this party stresses the importance of creating an immigration policy that is merit based and that will take into account Canada's economic needs. The Alliance is also, compared to other mainstream Canadian parties, stronger on security and deportation issues. In a policy document adopted in May 2002, it states, "non-citizens of Canada who are convicted of an indictable crime, or who are known to engage in serious criminal activity will be deported." (Canadian alliance, Policy Declaration) Further, the same document argues that, "To ensure fairness, we will quickly deport failed refugee claimants and illegal entrants, and will prosecute those who organize and profit from abuse of the system."

As noted earlier, the terrorist attacks on the World Trade Center and on the Pentagon have hardened the public's reaction toward immigrants in Canada. This, given American pressure for harmonization, will probably result in a stricter Canadian immigration policy. Already at the end of June 2002, a new and in some ways stricter Canadian policy came into force.[2] The safe third agreement, which was recently signed by Canada and its neighbors, fits into the same pattern. However, despite those facts, Canadian political parties have not yet acted in a way that would raise expectations that immigration would become, in the future, an important issue of any of these party platforms. In the same way, even if the Canadian provinces which assume a large part of the immigrants' integration cost (housing, health care, education etc) have complained, from time to time, about this increasing financial burden, immigration does not appear to be a key issue of any provincial party platform.

In France, beginning in the 1970s and continuing into the 1980s, political discourse over immigration and citizenship sharply divided exclusionary and inclusionary forces. The Front National, established in 1972, had remained a fringe group until the immigration issue gave it the chance to capitalize on public anxieties about "French identity" by stressing fears about an invasion of foreigners. The 1981-84 Socialist reforms (noted above) facilitated expression of immigrant claims but also focused public attention on the scale of illegal immigration and thereby unintentionally prompted a backlash and provided a foothold for the far right (Hollifield 1994, 163).

The FN experienced its first success in local elections in 1983, then in the European elections of 1984 in a negative economic context and a declining popularity of the Socialist government. These victories provided a breakthrough that the FN never relinquished (Perrineau 1989 41-62). In preparation for the 1986 legislative elections, the socialist coalition reinstituted proportional representation to prevent an electoral disaster for itself, but at the same time gave the FN an opportunity for national representation.

The Front National successfully crystallized anti-immigrant feelings with Le Pen, stressing "the unassimilibility of immigrants, the dangers of excessive cultural heterogeneity, the social strains and economic costs of immigration, and the prospect of Islamic fundamentalism and inter-ethnic strife" (Brubaker 1992, 76). In its program, the Front National advocated, "stopping all immigration, expelling foreign workers, and revising the nationality law to make it more difficult for the state to attribute citizenship to second-generation Algerian immigrants" (Hollifield 1992, 191).

A diffuse public antipathy against foreigners provided a platform for the FN to consistently win about 15% of the vote nationally. Elections between 1984 and 2002 have repeatedly demonstrated the persisting nature of the FN's core electorate and the electoral success of Jean Marie Le Pen has ensured that immigration would remain a source of polarization from which other parties could not escape. Urban areas with large foreign origin populations, including much of the largely communist industrial "Red Belt" around Paris, experienced increasing ethnic confrontations. Communal officials began pushing for exclusionary measures, including encouragement of temporary residents to return home. This marked a break with the PCF tradition of solidarity with (European) immigrant groups (Schain 1997, 261-4).   On the other side, inclusionary movements in defense of civil rights and minorities, such as S.O.S. Racisme, France Plus, FASTI (Federation of Associations of Solidarity with Immigrant Workers, GISTI (Group for Information and Support of Immigrant Workers) and MRAP (Movement against Racism) have sought to contain racism and to improve the image of immigrants by showing how these new comers are enriching French culture and economy (Hollifield 1992, 14).   The response of establishment parties, both to changing public perceptions and to changing patterns and levels of immigration, has also been critical to transforming the politics of immigration. Partly out of fear of the threat posed by the Front National, other  parties, notably the Gaullist RPR and other conservatives, have advocated a tightening of immigration controls and a more rigorous naturalization policy.

In February 1997, the surprising victory of the FN in Vitrolles outside Marseilles prompted new anxiety within governing circles, leading to the controversial loi Debré, passed March 1997.   The persisting centrality of the immigration issue again became obvious in the partisan battles between right and left during the 1997 legislative election campaign and more recently at the presidential election which placed Le Pen in second position on the first ballot.

In Germany, the arrival of millions of guest workers and their families spanning more than two decades produced surprisingly little public reaction. Although tensions surfaced in the 1980s, the "foreigner" question became particularly politicized in the 1990s with the opening of borders. A resurgent far right had surfaced in Germany at the end of the 1980s as the Republikaner (or REP), a splinter off the nationalist wing of post-war German conservatism, unexpectedly won 7.5% in Berlin and 7.2% in the European elections of 1989.   Following German reunification, the far right appeal evaporated, and the 1990 Bundestag election gave no reason to think a revival of extremism to be at all likely.

The euphoria of unification, however, faded when the shock effects of the eastern industrial collapse and the enormous costs of economic restoration in the new Länder became obvious.   Coincidentally, the collapse of the Iron Curtain allowed a sudden influx of asylum-seekers, peaking at some 438,000 in 1992. As numbers increased, the percent of those granted asylum declined (from about 19 percent in the 1980s to only 5 percent in the early 1990s).   Because the vast majority of those rejected remained in Germany without the right to work, they remained heavily dependent of welfare benefits.

Restrictions on employment failed to deter an influx that was driven by exogenous conditions.  This fueled the public's belief that asylum laws were being abused by "economic refugees" taking advantage of a constitutional loophole. There followed by a wave of attacks on foreigners, with the frequency of violence intensifying in both east and west.   During 1992 some 2,285 extremist attacks on foreigners were recorded.   The crisis atmosphere and the apparent incapacity of governments to respond to emergency conditions created a climate conducive to the nationalistic, racist appeals of extremist parties (Veen et al 1993, 13-21; Roth 1994; Kuechler 1993).

Running through much of the REP agenda were nativist slogans like "Germany for the Germans" and "The boat is full". Concretely, the party program advocated stopping asylum-seekers, stricter restrictions on citizenship and containment of housing and welfare costs associated with the influx of foreigners (Lepszy 1993, 101-6) The typical far right voters have been found disproportionately among younger males with low levels of education. Based on the 1992 Baden-Württemberg election, it is estimated that an amazing 40 percent of REP voters were blue-collar, often unskilled workers (Veen et al, 29-40; Minkenberg 1993; Saalfeld, 178 ). Only a minority of REP voters could be described as ideological extremists. An estimated two-thirds were populist protesters expressing frustration. Although the REP and French Front national share a potential for catch-all extremism, unlike the FN, support for the Republikaner faded by the mid-1990s.

Extremist outbursts notwithstanding, it is possible to overstate public hostility to foreigners. As opinion polls show, immigration/ asylum issues have not normally ranked at the top of popular concerns. (Politbarometer Reports, 1992-94). The salience of the Ausländer question peaked in 1992-93, and thereafter no significant swing towards extremism occurred. Resentment against asylum-seekers and foreigners must also be weighed against a broad public revulsion against brutality opinion data have shown that citizens accept the presence of foreigners as appropriate, although support for multi-cultural integration remains weak (Thränhardt 1994). Generally, support for extremist parties in Germany has proved to be sporadic and fragmented, especially when compared to its durability in neighboring countries (France, Austria, and Italy).

**Table 10.2**     **Politicization Patterns**

|  | **Mobilization** | **Polarization** |
|---|---|---|
| **France** | High salience, stable feature of political discourse (Question of identity, xenophobia) | Partisan Left-Right division, presence of strong anti-foreigner party |
| **Germany** | Momentarily high salience (xenophobia spe. 1991-1993, sporadic violent attacks against foreigners and eastern immigration) | Partisan divisions but capacity to compromise; failure of far right to establish a core |
| **Canada** | Low salience | Limited, a submerged issue, but basis of support for Reform Party |

**Interpretations**

Our survey of immigration and citizenship permits some preliminary interpretations regarding the consequences of trends in immigration policy for politics. A first obvious point is that this issue sector can no longer be confined to administrative agencies and closed ministerial decisions. Immigration and citizenship have moved from peripherality to centrality. Public opinion, parties and legislatures are now directly involved. An expanded transparency means greater visibility of immigration and citizenship, as political debate has widened. Our comparison also indicates that politicization of immigration and citizenship is more entrenched and has greater impact in some countries than in others. Generally in France, we see a pattern of political linkage along partisan lines. In Germany, where the governing majority remained stable from 1982 until 1998, policy shifts have been gradual. The watershed 1998 election brought to power a socialist-green coalition, marking a crucial turning point in immigration and citizenship policy. Its new agenda portended significant changes in citizenship and immigration laws

As mentioned earlier, Freeman's thesis stating that (1994,881) settler nations will be "relatively immune to sharp swings in direction", while nations, which only in the post-war era have become lands of mass immigration, will experience "highly volatile and conflictual" politics is confirmed by the difference between Canada and France. Policy change in Canada, compared to Europe, has remained relatively unaffected by exogenous or endogenous developments, and hence has experienced fewer and softer immigration shocks. The political effects in Germany, however, appear less conclusive with fluctuations in periods of political intensity. Consistent with the general proposition advanced by Cornelius, Hollifield and Martin, we also observe that public and elite perceptions of policy crisis may create pressure in favor of greater exclusionary instruments of control. It is also true, however, that such tendencies have been qualified/softened by national traditions and judicial/constitutional rulings that often have struck down measures expanding powers of state control. (For more details, see Jacobson, 1997 and Messina, 1995.)

Further, we note marked differences in the extent of public arousal. In France and Germany, immigration/citizenship has hit sensitive nerves. The French political debate has been particularly moralistic and filled with symbolic aspects touching on the threats to and nature of French identity. Divisions are deeply entrenched and directly represented in partisan polarization. The persisting centrality of the immigration issue is clear in the partisan controversy during the 1997 legislative election campaign and the 2002 presidential election. Germany, too, has experienced recent phases of popular anxiety in which symbols of identity have sparked debate, but partisan divisions have remained constrained, with the notable exception of the far right parties at the height of concern about asylum. Unlike France, nativistic reactions proved ephemeral. By 1997, German politics was increasingly preoccupied with rising joblessness, fears about a loss of competitiveness and the impending prospects of a European single currency, leaving little no space for debate about the status of foreigners.

In Canada, partisan polarization has been weak and symbolic effects have been hard to find. No party has made immigration a primary issue, and immigration has not surfaced as a significant point of debate in the 2000 Canadian parliamentary election. Despite the fact that there is no strong partisan politicization in Canada, the general public, mostly in bigger Canadian cities such as Toronto, Montreal and Vancouver, is becoming more and more anxious about immigration from non-traditional sources and its related cost (social services, housing, language courses etc.). A political willingness to attract more economic immigration while limiting family immigration and illegitimate refugee demands seem to characterize the actual and future governmental actions in Canada. The events of September 11 and the possible formation of a security perimeter could also push Canada towards more restrictive immigration policies.

We should also note that even if Germany, France and Canada have different history of immigration, we can foresee a beginning of convergence of immigration and citizenship policies even between the two contrasting German and Canadian cases. While the German immigration and citizenship policies are becoming more open, Canada's immigration policy is tending to take a more restrictive path. Despite the fact that important differences remain, this somewhat confirms Patrick Weil's thesis stating that "all stable, democratic nation states with immigrant populations have moved in the same legislative direction" (Weil, 2001, 34).

As September 11 has shown, no national system of immigration control can remain immune from international pressures. For France and Germany, European integration has established a unique and permanent external dimension to the politics of immigration. The founding principles of non-discrimination and free movement of peoples, enshrined in the 1957 Treaty of Rome, legitimize involvement in such matters, but in the first three decades, pressure for supranational policy development remained primarily within economic spheres.

In the 1980s, progress in completing the single market minimized or eliminated most internal non-tariff barriers. This facilitated an open labor market (although EU labour mobility remained far below levels found in the United States) and implied the eventual removal of internal borders. This was largely achieved through implementation of the Schengen Accords in the late 1990s. The TEU (Maastricht Treaty) cautiously advanced European authority to control migration flows with the establishment of the new policy domain of Justice and Home Affairs (Pillar 3). The Amsterdam Treaty and related EU summit decisions solidified this trend.

Additional impetus for Europeanization should be attributed to external developments. The opening of eastern borders produced unexpected waves of refugees and asylum-seekers fleeing economic distress and civil war. The tougher immigration controls in place by then also encouraged those seeking entry to take advantage of liberal asylum provisions. From the mid-1980s to the early 1990s, asylum applications rose tenfold (to 680,000 in 1992), with Germany accounting for 75 percent of the total. This new migration crisis exposed the need for a strengthening of external frontiers and increased pressure for stronger Euro-level instruments of control and a common Europe-wide policy response. Popular concerns over illegal immigrants, drug trafficking and organized crime served to heighten the political sensitivity of migration control issues.

In general, Europeanization has gradually made inroads, and there has been some convergence in national policies. However, the EU treaties provide a weak intergovernmental foundation for European responses to problems associated with trans-border population movements. The trend towards a Europe-wide policy has been consistently constrained by the strength of national interests in protecting their sovereignty in immigration and citizenship domains. This has prevented effective harmonization, cooperation and policing (Brubaker 1992, 21-7). As a result, the place of these issues on the European policy agenda remains unsettled. Migration pressures and their political consequence have become Euro-issues without, as yet, having produced Euro-solutions.

# Appendix 10.1

## EVOLUTION OF THE IMMIGRANT POPULATION
## IN FRANCE, 1921-1999

| YEAR | 1921 | 1931 | 1946 | 1954 | 1968 | 1975 | 1982 | 1990 | 1999 |
|---|---|---|---|---|---|---|---|---|---|
| Total population[1] | 38,798 | 41,228 | 39,848 | 42,781 | 49,756 | 52,599 | 54,296 | 56,652 | 58,521 |
| Immigrant population[2] | 1,429 | 2,729 | 1,986 | 2,293 | 3,281 | 3,887 | 4,037 | 4,166 | 4,310 |
| Immigrant population as % of total | 3.7 | 6.6 | 5.0 | 5.4 | 6.6 | 7.4 | 7.4 | 7.4 | 7.4 |

1. Residents in metropolitan France (thousands).
2. Immigrants in metropolitan France (thousands).

*Source*: INSEE, Population Census.

**EVOLUTION OF THE IMMIGRANT POPULATION
IN FRANCE, 1921-1999**

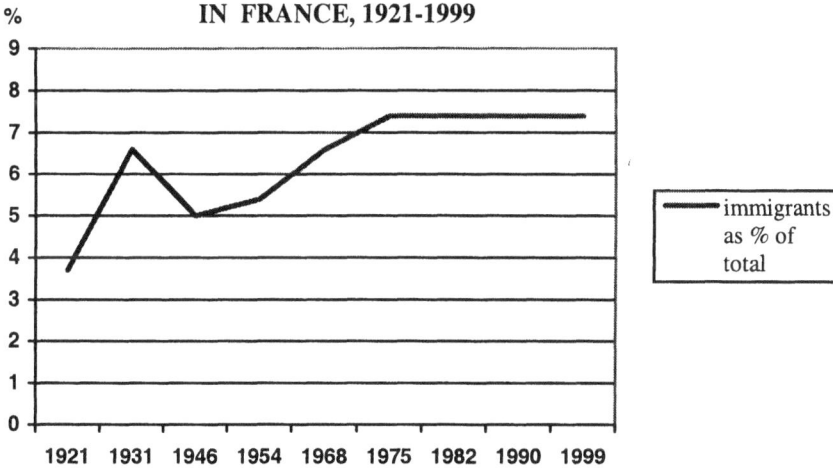

## Notes

1   Article 51 of the Basic Law stipulates that a state must cast its Bundesrat votes as a block. However, article 91 of the Brandenburg constitution indicates that the Minister-president represents his Land externally.
2   For instance, the new immigration and refugee act increases both arrest powers and inadmissibility grounds for refugees.


## References

Anderson, Christopher G, and Jerome H, Black. 1998. "Navigating a New Course: Liberal Immigration and Refugee Policy in the 1990s", in *How Ottawa Spends; Balancing Act: The Post-Deficit Mandate*, Toronto: Oxford University Press.

Ashford, Douglas E. 1982. *Policy and Politics in France; Living with Uncertainty*, Philadelphia: Temple University Press.

Atkinson, J. 1988. "Immigration in Two Federations: Canada and Australia", *International Migration*, 26, 1: 5-31.

Bade, Klaus. 1994. "Immigration and Social Peace in United Germany", *Daedalus*, 123, 1: 85-106.

Baldwin-Edwards, Martin. Martin A. Shain. 1997. "The Politics of Immigration: Introduction", *Western European Politics*, 17, 2: 1-16

Brubaker, Rogers. 1992. *Citizenship and Nationhood in France and Germany*, Cambridge: Harvard University Press.
http://www.canadianalliance.ca/yourprinciples/policy_declare/index.html

Citizenship and Immigration Canada. 1996. *Straying the Course* (1997: Annual Immigration Plan). Hull: Minister of Supply and Services Canada. http://www.cic.ca

Chandler, William M. "Danger on the Right? Assessing Extremism in United Germany." Paper presented for the Annual Meeting of the Canadian Political Science Association. 12-14 June 1994, Calgary.

Cornelius, Wayne A. Philip L. Martin. James F. Hollifield, eds. 1994. "Introduction: The Ambivalent Quest for Immigration Control", in Cornelius et al. *Controlling Immigration; A Global Perspective*, California: Stanford University Press.

Dirks, Gerald E. 1995. *Controversy and Complexity: Canadian Immigration Policy during the 1980s*, Montréal and Kingston: McGill-Queen's University Press.

Ehrmann, Henry W., Martin A. Schain. 1992. *Politics in France*, New York: Harper Collins Publishers.

Ezra, Esther. "The Undesired: Exclusion (and Inclusion) in Migration Policy-Making in Europe", *Revue des Affaires Européennes*, Vol. 1, no 2. (Avril 2000): 7-37.

Forschungsgruppe Wahlen, Politbarometer, Reports, 1992-96 (Mannheim).

France, http://www.brook.edu/fp/cusf/analysis/immigration.htm

Freeman, Gary P. 1994. "Modes of Immigration Politics in Liberal Democratic States". *International Migration Review*. 29: 881-902.

Frantzioch-Immenkeppel, Marion. 1996. "Die Vertriebenen in der Bundesrepublik Deutschland", *Aus Politik und Zeitgeschichte*. B28/96: 3-13.

García y Griego, Manuel. 1994. "Canada: Flexibility and Control in Immigration and Refugee Policy", in Cornelius et al. *Controlling Immigration:A Global Perspective*. California: Stanford University Press.

Hawkins, Freda.1989. "Canadian Immigration and Refugee Policies", in Painchaud, Paul, eds. *From Mackenzie King to Pierre Trudeau; Forty Years of Canadian Diplomacy 1945-1985*, Québec: Les Presses de l'Université Laval.

Henson, Penny and Nisha Malhan. 1995. "Endeavors to Export a Migration Crisis: Policy Making and Europeanization in the German Migration Dilemma", *German Politics*. 4, 3: 128-44.

Hollifield, James F. 1992. *Immigrants, Markets, And States; The Political Economy of Postwar Europe*, Cambridge: Harvard University Press.

Hollifield, James F. 1994. "Immigration and Republicanism in France: The Hidden Consensus", in Cornelius et al. *Controlling Immigration: A Global Perspective*. California: Stanford University Press.

Jacobson, David. 1997. *Rights Across Borders; Immigration and the Decline of Citizenship*. Baltimore and London: The Johns Hopkins University Press.

Kuechler, Manfred. 1993. "The Germans and the 'Others': Racism, Xenophobia, or Self-Defence?" Washington D.C., APSA Annual meeting.

Laghi, Brian. "Ottawa wants immigrants with better education", *Globe and Mail*, Toronto. 07/01/98: A1 and A5.

Le Moigne, Guy. 1995. *L'Immigration en France*, Paris: Presses Universitaires de France.

Lepszy, Norbert. "Die Republikaner", in Gerhard Hirsher. ed. *Represantative Demokratie und politishe Partizipation*, Munich: Hanns-Seidel Stiftung.

Lévesque, Lia. "Sondage Léger Marketing: Le Canada doit être plus sévère en matière d'immigration", *Le Devoir*, 5 novembre, 2001, A5.

Martin, Philip L. 1994. "Germany: Reluctant Land of Immigration", in Cornelius et al. *Controlling Immigration: A Global Perspective*, California: Stanford University Press.

McCarthy, Shawn. "Common currency Favoured in survey", *Globe and Mail*, November, 7, 2001, A10.

Meier-Braun, Karl-Heinz. 1995. "40 Jahre 'Gastarbeiter' und Ausländerpolitik in Deutschland", *Aus Politik und Zeitgeschichte*, B35/95: 14-22.

Messina, Anthony M. 1995. "Immigration as a Political dilemma in Britain: Implications for Western Europe", *Policy Studies*, 23(4): 686-698.

Ministère des Communautés Culturelles et de l'Immigration du Québec. 1991. Accord Canada-Québec Relatif à l'Immigration et à l'Admission Temporaire des Aubains. Québec: Editeur Officiel du Québec.

Minkenberg, Michael 1993, "The Far Right in Unified Germany", Washington, D.C., APSA annual meeting.

Nevitte, Neil, et al. 1994. "Electoral Discontinuity: The 1993 Canadian Federal Election", *International Social Science Journal*, 146: 584-599.

Opitz, Peter J. 1996. "Flucht, Vertreibung, Migration 1945-1995", *Aus Politik und Zeitgeschichte*, B44-45/96: 3-16

Perrineau, Pascal. 1989. "Les étapes d'une implantation électorale", in Mayer and Perrineau. *Le Front national à decouvert*, Paris: Presses de la Fondation nationale des Sciences Politiques.

Philip, Alan B. 1994. "European Union immigration Policy...", *Western European Politics*, 17, 2: 168-91.

Roth, Dieter. 1993. "The Volksparteien in Crisis? The Electoral Successes of the Extreme Right in Context", *German Politics* II, 1, 1-20.

Safran, William. 1991. *The French Policy*, New York: Longman.

Saalfeld, Thomas. 1993. "The Politics of National-Populism: Ideology and Policies of the German Republikaner Party", *German Politics* II, 2 (August), 177-199.

Schain, Martin. 1997. "Immigration and Politics", in Peter Hall et al., eds, *Developments in French Politics*, London: Macmillan, 253-68.

Thränhardt, Dietrich. 1994. *After the Guest Worker Age. Social, Economic and Political Citizenship for Immigrants in Germany*, Chicago, Europeanists' Conference.

Tiersky, Ronald. 1994. *France in the New Europe; Changing Yet Steadfast*, Belmont: Wadsworth Publishing Company.http://www.unhcr.ch

Veen, Hans-Joachim et al. 1993. *The Republikaner Party in Germany*, Westport: Preager.

Weil, Patrick. 1991. "Immigration and the Rise of Racism in France: The Contradictions in Mitterrand's Policies", *French Politics and Society*, 9, 3-4, pp. 82-100.

Weil, Patrick. 2001. "The history of French nationality: a lesson for Europe", in *Towards a European Nationality*, New York: Palgrave Publishing.

Weil, Patrick. 2001. "Access to Citizenship: A Comparison of Twenty-Five Nationality Laws", in *Citizenship Today: Global Perspective and Practices*, Washington: Brooking Institution Press.

Weiner, Myron. 1995. *The Global Migration Crisis, Challenge to States and Human Rights*, New York: Harper Collins.

Wihtol de Wenden, Catherine. 2000. "La dimension européenne des nouvelles lois françaises sur l'immigration et la ciotyenneté", R.A. E.-L.E.A. 88-93.

Wihtol de Wenden, Catherine.1994. "Immigrants as Political Actors in France", *West European Politics*, 17, 2: 91-109.

# Index

For Product Safety Concerns and Information please contact our EU
representative  GPSR@taylorandfrancis.com
Taylor & Francis Verlag GmbH, Kaufingerstraße 24, 80331 München, Germany

www.ingramcontent.com/pod-product-compliance
Lightning Source LLC
Chambersburg PA
CBHW070406270326
41926CB00014B/2718